Building Holy Relationships

Prayers, Sermons, and Other Writings by Lloyd H. Knox

Edited by Chet Martin with Ruth Sparrow

BUILDING HOLY RELATIONSHIPS
Prayers, Sermons, and Other Writings by Lloyd H. Knox
Edited by Chet Martin with Ruth Sparrow

Other Scripture versions cited are: King James Version (KJV); The Living Bible (TLB); The New Testament in Modern English (Phillips); New English Bible (NEB); Goodspeed, An American Translation (Goodspeed); and the Johnson Relational Paraphrase (Johnson).

Scripture quotations marked (LHK) are Lloyd Knox paraphrases.

As is the case with many pastors, especially in decades past, Dr. Knox did not document his sources as well as we now wish he had. These selections are presented much as they were found in Dr. Knox's files; therefore, some of his sources are not cited.

ISBN 0-89367-266-2

Light and Life Communications
Indianapolis, IN 46253-5002
Printed in the U.S.A.

"Relationships, that's really all that life's
about — our relationship with God
and our relationship with others."

Lloyd H. Knox

Lloyd Knox at Petra, 1990

Contents

Editor's Note: After hours of thought, I decided to present these selections from Dr. Knox's works in a simple alphabetical order, rather than attempt to categorize the writings as sermon, article, or liturgy. One reason for this: Dr. Knox rarely used any of his writings for a one-time purpose. Sermons became articles, papers became sermons, and so on. His writing reflects him: impossible to place in a conveniently labeled category!

Appreciation

Sincere thanks to the following persons whose generous contributions made the publication of this book possible:

Supporter

Ms. Christine C. Ames
Rev. and Mrs. Donald Bateman
Miss Vera A. Bethel
Bishop and Mrs. W. Dale Cryderman
Mrs. Winifred Howson
Dr. and Mrs. V. James Mannoia
Mr. Nelson Morton
Rev. and Mrs. Dean A. Parrott
Mr. and Mrs. Virgil L. Raley
Rev. and Mrs. Earl R. Schamehorn, Sr.
Mr. and Mrs. W. R. Sparrow
Dr. and Mrs. Frank Thompson
Rev. and Mrs. Lorne C. Ball
Rev. and Mrs. Roscoe E. Bell
Mr. and Mrs. Timothy J. Burkhart
Ms. Sharon E. Howson
Mr. and Mrs. Carl V. Jackson, Sr.
Rev. and Mrs. Chet Martin
Rev. and Mrs. Ronald O'Neal
Mr. and Mrs. Neil E. Pfoats
Mr. and Mrs. Howard Rose
Bishop and Mrs. Richard D. Snyder
Miss Ora Ann Sprague
Dr. and Mrs. A. H. Mathias Zahniser

Memorials

To Bishop Leslie R. Marston, who hired Lloyd Knox as Publisher, by Jack and Evelyn Mottweiler

To Helen L. Simpson by Thomas B. Simpson

Friend

Dr. Robert A. Briner
Dr. and Mrs. Joseph L. Davis
Mrs. Isabelle J. John
Dr. and Mrs. Bruce L. Kline
Dr. and Mrs. Wayne McCown
Kenneth and Jean Pletcher
Dr. and Mrs. Donald Riggs
The Snyder Foundation, Inc.
Dr. and Mrs. W. Richard Stephens
Mr. Craig W. Tidball
Dr. and Mrs. Elmore L. Clyde
Bishop and Mrs. Paul N. Ellis
Dr. Donald M. Joy
Mrs. Esther R. Lyon
Mr. and Mrs. Albert A. Moore
Mr. and Mrs. Porter Polston
Mr. and Mrs. William K. Sittig
Mr. and Mrs. Melvin J. Spencer
Dr. Catherine Stonehouse

Associate

Dr. David Bogdanoff
Free Methodist Church in Canada
Mr. and Mrs. Carroll D. Porter
Rev. and Mrs. Arden L. Reed
Mrs. Sylvia Tugan
Rev. and Mrs. Donald H. Bowen
Mr. and Mrs. Walter Knox
Rev. Sue Ellen Porter
Dr. and Mrs. Stanley B. Thompson
Rev. and Mrs. K. M. Walton

Co-Publisher

Dr. and Mrs. Leroy W. Kettinger
Dr. and Mrs. Edward Knox

Others

Rev. and Mrs. John M. Baker
Rev. and Mrs. Carl Rice
Miss Gertrude Haight
Mr. and Mrs. G. Edward Smiley

Note of Appreciation

Ruth Sparrow wishes to thank three wonderful women for their invaluable assistance with Dr. Knox's manuscripts: Tressa Martin, copy editor at the Free Methodist Publishing House for twenty years during Dr. Knox's tenure as publisher; Edith Simcoe; and Sherry Benson. All were longtime friends to Dr. Knox. These notes of thanks are particularly appropriate, as Dr. Knox felt strongly that women should have important roles in the church.

Chet Martin wishes to thank Rev. Roger Johnson for introducing him to Dr. Lloyd Knox; Dr. Ed Knox for trusting his father's papers to someone he didn't know; and Mrs. Carol Gates of Columbus, Indiana, for her personal assistance throughout the months of this project.

Both Ruth and Chet wish to thank Craig Tidball of the Free Methodist Foundation, whose advice and counsel have been invaluable in the financing of the project. Most of all, Ruth and Chet wish to thank each other; *Building Holy Relationships* has been a labor of love, and we have appreciated working with one another.

Foreword

In this book, friends and colleagues of the late Dr. Lloyd H. Knox offer a choice selection of his preaching and writing ministry. His secretary of many years, Ruth Sparrow, has preserved his papers and made them available for publication. The Reverend Chet Martin has edited them with loving care and deep appreciation of his friend, Dr. Knox.

For more than four decades, Lloyd Knox served the Free Methodist Church with distinction as pastor, teacher, publisher, lecturer, and writer. He was a creative and forceful leader in every field of endeavor. For twenty-five years, he served as the publisher of the denominational literature. In this capacity he developed the Christian education materials to the highest quality the church has known. He inspired and led in cooperative endeavors with other denominations in the publication of carefully graded study materials.

Dr. Knox was known for his strong preaching ministry. He was profoundly concerned with Christian theology. He knew, however, how to proclaim biblical truth with evangelistic fervor. He preached for decision. He instructed young pastors to ask themselves, when preparing the sermon: "What is it I want these people to decide?" The sermons selected here well illustrate the power of his pulpit ministry.

As a publisher, Dr. Knox was a practical visionary. He saw the big picture, and he knew how to get things done. He inspired and enabled his assistants. He chose persons in whom he saw exceptional talent and potential. He offered motivation and assistance in their continuing education. From his office many have moved forward into positions of significant leadership in the church.

A strong competitive leader in publishing, Dr. Knox saw himself, however, as a generalist. "Our total mission is bigger than any segment of our ministries," he told an interviewer at the time of his retirement in 1979. He wanted to be remembered as "one who had a concern for the total church program."

The selected works of Dr. Knox will benefit "the total church program." His writing will inspire this generation of Christian leaders, clergy and laity, alike. His concerns for the church are relevant today.

Dr. Knox cautions against all that is cheap and thin in Christian worship and discipleship. He pleads for "holy love" in evangelism and in the spiritual instruction of new disciples. His challenge to holy living is both biblical and realistic. His long view of the ministry and mission of Christ's church will keep his work contemporary for many years to come.

Paul N. Ellis
Lakeland, Florida

Tributes

I *might* still be a Free Methodist pastor today if I had never met Dr. Lloyd Knox, but I would *not* be the Free Methodist pastor I am if I had never met him — a man I always called Pastor, right up until my final telephone conversation with him, just a few days before his death.

Once, I mentioned to a member of our academic circle that in terms of theology, I might best be termed a Knoxian. His reply was that that distinction might have been more acceptable a bit earlier in our denomination's history than it would be today; my reply was that that did not matter to me in the least.

Now it would be fair to ask what that distinction means to me. Being mentored by Pastor Knox has shaped me in many ways, some of which I cannot articulate, some of which I may not even recognize. But there are several effects of his pastoral leadership and mentoring that I can identify and affirm.

He made me *think*. Dr. Knox was my pastor during a brief supply experience at the Meadowood church in Elkhart, Indiana. The church had, in the previous year, undergone a wrenching division that left scarred and pained people in its wake. He walked into a church of about thirty-five, that had been a church of about 175 just a year before.

We were hurting, amazed and shocked by all that had happened in so short a time, and worse, we were used to preaching and teaching that simply reiterated that which we already knew. Without meaning to be hurtful in any way, I remember that we were used to manipulation and artificial emotional highs that did not produce the fruit of the Spirit and maturity. And here came this brilliant man, gangly and grandfatherly, who did not do things the way we were used to at all!

He insisted on calling the foyer the narthex. He started the service with the "Doxology" and had us sing an unfamiliar song after the offering. His sermons were often two- and three-parters. If you didn't listen, you didn't learn. If you didn't think, you didn't grow.

So I listened. And I thought. One day, when studying Romans, I called him on the phone and said excitedly, "I think I understand predestination and election now!" I'm sure he chuckled inwardly, but he asked me what my understanding was. I told him, and he beamed over the phone at me. "That's right," he said. "That's just what the Bible teaches, it's what Wesley believed, and I think you're right, too." I doubt that receiving Wesley's own seal of approval could have meant more to me than receiving a word of commendation from my pastor, my teacher.

He helped me understand *grace*. "I see grace as a river, everflowing from God," was one of the last things he told me, the October before he died. I had wanted to stay with him during the Greenville Minister's Conference, but those scheduling the event felt that his health was too precarious. They placed me in a different home. But I didn't unpack my car, and soon after arriving there, I saw Pastor Knox near the Armington Center, and he called out to me, voice still strong, "Where are you staying?" I told him what had transpired, and he said, "You're staying with me."

During those days, I accompanied Dr. Knox to as many events of the conference as he could handle and talked with him at his home about the ones he felt he had to skip. I was able to enjoy a conversation between him and another of my personal preacher heroes, Douglas Crossman of Great Britain.

But during that entire time in October, Pastor Knox spoke more of grace than anything else. He felt he understood it better then than ever before. Perhaps that had something to do with recent events in his life. I think he always understood grace.

When he was in Elkhart, my younger half-sister was living with me. She had deep emotional hurts that made me fear for her personal safety and well-being, so I encouraged her to talk to our pastor. She did, and she told him some family history that, well, embarrassed me. I was embarrassed about what he now knew, and for the first time, I felt uncomfortable when I saw him. He came over to our home, played with our son Zack, and then, without any prompting, began to tell me some family things that had embarrassed him. He said, "You see, we all have skeletons. Don't worry so much about yours." I don't know how theologically sound this is, but I tell you: that was grace extended to me.

A young man who had never been able to really receive forgiveness in any way other than intellectually began to receive it and to have a glimmer of hope that God really accepted him. Now a pastor, I hope I communicate grace with the same effectiveness.

Pastor Knox taught me about *commitment*. I never met Mrs. Knox. She was already in a nursing facility when he came to Elkhart. I know that he lived in New York and then in Illinois while she remained in the home near Winona Lake. But when Pastor Knox was in town, he always visited his wife, though the progression of her Alzheimer's meant that she did not know who he was or, finally, even that he was there. When he wasn't in town, Mrs. Knox was never far from his heart. He loved her deeply and regretted her loss.

Finally, I would say that my pastor taught me *self-confidence*. He had no persona to protect, no image of staidness or sternness to maintain. "Too many people are petrified instead of sanctified," he would say. Several who attended a mid-1980s J-term class on Ephesians taught by Dr. Knox in Winona Lake at the Friendship House will never forget the camaraderie we had with him and the easy self-assurance he modeled. He knew himself, his talents, his abilities.

During my stay with him that last October, he was talking about some recent experiences. "I was wrong," he said, and "Well, there's no fool like an old fool." Some very private comments made during that conversation will never be revealed by me, but I did learn more from my pastor, mentor, and friend. It's human to be wrong. It's human to mess up. Best of all, it's good to be honest about it when you do.

Now Dr. Knox was not perfect. His feet were firmly anchored to this planet. One time, when I visited him in Winona Lake, I remember that he was particularly grouchy. I don't know why, and he never told me. Maybe he didn't even know he was being grouchy, or maybe he thought I was the one off-key. Perhaps I was. What I learned from Pastor Knox was, however, learned within the context of humanness.

I have been honored to work with his papers, but I do not want any reader to think that my role has been more than it was. Dr. Knox wrote so well that editing needs were minimal. I was glad to have a hand in the selection process. Dr. Knox's longtime secretary and friend, Ruth Sparrow, deserves the greater praise for this book. Her hours spent on it were innumerable. She has been extremely patient working with me, and I want to thank her here.

And thank you, Pastor Knox. You continue to enrich my life. I look forward to our reunion in heaven, when my understanding of the things of God might finally approach yours.

Chet Martin

Eighteen years ago (June 1979) I wrote the following letter to Dr. Knox upon his retirement as publisher:

Dear Dr. Knox:

Bishop Bastian asked me to put in writing for him some of your "strengths, special abilities, and graces." This is what I gave him:

Is an excellent administrator.

Has great vision — to me he always seems to go beyond the immediate subject under discussion and considers aspects others might not think of.

Is a logical thinker and articulate. (I am constantly amazed at how from notes on a small index card he can dictate, for instance, a three- or four-page document, have it well-worded and in proper order. Too, he can read a letter requesting, for instance, technical business information or regarding a theological matter and dictate an immediate reply which is logical, clear, and appropriate. This is an ability that constantly amazes me.)

Is totally committed to whatever task he is assigned to do and takes prompt action.

He is not an opportunist, not a politician — quite the opposite!

He can quickly change his mind if some line of action is wrong and he believes another is better. Doesn't worry about losing face. It's easy for him to say that he is wrong and that another person is right.

Is very straightforward, not two-faced. Many employees and others seek his counsel for they know that he will be honest and that he has their interest at heart.

Is prudent in all his dealings, in his personal business as well as that of the publishing house.

> An outstanding feature is that he is very tenderhearted — is empathetic, cares about persons.
>
> It has been a sincere pleasure to work for you for twenty-five years, save three months. May your years in Spring Arbor be as successful and fulfilling as your nearly twenty-six years with the publishing house.
>
> Sincerely,
> Ruth M. Sparrow

I think of an incident that occurred in 1960 — a few years after he was appointed publisher — which to me characterizes his unusual insight, the fact that his mind was always "in gear," and his great concern for the advancement of the church he loved.

On that day, precisely at eight o'clock, he strode into the office and said, "I have something to dictate." When he began, he said, "Entitle this 'A Philosophy of Investment.'" And without any written notes, his creative and problem-solving mind brought forth in a well-organized manner, new insights and different methods for handling the church's investments.

The money handled by the Investment Committee, the tithes and offerings of the people, he referred to throughout the article as "God's money." And since it was God's money, for one thing, he advocated taking the risk and lending money at greatly reduced interest rates to new and struggling churches, rather than investing in secular organizations seeking higher monetary dividends.

He vividly envisioned the far-reaching results and benefits to numberless unchurched persons, and at the same time greatly building up and advancing our church.

I remember my enthusiasm mounting as he dictated and eagerly asking when he finished, "Who do you want to send this to?"

He answered, "No one. That's not my area. Just type it and put it in the file." (The finished article amounted to two and one-half pages, single spaced!)

I shall always remember "Mr. Knox" as a great man.

Ruth M. Sparrow

Lloyd Henry Knox was born a British citizen in the small town of Brantford, Ontario, to a farming couple on Valentine's Day 1914. He died in Reston, Virginia, on the outskirts of Washington, D.C., on January 3, 1994. In the intervening 80 years my immigrant father lived through two world wars, a great depression, a cold war, and the most astonishing period of change in history.

He left me a legacy, a priceless legacy of memories, great gifts, and a pattern of thought and action. I want to share some of my thoughts about what my father meant to me, because his going has left an enormous hole in my life, and I need to understand what it means as the rest of the Knox family picks up the skeins of life and goes on.

He did not go easily that last night. He was in great pain. His heart raced as he struggled for breath. At times he was right there with us as we gave him additional doses of morphine in an attempt to ease his pain. At other times, he seemed to be somewhere else in time replaying bits of the past. Once, he sat straight up in bed and stared seriously at me, saying with wonderment, "I just learned I have a mission. I didn't know I had a mission."

Another time he told me that the French were mixed up in it somewhere. And, of course, I had always expected that the French were indeed mixed up in it somehow. I gave him a few drops of morphine, and he said thoughtfully, "I don't see the strategic sense of this." Which was a bit shaking to me as a semi-competent nurse doing my best in an unfamiliar role. Again, this must have been a memory from an event in the past. But, I thought that these words caught the man — he had a mission which he served faithfully for a lifetime. And, he never forgot the context, how to place action in intelligent perspective.

He was such a strong man. After he died, I kept looking at him expecting him to start breathing, acting, moving, thinking. It was such a shock that he didn't.

I remembered less than four years ago, our riding horseback together into Petra, whose rose-red cliffside monuments were "as old as time"; walking together on the Street Called Straight in Damascus and staying overnight in a Syrian nunnery as we discussed his early days in Canada; exploring Iraq al-Amir, a ruined palace in a valley south of Amman; looking for papyrus in Cairo; taking photographs in the Mosque of Ibu Tulun. We walked, two historians, in Jordan, where Roman legionnaires had walked two thousand years earlier, just as we had walked in England along Hadrian's Wall in 1983, and marveled at the sweep of an empire from Scotland to the great Syrian desert. There was never a more satisfying tourist in the world, taking it all in with wonderment and appreciation. And, it wasn't just the ancient Near East he would gawk at.

He had driven us to the malls of Warsaw, Indiana, to point out in stupefying detail the latest commercial marvels of northern Indiana. As an audible appreciator of human and divine endeavor he had few peers and no betters. What a pleasure to take him to see your favorite places and hear him exclaim with you about its beauty. What a pleasure to discuss with him your precious ideas and hear him take them seriously. Oh, how I miss him!

He never lost his zest for ideas and places. The last time we returned from radiation treatment on his spine we talked about our impressions that we were in the midst of a great social, global upheaval that was sweeping our society and time. He told me he thought we were on the verge of a great sea of change in ideas and social organization, and he said it was so interesting he hoped to see part of it.

He had that kind of mind. Hopeful, upbeat, curious. Among his papers that he brought with him to Reston were several pages of notes on "Reasons for Christian Hope." Hope ... to the end.

What did I inherit from my father? A love of ideas, a love of books. An orientation toward service. A bent toward working with and within organizations. A belief in the family.

And a code. This is really hard to pin down, but I have caught glimpses of it in my actions as I grew up. Most men of a certain age, I think, will recognize that we adhere to a code. Show compassion to the weak and needy. Have contempt for those who use others spitefully. Put the group before the individual. Give others credit when due. Act modestly. Talk is cheap; get down into the trenches and work shoulder to shoulder with the real workers. Don't ask for pity. You may weep, if you must, but don't allow yourself to appear weak. Comfort others, but take the pain without complaint. Be honest. Tell the truth, but be supportive. Tell yourself the truth. Do not take unfair advantage of others. Don't blow your own horn; only weaklings and cowards do that. Play for the team to win. Lead but efface yourself when possible. Be responsible. I could go on at length to catalogue all the elements of the code, but I think you get the idea.

It was a harsh and demanding code; one very hard to live up to, but one he never relaxed on. On his notes on "Reasons for Christian Hope," he repeats a theme he spoke to me about probably 40 years ago. In the physical realm there are laws that, were we to defy them, would break us. Try, for instance, to act against the law of gravity. It's the same in the moral world. There are laws there that will just as surely leave us broken as though we had tried to step off a high cliff, not expecting gravity to act as implacably as it always does.

This was one of his great lifelong themes. I admired him for his attachment to principle, for his great strength of character. At times it cost him dearly, and it cost me, Walter, and Sylvia as we grew up.

I also admired him for his lifelong devotion to his mission. This was truly central to his being. Devotion to God and to his church. This was no lip service but total dedication and sacrifice on the altar of the mission to God. This was my father — a man of great enthusiasms spending his energies in the service of his life callings.

He fit the ideal described by Teddy Roosevelt: "It is not the critic who counts, nor the one who points out how the strong man stumbled or how the doer of deeds could have done them better. The credit belongs to the man who is actually in the arena, whose face is marred by dust and sweat and blood; who strives valiantly, who errs and comes up short again and again; who knows the great enthusiasms, the great devotions, and spends himself in a worthy cause; who, at best, knows in the end, the triumph of high achievement; and who, at the worst, if he fails, at least fails while daring greatly, so that his place shall never be with the cold and timid souls who know neither victory nor defeat."

I must tell you that this attitude toward life is not always appreciated in large organizations where the motto "Make No Waves" is emblazoned over the entrance. Indeed I am astonished at my father's successes. Because if anyone ever merited the name

Wavemaker, it was Lloyd H. Knox. He had little time for fools, dull functionaries, or timewasters. His intelligence was penetrating, his mode of speech direct and to the point, and his choice was ACTION, every time. Never mind that he was as hard on himself as he was on anyone else, his great strength was also his greatest weakness. Some years ago I took part in a management exercise in which my fellow managers and I were closely observed in action over the course of several hours. This was the feedback concerning my management style: "You are focused on getting the job done and you see the future implications of action very clearly, and you will pick up the bodies later." Some part of me was proud of that assessment. I said to myself, "Ah, you are your father's son."

One of Dad's good friends and colleagues wrote to me last week: "I watched your Dad mellow across the years of his ministry, enabling him to minister to hurting people with an empathy that came from the crucible of his own personal sorrow. I thank God for the memories." Exactly, and said brilliantly. He changed. The price was pain.

My family and I would like to express our appreciation to the entire Greenville community for their love and support of my father in the last years of his life. Thanks to Pastor Hendricks for pulling the memorial service together with the able assistance of Dr. Harriette Whiteman.

I have known Harriette as long as I remember life. She taught English to Dad when he was in college and she taught me. She and Lester Whiteman, who seemed to visit Dad daily, are special people.

Emily and Al Moore, I believe, helped keep Dad together over the past years. I don't know what he would have done without them.

And the Simcoes, Riker and Edith. He loved to spend time with them. And Steve and Beverly Toomey, his next-door neighbors, who showed so many special kindnesses over the last year and shared with him the "best Thanksgiving" he could remember.

To Ruth Sparrow who flew to Reston to help us care for Dad — though he lived only twelve hours more. I am grateful. And a cast of thousands more in Greenville. Sometimes it seemed when we were visiting him at the hospital last year that all the city coursed through the room, as I'm sure it seemed to his doctor, Dr. Tom Dawdy.

Despite all the pain and travail late in life, Dad was a fortunate man. He had you, and many more like you around the country, for friends.

And, I too am fortunate. He was my father. I shall miss him. He was a lovely man.

Ed Knox

My friendship with Lloyd Knox lasted more than seventy years, and ended — except for a rich store of memories — only with his death. We met in Spring Arbor in 1923 where my father had been the baccalaureate speaker.

The following year my family moved to Spring Arbor. There I found a wonderful group of playmates that included Lloyd Knox, already nine. I was still eight. Lloyd was always immaculately dressed and freshly scrubbed. The other boys, usually in well-worn and not very clean overalls, teased Lloyd, wearing freshly pressed khaki shorts, about his "stove-pipe" pants.

Lloyd's father finished his belated education and had been assigned to a pastorate in the Michigan Conference. During the next few years I caught glimpses of Lloyd occasionally at a camp meeting or conference.

But in the summer of 1933, just before I went to Greenville to finish college, I was traveling with a Spring Arbor girls' quartet. We were assigned to sing at Rev. Earl Knox's church at Benton Harbor, Michigan.

Just as we were leaving, Lloyd, now nineteen, appeared to tell us "hello" and "goodbye." He had finished high school with honors, and — with the Great Depression being at its worst — had postponed college, preached at a mission, supplied the pulpit of another small church, went to business college, and worked at the local A & P store to aid in his parents' support and to try to put away a little money for college.

I went to Greenville, graduated, and got a job at the 1935 General Conference, the first one held at Winona Lake. There Dr. LeRoy Lowell invited me to join the Spring Arbor faculty as the professor of English and speech for the junior college. Salary was $310.00 for the year. Both frightened and delighted, I accepted.

When school opened, I found myself, still not quite twenty-one, facing a Freshman Rhetoric class of about forty, most of whom were older than I — among them Lloyd Knox.

Lloyd was a brilliant student and worked hard. He also was active in speech events and took a number of prizes! One of his proudest memories to the end of his life was Spring Arbor's smashing victory in a debate with Houghton College — on their turf — and with Stephen Paine, later the president of that college, as their coach! And Spring Arbor had only *me*. Fortunately, I was twenty-two by then.

Lloyd played pranks, which tickled his memory to his last days. Once he became very irritated with me. I don't remember what it was about or what he said. What I do remember is that a few days later, during my class, Lloyd asked for the floor, stood, and made a public apology to me before the whole group! I never forgot that day!

After junior college Lloyd married my best friend. I was maid of honor at their wedding — the first church wedding ever at Spring Arbor. A year later I was married there, with Harriet Knox as my matron of honor.

Then General Conference came again. The Knoxes came from their parish, "Petersburg, Prairie, and Town Line," and stayed with us in our one-bedroom apartment in Winona Lake. They had by then endured the tearing sorrow of the death at birth of their first-born, little Paul.

A few years later, when Lloyd was pastor at Ferndale, Michigan, we moved to Ferndale for the wartime work opportunities for my husband, Lester, and for my continuing graduate study. These were wonderful years of fellowship with both our growing families.

And how we did enjoy Lloyd's preaching!

But things kept changing. I returned home from teaching summer school at Greenville to find that the Knoxes had accepted the pastorate at Rochester, New York. And before many years they were at Winona Lake, with Lloyd as publisher. And how well he took to his new position!

Our return to Greenville was timed so that I had the privilege of teaching two of the Knox children. Lloyd continued to distinguish himself in his career, holding many important positions, traveling, receiving a doctorate from Asbury Theological Seminary.

All too soon came Lloyd's retirement and his wife Harriet's terrible illness, throughout which we managed to stay in touch.

Then Lloyd became our pastor again, at Greenville, to our great joy. We were able to be with him a great deal during his final illness.

Lloyd Knox's passing was a great loss to Free Methodism. He was a preacher, scholar, and leader, the likes of whom we don't see often. I have known many of the giants of our denomination, but of them all, none loved the Word, the study of it, and our denomination more than did Dr. Lloyd Henry Knox.

Harriette Warner Whiteman

I Am

I am a Christian who loves Jesus Christ.
I wonder if animals will be in heaven.
I hear Jesus say, "Well done, my good and faithful servant."
I want to read God's Word and know His promises.
I am a Christian who loves Jesus Christ.

I pretend Jesus is on earth, and I ask Him for advice.
I feel the power of prayer.
I touch His robe; it's the softest feeling I've ever known.
I worry about my brother's relationship with God.
I cry when I think of people facing eternal hell.
I am a Christian who loves Jesus Christ.

I understand a little more every day how awesome God is.
I say to my sister and my grandparents in heaven,
"I love you, and I'll be with you some day."
I dream that everyone will be saved.
I try to be an example to others.
I hope God uses me in many ways.

Brandy S. Knox (12)
Granddaughter of Lloyd H. Knox

Access to Resurrection

That great book of Ephesians! ... *his incomparably great power for us who believe — that power is like the working of his mighty strength, which he exerted in Christ when he raised him from the dead and seated him at his right hand in the heavenly realm* (Ephesians 1:19-20, NIV).

A man by the name of Johnson put out a relational paraphrase of Paul's letters, and he translates Paul as pleading that "you will be aware of the incredibly immense strength which is available to us." You see, we have access to Resurrection, to the strength and power God demonstrated in Christ when He raised Him from death and gave Him supreme authority! I want to ask four questions:

1. What is this incredible power?
2. Who is the power for?
3. What is the power to do?
4. How do we gain access to this power?

What is this incredible power?

Verse 19 in that first chapter of Ephesians employs five words to build and expand our vision of the power that is designed for our use and designed to be channeled through ordinary Christ-persons, ordinary believers.

First, Paul uses the Greek that we translate "greatness." Literally, it means "very tall indeed." But then I note there is a word that is significant and precedes it. It is the word "excelling," or "immeasurable." I think that what Paul is trying to say to us is: "Our God is BIG, BIG! Immeasurably BIG! Let's not make Him small!"

How big is your God this morning? The bigness of God is a bigness of grace and a bigness of power, and that's the second main word that Paul uses here. It is the word from which we derive "dynamo" and "dynamic" and "dynamite."

The third word is the one from which we have energy. It indicates working and effective action, and it is always used of supernatural beings. It is often translated "operation working."

The fourth word is "might," which suggests strength and intensity as opposed to weakness.

And the fifth word is "strength," and it is strength with a particular connotation. It suggests over-mastering, ruling power.

Paul simply exhausts the Greek language to try and get us a picture of the kind of power that he wants us to be acquainted with.

Who is the power for?

It is clear that Paul has exhausted this rich Greek language resource to paint a picture of the power of God operating in, available to, and flowing through Christ-persons, and flowing outward from a believer in Christ to the world around us.

Paul seems very intent that we shall not glide past this point in the prayer, for he is on his knees, praying. It is a deliberate effort to give us a picture that will have maximum impact on his Christian reader friends. Paul is always sensitive to the power of illustrating words. I wonder what the impact must have been on the first congregation that read these words.

But Paul has by no means finished making a point, making a point on his knees. Now he wasn't doing what I've known some people to do, and that is to pray at someone else over the Lord's shoulder. That is not what he's doing.

But he's not through praying. And his praying for us becomes preaching, doesn't it? The best is yet to come in the words of Paul. This dynamic God power which is exceedingly great in its effective operation and strength did a specific, historical, objective, concrete thing which is of the utmost importance to our everyday lives, right now!

That great power of God raised Christ Jesus, the Messiah, out from among the dead ones and seated Him at the right hand of Him who is in the heavenlies and established His authority, His power, and His lordship on a cosmic scale which extends to us here in Greenville, to this congregation, this morning — to the Church of Jesus Christ, to the cosmos, and to the age which is yet to come!

That very same power — God takes that power and aims it, takes that energy and aims it in our direction! He brings it right to us! He brings it to the point where we can tap into that power! We have access to Resurrection! I have access to Resurrection! As an individual Christ-person we have access as the organism of Christ on earth, His body!

What is the power to do?

When individual Christians are put into the Body of Christ by the power of God, the church becomes God's instrument in the world for achieving God's ultimate and full purposes! Johnson translates 1:23: *"In the midst of creation, he guides the church, his body, which fulfills his intention as he, Christ, fills the whole wide universe."*

Talk about a mighty concept, talk about a mighty reality — this was something surging powerfully through the soul of the Apostle Paul. And as he prays, he has the hope that as these words are read they will surge with power through us.

Paul raises our personal and corporate vision and expectations to unimaginable heights. He gives positive and possibility thinking in its ultimate form. So let's ask — how big is your God? We not only have a big God this morning, but we have a God with big power to be expended on us!

What is this power for? It's made quite clear that it is power used in line with the announced purpose of God for us in the earlier part of the chapter — mainly that we should be holy! Great dynamic power!

And I'm telling you that in the kind of world we're living in we shall have to have Resurrection power if we are going to be moral and if we are going to be spiritual, that we should be holy and blameless and loving.

Christians, you can't be loving without the power of God. And you aren't. And I'm not. We need this Resurrection power to make us loving, to make us holy, to make us blameless. It is not the promise for power for some spiritual spectaculars or for some ecstasies to be consumed by ourselves.

It is moral and spiritual power! It is transforming, character-changing power! It is radical life-changing power! It is coping power, in the midst of the struggles of life! God purposes to make us Christ-persons in a Christless world. He aims to make us mature in Christ. He aims to impart copability to us.

He determines to develop in us pull-power and love power in our individual and in our corporate lives. Power for radical change is the sort of thing Paul is suggesting here.

When I first read Johnson's translation of verse 20, *"access to Resurrection,"* it came at a moment when I needed that word. And when I read it I was overcome. I was overcome intellectually. I was overcome emotionally. Something happened to me deep within. I was shocked with the boldness and the promise of the assertion.

It may be that this hit harder because I was in an experience where I had an overwhelming sense of my own weakness. I so desperately needed courage. I so desperately needed copability and understanding, and love and joy and on and on. You name it, I needed it. And that phrase has helpfully haunted me, and I hope it will you, with its utter audacity.

Access to Resurrection power! The truly inspired Paul has extended our vision, lifted our horizon, raised our hopes! He points us to the fuller dimensions of reality! I need access to Resurrection to make all this a part of my life as I live it amid its stresses and its distresses and its fears and its sorrows and its defeats and the attacks of the Enemy.

I need Resurrection power — power prayed for and therefore promised is designed to impact on my life, our lives, in specific ways. What impact has that power had on you — this week? Perhaps our petitioner, Paul, is our best witness. He testifies about the impact of this power on his life.

"What, Paul, do you say this morning?" Let's bring him on. "Please, Paul, will you give us your testimony? You're talking about having access to Resurrection power. What do you know about it?"

Let's hear him speak: *"I have learned to be content whatever the circumstances may be. I know how to live when things are difficult, and I know how to live when things are prosperous."* (I know how to enjoy T-bones and pizzas.) *"In general and in particular I have learned the secret of facing either plenty or poverty. I am ready for anything through the strength of the One who lives within me"* (Philippians 4:11-13, Johnson).

Those are powerful words. He could not have said that unless he had access to Resurrection power. Resurrection power made Paul adequate, made him adaptable. What brought him to this point? Well, you know that Paul was one day confronted on a bloody mission to Damascus. Christ arrested him and Christ changed him.

Paul felt he had been raised from a very real death, a death from which trespasses and sins had cut him off from real living. The direction and quality of his life was changed from that moment on. Again he testifies, *"Whatever gain I had* [in the old life] *I count it as lost for Christ's sake. Indeed, I count everything as lost because of the surpassing worth of knowing Jesus Christ, my Lord."*

He goes on, *"For his sake I have suffered the loss of all things and count these as refuse* [garbage] *in order that I may gain Christ and be found in him, not having a righteousness of my own based on the law but that which is through faith in Christ, the righteousness from God which depends on faith, that I may know him and the power of his resurrection, and the fellowship and to share in his sufferings becoming like him in his death and experience resurrection as he did"* (Philippians 3:7-11, Johnson).

The death and resurrection of Jesus Christ is never a moment away from the everyday experience of the Apostle Paul. So there we have the secret of the driving force of Paul's life. And we find the answer to the question, "What is this Resurrection power for?"

Well, let's pursue yet another question.

How do we gain access to this Resurrection power?

Imagine, if you will, those monstrous electric power lines that cross our nation's landscape carrying immense power, high voltage. Look at them. They just lie there not doing a single thing. There's nothing in their appearance to suggest the immense power that is flowing through those lines.

They're not jumping up and down, excited. They're not doing anything ecstatic — they just lie there. You drive under those wires and you find things happening to your radio, and you know that something's up there. With all the insulation, still some of that power escapes and interrupts the airways, impacting on my radio.

Once again, imagine that you have never seen such lines before, they've never been there before, but you're told that these new lines carry an invisible source of power. Someone said that we ought to call it "electricity." And you're told that if you knew how to do it, you could gain access to that power and it could do some very marvelous things for you and for others.

Why, there's power enough in those lines to drive huge printing presses (I've watched them), light large buildings, heat churches and cool churches and homes and make computers work and dry your hair and shave your whiskers and mow your lawns and cook your food and hundreds of other marvelous things — it can bring the world into your living room through providing the TV with the power it needs, make motors useful and drive food mixers and run refrigerators. Only one problem — you have to plug in.

Now is not Paul saying that there's a power like that which operates in another dimension of reality which impacts with just as great practicality in our daily lives? Thank God for the power now available for the external and material world. But let us now also thank God for the power which is near and accessible for the internal and for the spiritual world in which we live, as well as we live in the material.

The Resurrection power that raised Christ from the dead was most unspectacular in its operation, but not in its results. It's quiet, noiseless power. But it can raise the dead! It is a power different from and mightier than electricity, mightier than atomic power, mightier than volcanic power or hurricane power, or any other harnessed or unharnessed power within human experience.

This power is available for a particular kind of person and persons. It is for Christ-trusters; it is for believers. It is for believing strugglers — strugglers just like you, just like me.

How do we gain access? By opening entrusting faith. Right there is the power — by opening entrusting faith. **First**, I take the plug of faith and I push it into the receptacle of power and grace, and now it is no longer I, but it is the power transmitted to me working in me.

Second, we gain access by doing what Jesus did, so says Paul in Philippians. What did Jesus do? He emptied Himself by identifying with us humans, becoming a servant. You get power by being a servant, by emptying yourself, by obedience even to death. *"God therefore,"* Paul says, *"raised him, exalted him."* Why? Because of His obedience, because of His self-emptying. Paul said that to tell us the path to glory and the path to power.

Third, we must be willing to let the energy and the power be seen to be God's and not ours. The light of God, he told the Corinthians, is to be in us as earthen pots.

He then told just how this worked out. He said, *"Well, we're quite human. We experience every kind of pressure but we are not confined. We are often confused, but never totally immobilized; persecuted by man, we are not abandoned by God. Thrown to the ground by our opponents, we are not totally wiped out."*

"These negative experiences remind me that I am daily sharing," says Paul, *"the death of Christ while the inner resources which these experiences call forth manifest my participation in the Resurrection. During our life we constantly experience different kinds of death for Jesus' sake so that new dimensions of life he revealed may be expressed through us"* (2 Corinthians 4:7-11, Johnson).

Then at chapter six he testifies for the Christian brotherhood that by the power of the Resurrection realized now, *"We can endure with patience and fortitude an enormous amount of suffering of material needs, of emotional stress, even beatings, imprisonments, riots and numerous tasks performed through sleepless nights and foodless days."*

And this was a man who knew what he was talking about. *"We show that we are truly agents of God by the purity of our conscious intentions, by gaining more knowledge, by patient waiting, by kindness, by responding to the Holy Spirit, by having sincere love, by truths which we express, by the power of God we demonstrate, by using all the resources which are available through our right relation with God."*

(I'm still reading the Scripture.) *"We maintain our integrity in the midst of conflicting reports that we are honorable and dishonorable — reports that we are evil and that we are good. They say we are shysters, but we are genuine. Some persons do not know us at all, but God knows us very well.*

"Frequently at the edge of death, we are nevertheless quite alive. We suffer a great deal, but obviously hardship has not killed us. As God's agents we experience a lot of disappointment. We can always

find something to celebrate. We don't own anything, but we are enriching the lives of many persons. It may appear that we have nothing, but really we have everything" (2 Corinthians 6:4-10, Johnson).

But the first application of the words of our text is found in Ephesians 2:1 (Johnson): *"You he made alive. You were dead to God through trespasses and sins. You are now alive to God through Christ. You have had access to Resurrection."*

That's no less a miracle, let me tell you this morning, than the resurrection of Christ, that we come alive out of our sins and out of our trespasses — the very same power that makes us new creations in Christ Jesus. It is no less a power than that which hurled the universe into existence.

But the power that transforms us, Paul sees as continuing to transform us. It is a power which can be brought to bear on our persons and upon our corporate needs. It is the power that will make a reality out of the future which long ago was designed by the Father's love for His creation.

So this is a power flowing from God the Father's love, released by God the Son's death, made effective and practical for us by God the Holy Spirit's energetic and effective ministry in our personal life and in the life of the church. It is a power that can cause us to triumph over all powers of darkness so that the believing Christ-person becomes a wonder to himself.

May we have access to the power of the Resurrection. May we believing strugglers know the achievement possible by the power of His resurrection.

Assurance: Another Kind of Knowing

Therefore, brothers, we have an obligation — but it is not to the sinful nature, to live according to it. For if you live according to the sinful nature, you will die; but if by the Spirit you put to death the misdeeds of the body, you will live, because those who are led by the Spirit of God are sons of God.

For you did not receive a spirit that makes you a slave again to fear, but you received the Spirit of sonship. And by him we cry, "Abba, Father." The Spirit himself testifies with our spirit that we are God's children. Now if we are children, then we are heirs — heirs of God and co-heirs with Christ, if indeed we share in his sufferings in order that we may also share in his glory (Romans 8:12-17, NIV).

My grandfather, Henry Mellor, was raised in England and migrated to Canada. As a boy he was quite sickly, and he told me that his mother would say in the morning, "Harry (she called him Harry but his name was Henry), be sure you drink your ale."

Now it was a mother, uninformed, urging to help. There is, we know now, better dietary knowledge available. Today, I assume that a mother would more likely say, "Harry, be sure you drink your milk." But in that transition from ale to milk is involved a kind of "knowing."

How do we know the difference between the value of ale and the value of milk? We have had a great deal of dietary research involving analysis and identification of vitamins and involving something you've all heard of called "calories." You've heard the role of minerals in foodstuff, and we've assembled facts, and then we've interpreted facts so that we feel we are far advanced in knowledge through a specific kind of knowing.

Now my grandfather also came to Canada with another

kind of knowledge. It was a negative sort of thing, and it was this: that one could not be sure at all whether one belonged to the elect or to the damned. And he has recited for me that he lived a very uneasy and troubled existence with that kind of teaching, that kind of supposed knowledge.

Then he came under a different kind of teaching that taught from the Bible that one did not need to live under such a load of uncertainty, that the Bible had something more to say that had not been passed on, as yet, to him. He had been reading through glasses tinted — tinted by certain theological assumptions.

Now, he was told that he could know — he could know a very deep assurance that he belonged to the family of God. He could know that he was indeed a child of God, a son, that he was an heir, and that he had passed from death to life. And to his death he rejoiced — he literally rejoiced in that assurance and passed over the River of Death with that confidence.

My earliest memories, incidentally, of my grandfather (he and my grandmother were both professional tailors) are that his health broke and he was advised to go to a farm. This advice I've never understood, for he made a rather poor farmer. But he was a wonderful musician.

I can remember that the organ got played every morning down in the parlor. Some of you are not old enough to know what a parlor is, but in the parlor was the organ. And before the cows ever got milked, Grandpa went down and sang the great hymns of the church to the accompaniment of that little organ. I shall never forget that and am blessed by it.

Well, there are all kinds of knowing — knowing that is biblically informed, knowing that is chemically determined, that is biologically sure, that is astronomical knowledge — that we seem to think we know quite well. On and on we could go with the different kinds of knowing.

And while there are shared characteristics, likely between some of these ways of knowing, we simply know that you do not know all things in the very same way. There is knowing, for example, that comes through the senses of touching and tasting and smelling and seeing and hearing.

"How do you know?" we are asked. And we may respond, "Well, I heard and that's the way I know. I heard that bird and I know its call. I know it's a cardinal, or I know it's a crow, or I know it's an owl."

And then there's a thing that we call instinct, a kind of mysterious, built-in kind of knowing. There's the birds' unerring flight over thousands of miles at the right time of the year to repeatable stops and places. It's a mystery. The spawning of whales and fish — mysterious indeed. I've seen the ladders built jointly by Canada and the United States on the great Fraser River, where these steps are built in order that the salmon can go upstream to spawn. They will in fact give their life to try to get back, so ladders are provided for them.

Now there's a marvelous kind of knowing back of all of this, and we do not, I would point out, understand this even in any very complete way. And the examples of this sort of thing could be multiplied of course.

Then there is that equally mysterious and wonderful way of knowing that we call "intuition." (That's what women are gifted with.) "I intuit so-and-so." And you ask, "How do you know?" And I answer, "I don't know how I know, but I know." (I've always called that a woman's "ignition.") Intuitive knowledge, like other knowledge, can be wrong, but the existence of valid intuition, none will, I'm sure, deny.

Well, what can I know this morning about my relationship to God? Can we really know that we are, this morning, the children of God? Can we know that we are now sons rather than slaves of God? Can we know that God for sure has put His Spirit in our spirits? Can we really know that we have passed from death to life? Can we know that we are new-born in Christ Jesus?

Can we have the Scriptures called to our attention, believe what they say, and then have a conviction born that the promises of God regarding our salvation have become a living reality in our lives, a kind of unshakeable knowledge? Can we know for sure from deep within and by a "spirit of sonship" that we are crying out of a sure and a certified relationship, "Abba, Father," translated "Daddy, Father," and have the deep certainty within that this is a genuine, valid cry? Can we have an inner confidence as sure as the child who is certain and secure in the sense of belonging to father and to mother and to family — not a shadow of a doubt with that child?

If we cannot — if we cannot, then I must inquire whether this highly touted communicating God is as real as His advertising claims! Well, the biblical answer to all these questions is a resounding, "Yes, we can know!"

The objective base for such inward and subjective knowing is the act of God's love in Jesus, the Christ on the Cross of Calvary. The word has been carried to us that Jesus loves us, that Jesus loves me, and that love includes the love of the Father, God. God has used His best form of communication, that of a Person — God Himself for me, God Himself for us.

We, the Bible says, are reconciled to God. I, as an individual, am reconciled to God. Both the personal and communal aspects are clearly in view.

Let's hear a few words of Paul from the second letter that he wrote to the Corinthians, the first chapter, verses 21 and 22 (NIV), where he says: *"Now it is God who makes both us and you stand firm in Christ. He anointed us, set his seal of ownership on us, and put his Spirit in our hearts as a deposit, guaranteeing what is to come."*

Now that entire word, will you note, has the sound of sureness. The world may shake, circumstances may change, our feelings may vary. We may have times when we're up and times when we're down, but it is God's intent to make us stand firm to not lose heart.

We are to stand firm, not in our own knowledge or in our own ignorance. We are to stand firm in a relationship to Christ, in Christ. The strength of our relationship provides the strength of our stand.

Do I know, can I know my relationship to another human being? Can human spirit engage with another human spirit and come to a sense of security in that relationship? If that is true, then God, who is personal, I more than suggest to you this morning can be known, can be real, and can assure us. To Him we can be related and firmly related.

But there's more in the Corinthians passage. It more than hints; it speaks at our way of knowing. He gives, Paul says, an anointing. He sets His seal of ownership on us. He puts His Spirit in our hearts. Now surely Paul would not have written those words unless he had an inward assurance that that was indeed true.

Well, the first thing I note here then is that he means that assurance is the gift of knowing. We can't go to the lab or the forest or the mountain or the moon for this knowing — we can't do it. God places His kind of a receptor within me, a receptor for knowing, of being in relationship with Himself. And He has made us more than animal, more than instinctual.

He has made us a personal spirit and thus is opened a two-way communication channel. God is forever trying to keep this channel unclogged, unjammed, so He can assure us and continue to assure us of our belonging and to whisper to us His will for our lives.

Tell me, just how do you go about knowing? How do you go about being in relationship with another human being? We can't be told all there is to be told about that, but we somehow share enough of a likeness of being that a relationship of depth and of meaning is possible — and we've experienced it.

So to us has been given this incomparable likeness to the King of the Universe, the Father God that we can know.

The Romans passage also says it is this gift in our hearts, in our inmost deepest self, that comes to us as a deposit, a down payment guaranteeing what is to come. He has set his seal of ownership upon us. He has put His Spirit in our hearts and this becomes the down payment, the deposit, the guarantee of what is yet to come.

And what is it that is yet to come? I do not know the full answer for that, and if I did, or you did, it would take half of the excitement, I think, if not more, out of the promise of God. It seems to me that God is saying to us, "I have some exciting things ahead for you, but I want to give you a foretaste, a down payment, and the more you walk with Me, the more you will enjoy your walk, and the more you will enjoy your assurance that I am yours and you are Mine."

Relationships can be exciting. They can also be surprising, and so whatever lies out ahead for the assured, I'm sure will be both surprising and exciting and consummately satisfying. A growing, developing relationship means a growing assurance, a growing knowing.

I can feel loved and accepted now, but with the passing of the days a sense of belonging and a sense of seurity grows and grows and grows so that I become surer, not only of Heaven, which to me is not the thing I think about. I may be getting closer, but I don't think much about it. What I think about is my relation to Him which in Heaven shall be but an extension of that which I've begun here.

And as I come closer, I become (grow) surer, because He walks with me and He talks with me and He assures me that I am His own. This then is the wonder which is beyond all wonders that the Scriptures hold out to us this morning, that I can know God and that I can be known of God. And I can be assured that I belong to Him personally, and that I belong to Him with us corporately.

So we can know. There comes the testimony of the Holy Spirit to our human spirit, an inward and deep and reliable impression of the soul, a kind of conviction that the Spirit of God now witnesses directly with my spirit that I am a child of His.

I know, and this is important to accent, that I am a member of a family, a new family, the family of God. I have an assurance of my relationship both vertical and horizontal. Strange that we often make this so personal that we in effect deny its communal dimensions. We are born into a family, and we need that family.

I have very great difficulty understanding those who read the Bible and then go and worship all by themselves out in nature and never find themselves in communion with others who know God. Because it seems to me that the Scriptures are quite clear that we cannot grow and develop a relationship with God in Christ in separation from the body.

We not only have an individual asssurance but our assurance is reinforced in the body of the assured. To think otherwise is a kind of an arrogance, but even worse we by that effectively block the full development of a growing assurance. And we ought not do that.

With the kind of assurance that the Bible offers and that I'm talking about this morning, I find that I am delivered from fear. I am delivered from faltering. I am delivered from distrusting and have peace, the peace of an inward, confident knowing.

The whole of the person may be involved in this kind of knowing, but it is more than mind on mind, it's more than body to body kind of knowing. There is a capacity for God. Our human spirit is built as a receptor of the knowledge from the Spirit of God himself.

But indeed it is my human spirit that is the receptor, that is the responder. My human spirit does not initiate. My spirit responds. John sees a parallel when he says that God loves us first and then we respond in love, and that we seemingly cannot respond unless we become aware of the fact that He does indeed love us.

God is always the great initiator. He is here this morning. God has been the great communicator here this morning. He's communicating to you, and I have the confidence that your receptor is there, it's in place, and let's trust its channels are open so that we hear God saying to us, "If you have any doubt about assurance this morning, you may have that doubt removed. I want to assure you that you're forgiven and that you are now Mine and that life has been changed."

God, again I say, is the great Initiator. He is the great Communicator. He is the great Lover of our souls.

Now it may well be that there is an analogy or else — and I don't know for sure — there's a thin line between intuition and this business of the Holy Spirit's communication with our spirit. We're in an area here where it's difficult to explain, but where we would lift your expectation that you are so built by God that you can know Him and that you can be assured of Him in your life.

However, we understand it based on biblical promises. Its clear word to us is that the promise of the Holy Spirit speaking to our spirit is a kind of unshakable knowing. It is reminiscent of the blind man that Jesus caused to see, and he was harrassed by cynical questioners and yet in the midst of all that he remained unshaken for there was one thing he knew — "once I was blind but now I see."

Get on with all your cynical questions. I know that I have passed from death to life. I know that I'm a child of God. I once was blind but now I see. And so this unshakable assurance based firmly on the sure word of God rises from its base to soar and to rejoice in a great inward reality.

For those who know not this kind of knowing this morning, John Wesley, the great advocate of assurance, had not only sympathy but he had understanding for those who do not know, who do not have this assurance, and he longed for people to experience that leap from obedient slaves to loving, secure, and knowing sons.

As it appears, the New Testament points and proclaims and invites to this same kind of knowing. Faith is the handle that we have, that we turn in response to the Father's voice in promise, if not in entreaty.

Faith alone, says Wesley, is that evidence, that conviction, that demonstration of things invisible whereby the eyes of our understanding being open and divine light poured in upon them we see the wondrous things of God's love. This conviction, this assurance, rises above our feelings and yet is not forever removed from them.

Luther, I think, was quite right when he said feelings may say to us, "You are a sinner." But he said we have a ready reply, "I know, I know I'm a sinner, but Christ Jesus forgives sinners."

Let me conclude with the famous Aldersgate Street experience of John Wesley. I only wish to quote the second paragraph of his report which is seldom provided in any quotation. Well, you remember the story. "In the evening I went very unwillingly to a society on Aldersgate Street where one was reading Luther's preface to the Epistle to the Romans." (I've always thought that intriguing, that marvelous book of Romans. He was only reading the preface.)

"About a quarter before nine" (Here's the precise Wesley. He'll even tell you down to the minute.), "while he was describing the change which God works in the heart through faith in Christ, I felt my heart strangly warmed." (Now that's the quotation that is used again and again, "I felt my heart strangely warmed.") "I felt I did trust in Christ, Christ alone for my salvation and an assurance was given me that He had taken away my sins, even mine, and saved me from the law of sin and death." (Which is picked up from Paul in the seventh chapter of Romans.)

Now let's correlate the word *strangely* that he uses with his next paragraph. "It was not long," says Wesley, "before the enemy suggested 'this cannot be faith for where is your joy?' Then was I taught that peace and victory over sin are essential to faith in the Captain of our salvation; but, that as to the transports of joy that usually attend the beginning of it, especially in those who have mourned deeply, God sometimes giveth, sometimes withholdeth them (the transports, the ecstasies), according to the counsels of His own will."

Now Wesley is saying that there is usually the accompaniment of feeling, but not always. And what is more important, the inner certainty of assurance rises above the vagaries of our unreliable feelings.

If you read through Wesley you find somewhere in his diary that he recorded that he went to bed feeling just great but he'd had a terrific meal that night. He woke up in the morning and recorded in his diary that he had felt he had hardly any religion at all.

Well, feelings are not a very good thing to go by. He probably would have felt more religious if he had eaten better — and maybe some of you would, or maybe I would, too.

May no one be content with a hand-me-down religion. I think that is what I want to say to you this morning. Let no one be content with something handed down that is only lodged here from your parents or your Sunday school experience, or from whatever. No one should be content with a hand-me-down religion. It just won't work.

Assurance is based on a first-hand experience, a direct encounter — an encounter with Christ who is alive. Assurance then is the product of a living encounter with a living Lord. It forever frees us from believing only what is intellectually passed to us, from parents or others, to the freedom of personal certainty.

The Spirit of God wants this this morning — to grant to each person who is here just such a sense of assurance and security. As I preached last Sunday, forgiveness is no illusion. It is a reality. And so I preach to you this morning that assurance also is the equal and the corresponding reality to forgiveness of sins.

> Jesus Lover of My Soul, Let me to Thy bosom fly.
> While the nearer waters roll, While the tempest still is high;
> Hide me, O my Savior, hide, Till the storm of life is past;
> Safe into the haven guide, O receive my soul at last.
>
> Other refuge have I none; Hangs my helpless soul on Thee;
> Leave, ah! leave me not alone; Still support and comfort me.
> All my trust on Thee is stayed, All my help from Thee I bring;

Cover my defenseless head With the shadow of Thy wing.

Thou, O Christ, art all I want; More than all in Thee I find;
Raise the fallen, cheer the faint, Heal the sick, and lead the blind.
Just and holy is Thy name, I am all unrighteousness;
False and full of sin I am, Thou art full of truth and grace.

Plenteous grace with Thee is found, Grace to cover all my sin;
Let the healing streams abound, Make and keep me pure within.
Thou of life the fountain art, Freely let me take of Thee;
Spring Thou up within my heart, Rise to all eternity. Amen.

Charles Wesley

Backslider

Editor's Note: The following was printed in *Light and Life* Magazine, under the name Henry Lloyd.

My friend's face was a sorry mess. Battered. And ribs were broken. He could not stand straight. He was in pain. A friend of my friend was already there when I arrived. As it developed, he was a better friend for the moment than I could possibly be. Both were members of Alcoholics Anonymous — one a faithful member, the other a backslider.

I just listened.

"Joe (that's my friend), you know what's wrong. You haven't been attending meetings."

Long pause.

"Every time you quit attending the same thing happens. I'd think you'd learn."

Pause.

"You know the value of the meetings. You know you can't do this alone."

My subdued friend said, "Yeah. Yeah, seems like it."

"You know, Joe, you don't need sympathy."

"Well, I don't get any around here."

Long pause.

"Joe, there's something else. You can't go to those meetings and argue and get any good out of it. You got to go with the right attitude. You can't have a chip on your shoulder. You just can't receive any good that way."

Long pause. No response, but you can feel the message hit — thud.

"You know, Joe, I couldn't miss the meetings or go with a wrong attitude without ending up just like you are now. Man, in three weeks I'd be in trouble."

Here was one alcoholic identifying with another. It was cold turkey, straightforward medicine. Tough, realistic therapy.

The friend of my friend just stayed on. Not too many words, but a presence. Not sympathetic. And yet it was help — the kind needed. The kind understood. The inescapable brutal kind of help that was the mark of a genuine, concerned, caring kind of friend. No whine or whimper. A straightforward challenge to change behavior.

I don't know what my friend will do. But I join his other friend in hope.

But something more. I felt somehow I had been witness to a profound lesson for those of us who go to other kinds of meetings, in other kinds of settings. I thought about the attitude I take with me. I thought about the value of regularity. I pondered the support, the confirming I receive. I wondered who — what backslider — I could nudge back into the fold.

In fact, I'm still thinking about that experience and about the work and life of the church. Somehow I haven't finished my thinking. Thought you might like to "think along."

Biblical Grounds for Divorce

The prior consideration asks: (1) How should we understand "biblical" and (2) what constitutes "marriage" in the biblical sense?

What Is "Biblical"?

The primary source for understanding and interpretation is the relevant material in the Old and New Testaments. This is true regarding any issue.

There are other generally agreed upon hermeneutic/interpretive principles. For example: work should proceed from that which is clear. No doctrine should be based on unclear passages. Debatable translations in specific passages should be avoided along with ambiguities.

The context is of primary importance.

The cultural/historical conditions must be known and taken seriously. It must be asked how words used centuries ago in very different situations apply now. What unchanging principles apply now and universally?

A further question may even then be asked, "Can the application in one contemporary situation vary from another?"

In the pursuit of sound interpretation it may also be important to be sensitive to the silences, to what is not addressed. The Bible is not a manual providing sets of specific rules governing every aspect of life. It does provide principles.

What Is "Biblical" Marriage?

A biblical marriage rests on the structure of creation: male, female. It is God's grand idea. It defines the primary relationship among human relationships. Along with the animal kingdom it serves a procreative purpose. But the first goal is companionship and communication. It was designed for completion rather than competition; for mutual love, respect and commitment. The partners were to be bone of bone and flesh of flesh. Indeed, they were to be "one flesh" (Genesis 2:23-24; Matthew 19:4-6).

Marriage is God's lovely way to combat loneliness, separateness and boredom. The marriage partners would be amazingly alike and yet wonderfully different. They would be suited to each other spiritually, intellectually, emotionally and physically. Both their likeness and difference in each area would add zest, excitement and fulfillment. The exploring of each other was designed for a lifetime of adventure. The partners were to be best friends and allies. They were to be mutually helpful.

Commitment is a key word. Three biblical elements compose the commitment: *leaving*, *cleaving*, and *knowing*. In the entire range of human relationships, marriage has priority. It puts the two, now made "one flesh" prior to "father and mother" or any other human relationship. Yes, even children, who are given as a temporary stewardship. The married now "cleave" to each other in the most interdependent relationship of life. They are more than roommates or playmates. They are absorbed in a total commitment without any mental escape clauses. "Cleaving" is neither a passive nor a smothering concept. It suggests an active, continuous cementing process. The third element is "knowing": intimate and growing knowledge of each other in all dimensions — spiritual, intellectual, emotional and physical. It all begins and continues in courtship — never-ending courtship! God's grand idea is to be translated into the consummate experience of life.

A Book About Relationships

The Bible is primarily a book about human relations. For me, the Bible, life and theology are best understood in relational terms. I find groups of any age agreeing that the nature and quality of human relationships are the foremost factors in providing a reasonably happy life.

The Eden story surely begins and accents the importance of relationships and in particular the male-female partnership. The tragedy of ruptured relationships follows quickly on the heels of Eden.

The concern of the Ten Commandments (principles) is for relationships: four vertical; six horizontal, with more than a hint that the vertical is key to the quality of the horizontal. Difference in situational application has always posed problems for individuals and institutions. By the time of Jesus, the Jews were under a burden of thousands of applications to life.

Jesus made human relations His mission. He embraced and refocused the Ten Commands. He put one word at the center: LOVE. He gave it three dimensions. This love is total, responsible respect toward persons: God, others, self. It is a rational commitment.

In word and action, Jesus made war on everything in individual or institution that violated this tri-directional love. He was harsh with religious hypocrisy. He opposed — even to the cross — all that demeaned and depersonalized. He judged rather than excused failures to love and called it sin. He did not excuse sin as a mistake. Yet, He also forgave. In Jesus, we encounter reality therapy. He lived and died to deal with our relational problems.

Examples of the relational character of the Bible can be vastly extended. One example is instructive: the sacrificial system. To us it is ancient and outdated and of little concern until we realize that every ritual had a relational goal — atone, repair, improve, restore. The visual-physical rituals were intended to impact on mind, spirit and behavior. They were like stories intended to influence attitude and act toward God and others. The message of the rituals was for the realities of day-to-day living.

It is significant that marriage is used as the supreme symbol of the relationship between God and His people Israel in the Old Testament and the church of the New Testament. It expresses the level of expected commitment. The commitment of one party (God) is utterly dependable and unwavering. But that does not prevent the possible tragedy of divorce. We will see that this becomes important in discussing biblical grounds for divorce.

Grounds for Divorce

The brief sections above on what is biblical, what is biblical marriage, and regarding the Bible as a collection of writings with relationships as the primary concern prepare us to think about the biblical grounds for divorce.

It is human to want things black or white, crystal clear, with no ambiguities, no doubts, no questions. But the great issues of life often deny us the comfort of dogmatism. So each generation experiences the never-ending struggle of applying unvarying truth and principles to varying life conditions, cultures, and understandings. What a relief if everything was spelled out so we always knew the best of the options life brings our way. The appeal of the dogmatic is almost irresistible.

A violation of the primary conditions of a biblical marriage should justify divorce. Specifically, if any other relationship is given priority and the situation will not yield to counsel or dialogue, an annulment or divorce seems a regrettable prospect. Failure to give priority to the marriage relationship clearly indicates a lack of the necessary commitment and effectively blocks the fulfillment of the necessary components of marriage: leaving, cleaving, knowing. In fact, this failure of commitment nullifies, by definition, a marriage.

It is clear that a biblical marriage commitment requires a genuine partnership. Without denying individuality, marriage requires shared decisions. Unilateral decisions on matters which properly affect both partners constitute a reversion to single (solo) performance and are an expression of a self-centeredness inimitable to a healthy marriage. The biblical marriage is denied. There is no true marriage. Lacking a priority of commitment and partnership there is no real marriage. Two are just living together. The sexual act does not in itself make a marriage a marriage. It is an element in the commitment. Rather, the holistic commitment of two persons (male-female) involving the spiritual, intellectual, emotional and physical areas of their lives constitutes marriage.

The Old Testament addresses the cause for divorce in the relationship of God and Israel. God and Israel were to live together in marriage. The commitment and fidelity of God remained constant. The commitment and fidelity of Israel was defective and often abandoned. Israel is accused of adultery, of whoring. Adultery is grounds for divorce. Yet the sexual act of whoring is not the target of God's denunciation. Adultery, we discover, had broadened application. And, indeed, this comes to the very heart and soul of a real marriage: unreserved commitment to the spouse and the development of a growing rather than diminishing partnership.

So here we come graphically to the grounds for divorce. It is a failed partnership and the nonexistence of a genuine commitment. It is an unwillingness to be a partner. Here is the real culprit. However, this is not the legal definition of adultery. Rather, it is the biblical understanding. Adultery tells the reality of a relationship which has been violated and is now nonexistent. Divorce is the consequence whether legal separation is pursued or not. It is the ultimate word for a preexistent reality.

Finally, the biblical attitude, pronouncement and concern regarding relationships adds another whole window on the subject of divorce. The clue is found in the Old Testament's Ten Commands and the key words of Jesus on all interpersonal relationships. At the base of both clues to Christian attitudes is respect and responsibility. It has negative and positive application to all human relations and certainly to the priority relationship of marriage. In passing, we should observe and emphasize the institutional as well as the individual application.

POSITIVELY, there is in the "commands" and in the condensation/translation of Jesus the call for positive support, concern, care and love for persons. There is an implicit call for sensitivity to the self-esteem of others.

NEGATIVELY, abusive, demeaning, depersonalizing words and acts lead to the destruction of relationships. Domination by one without respect for the other's personhood in a disregard of the needs for partnership are divorcing attitudes and acts.

We generally recognize that abusive behavior is not limited to physical acts of violence. Often the non-physical abuse can be more destructive than some physical acts. And there is no way a case can be made for Jesus' support of such situations.

Yes, Jesus spoke against divorce. But His basic posture is not to be found in His declaration on divorce but in His plainly stated posture regarding all human relations. Jesus made war on all that is destructive in human relations. Place Him at the shoulder of a Christian counselor and it is not imaginable that He would not condemn abusive treatment in a marriage. It is impossible that He would not concur in a decision for one party to divorce when all attempts at repair were exhausted and the abuse did not end but continued and worsened. If a marriage COMMITMENT has never been consummated or has been violated, there must be some point at which divorce is the only way to protect both parties against bitterness, abusiveness, and the destruction of one or the other party. Consummation in this context does not refer to sexual intercourse.

Our Christian instinct has realized the validity of this approach to divorce. Our judgments, in practice, have long since tacitly approved divorce in situations set forth above. It is done with some vague apprehension. We are often unable or unwilling to provide a broad hermeneutic rationale for divorce other than sexual adultery.

Instinctively, we recognize our current culture in the way we think and apply biblical truth. We have done that for years in other cultures of the world. Jesus provides their precedent. His day was male dominated. Divorce was a male prerogative and grossly abused. Women were regarded as little more than chattel. Jesus, upon a direct question, faced but one aspect of His culture and the concern of divorce. Jewish men could divorce with the most flimsy excuse and with hardly any bother. So we must not stretch Jesus' opposition to divorce into a position so legalistic and inflexible as to permit male abuse of a spouse. Neither can Jesus' words provide endorsement of female abuse of a spouse. His primary position on relationships bars any such conclusion. Jesus' words simply do not cover all marital situations directly.

Over time, Jesus' basic attitude has brought women to a new level of recognized personhood. Jesus does not address our society on every subsidiary need. He does make clear the need for respect for every person in every relationship.

Most pastors have found that there are things worse than a dissolution of a marriage. Repeatedly, these questions have to be asked: How serious is the violation of the marriage relationship? Is there hope for change? What will do most damage to the personhood of the marital parties? The conclusion must attempt to apply Jesus' basic attitude regarding all human relationships.

Addenda

(Written while pastor of the Greenville F.M. Church for *The Marriage Book.*)

Marriage: A Grand Idea

Marriage is a grand idea. It is, in fact, God's idea. God created us male and female for completion rather than competition — for mutual love, respect and commitment.

The first goal of marriage is not procreation but companionship and communication. It is God's lovely way to combat loneliness and separateness. God designed creatures both amazingly alike and wonderfully different. It was a plan to meet both loneliness and boredom. They were suited to each other physically, intellectually, emotionally and spiritually. Both their likeness and difference in each area would add zest, excitement and fulfillment if exploring each other carried on a lifetime. They were to be friends and allies. They were to be mutually helpful. In fact, they were to be bone of bone and flesh of flesh.

May your marriage not only be a grand idea but a consummate experience.

Can God Be Trusted?

The famous J. B. Phillips wrote a book entitled *Your God Is Too Small.* Perhaps it needs a sequel entitled *Your God Is Too Mean.* There are current caricatures of God infecting Evangelicalism. I choose my words carefully. Some recurring emphases are, in my judgment, nothing short of blasphemy. There is a new flare-up of the idea that to include the prayer of dependence, "If it be Thy will," when asking for healing, undermines faith, cuts its nerve, provides it a crutch.

Is this really true? Wherever this view is pushed, very soon a condemning-censorious spirit inserts itself into the life of the church, adding a sense of guilt to the illness of those who remain unhealed. Is this Christian?

It sounds so utterly plausible to say that God wants everyone to be whole. Indeed, there is a truth in this; but it is not all of the truth. It is equally true to say that whether we are saints or sinners we live in a world in which the virus of evil is abroad and in which no saint is promised foolproof protection against his environment.

The issue is our view of God. Is our view sufficiently Christian? Can God be trusted? There should be no question in any Christian's mind that God has all the power necessary to do what He wants to do. But God has also accepted a less than perfect world for the drama of His purposes, which are morally and spiritually redemptive — looking toward a future redemption of the entire environment.

I recall reading in my youth the story of Madame Guyon, that wonderful Catholic saint whose story is a classic even for Protestants. She describes in detail how God knocked one prop after another away from her life so that she would learn the central lesson that "salvation is trust." The impact of this concept has never forsaken me. Increasingly I have felt confident in the love, the tender care, and concern of my heavenly Father. I cannot believe that He intends anything but good for me. But neither can I presume to tell Him what that good is. Nor can I assume a self-righteous arrogance which condemns my brother who, living in the same confidence, does not experience physical healing.

True, God intends nothing but good for us, but what is good for us embraces both time and eternity. But in time we live within an environment created both by God and rebellious man. God does not prevent our entrance into the world with unequal sets of chromosomes. He does not always interfere in the consequences of our environment.

Christ, the holiest of all, suffered and died. Paul, the greatest of all apostles, was not relieved from a thorn in the flesh. Both exemplified completely their unswerving confidence in the Heavenly Father. The Christian who demands that God heal the physical is, I fear, praying the prayer of the first Adam, which in essence was, "Not Thy will, O God, but mine be done." The first Adam put his own interests first. Our model is to be found in another garden and with the Second Adam who prayed, "Father, not my will but Thine be done."

Perhaps the unkind things that happen to us in life may be a test of our real confidence in the good will of the Heavenly Father. As a Christian I must, both from the point of view of the biblical record and from that of experience, conclude that healing is both *miracle* and *mystery.* Gladly I accept both aspects of His dealing with His children.

Someday we all must die, but in the meantime I can expect Him to make me whole in the sense of 1 Thessalonians 5:23-24: *"May the God of peace make you holy through and through. May you be kept in soul and mind and body in spotless integrity until the coming of our Lord Jesus Christ. He who calls you is utterly faithful and he will finish what he has set out to do"* (Phillips). And as His child I can ask for healing of any physical or mental disorder in complete trust that He does what is good and best. Hence, I trust Him for miracle but can be content with mystery.

A Case of Identity or Who Am I?

Save me, for I am yours; I have sought out your precepts (Psalm 119:94, NIV).

I call out to you; save me and I will keep your statutes (v. 146).

I will walk about in freedom, for I have sought out your precepts (v. 45).

Please identify yourself using from 50 to 100 words! What do you say? Name, occupation, marital status, education, age, accomplishments, failures?

Between 1953 and 1979, I could have said that I am the general publisher for the Free Methodist Church denomination, that I have done so and so, that I am involved in such and such organizations, that I have received certain recognitions — but would anyone know me by that attempt at identifying myself? Under some circumstances that is important to do, but it does not necessarily reveal who I am.

If you had worked with me, lived with me, you would likely skip all of these designations and labels and speak something more of personality, character, strengths, and weaknesses.

There may be those who never struggled with the matter of their identity. Others have and still do. Many never get to understand what goes on inside themselves, never understand themselves beyond the superficial, never feel secure in their identity, never achieve self-acceptance.

Dietrich Bonhoeffer, theologian and martyr under the Hitler persecution, was aware of his struggle for identity:

Am I really all that which other men tell of?
Or am I only what I myself know of myself?
Restless and longing and sick, like a bird in a cage,
Struggling for breath, as though hands were compressing my throat.

Yearning for colors, for flowers, for the voices of birds,
Thirsting for words of kindness, for neighborliness,
Tossing in expectation of great events,
Powerlessly trembling for friends at an infinite distance.
Weary and empty at praying, at thinking, at making,
Faint, and ready to say farewell to it all?

Who am I? This or the other?
Am I one person today and tomorrow another?
Am I both at once? A hypocrite before others,
And before myself a contemptibly woebegone weakling?
Or is something within me still like a beaten army,
Fleeing in disorder from victory already achieved:
Who am I? They mock me, these lonely questions of mine.
Whoever I am, Thou knowest, O God, I am Thine!

Thou Knowest, O God, I Am Thine!

The psalmist said, *"I am thine, save me!"* Psalmist and Bonhoeffer experienced a like struggle. Their one certainty? They belonged to God.

The struggle, the search for a satisfying identity, will never reach maximum fulfillment apart from the similar affirmations made by both psalmist and Bonhoeffer.

The lack of a satisfying sense of identity has certain common symptoms: sense of inferiority, low self-concept, image, esteem. Results are often feelings of loneliness, depression, sometimes anger, frustration.

One writer makes a valuable distinction for us. Self-concept and image are what we think, feel about ourselves — the attitudes we have about ourselves. While self-esteem is the evaluation we make of our "worth, competence and significance."

Well, how are you doing? If right now you feel like you are not doing so well, you may take some comfort — you have a lot of company.

Maxwell Maltz, a physician whose writing on this subject has become famous, declares an estimated 95 percent feel inferior. It is hard to escape some such feelings. Some such feelings may drive us to succeed. Too heavy a dose may drive us to despair and may, in fact, paralyze! Most humans struggle with a bundle of insecurities, even if they do not admit it.

Paul Tournier said that we tend to divide others into the weak and the strong as we observe them, and that we gather some personal strength because others are weaker than we are. And on the other hand we are intimidated by the strength of those we see as having superior strength. But he says the truth is that we are all more alike than different, that there is an external mask which hides this likeness.

Tournier, in *The Strong and the Weak*, says, "All men, in fact, are weak. All are weak because they all are afraid. They are all afraid of being trampled underfoot. They are all afraid of their inner weakness being discovered. They all have secret faults; they all have a bad conscience on account of certain acts which they would like to keep covered up. They are all afraid of other men and of God, of themselves, of life and of death. What distinguishes men from each other is not their inner nature, but the way in which they react to this common distress."

Each of us is damaged in some way in our "inner nature" and in our self-concept. This is due to the reception by parents and adults in our early life as well as by our peers. Very early our self-image is formed. That image is altered, gradually, by the experience with the widening circles of life as we move into maturity and experience its very own stages of development.

But, we must also note that we are likewise damaged by sin — sin of two kinds — inherited and acquired: the bent for which we have no moral accountability and the sins for which we are answerable.

Too few today are considering sin as the enormous factor it is in achieving or failing to secure a satisfying self-image. If we wish to care for ourselves properly, we must come to terms with this large factor in our lives.

Fortunately, there is help for this sin factor in our self-concept. The **first** part of that help is forgiveness; the **second** part is deep-cleansing of our subconscious by the ministry of the Holy Spirit; the **third** part is being taught to forgive ourselves.

Taken together, there is a built-in protection against continuing to commit the sins we have confessed, so that we do not live a life of confessing-sinning, so that this becomes the habitual posture of our life.

Hindrances to a Satisfying Identity

- Sin — above spoken to.
- Bad theology. Crucifixion misapplied, that implies death to our very personhood. Making a mess out of metaphor.
- Past experiences.
- Unrealistic expectations.
- Introverted thinking: I'm no good; nobody likes me; "they" like others better than me; etc. It is a sign that we are turning excessively inward.
- Cultural influences: status symbols; physical attractiveness — the TV myths.

Helps to a Satisfying Identity

The major helps are religious, theological, biblical.

- A biblical and sound theological perspective on our worth as humans. Creation, Incarnation and eschatological view.
- A biblical view on self-love. Not an attitude of self-centered pride, of superiority, of stubborn self-will, not an erotic or ecstatic self-adoration.

This involves a look at ourself which is realistic. We look at ourself with a concern about what that self is and can become. We look at self as worthwhile, as creatures of value to God and loved unconditionally by God who sees us as a gifted member of the body of Christ (if Christian), as bearers of a divine image. This becomes the basis for building self-esteem.

- Developing self-understanding. Why our acts, our attitudes? Self-questioning.
- Experiencing the genuine support, acceptance, and approval of Significant Others and the body of Christ.
- Realistic self-evaluation. List good traits, strengths, assets, weaknesses, inabilities, and less desirable features.
- Reexamination: Expectations, Goals, Priorities. Use short and long-range goals. Be realistic.

Insights of all sorts do help, but those of and about ourself are indispensable. But it is difficult for most of us to open ourself to ourself, much less to another. For often to do so is to produce dismay, shame. It may hurt and sear. And the more sensitive one is to God, the more keenly one feels his need.

Complacency is dispelled. Our hope is in belonging to *One*

who is able! Our hope is in belonging to *One* who knows us — warts and all — yet accepts, understands, forgives, and stabilizes our next steps. Yes, He will mature us if we permit! Make us whole persons!

While difficult to open ourself to ourself, to others, and even to God, we must. We can make a start by opening ourself to God. The psalmist's confidence is in the commitment he has made to God — *"I Am Thine!"*

Furthermore, the psalmist has responded to God on a continuing basis — *"I have sought Thy precepts."* Included is a promise *"to observe Thy testimonies."* He also believes the results are predictable: *"And I shall walk at liberty."*

The only free man is the man who belongs to God. Then whatever self-confidence, self-assurance he achieves, he recognizes as derived. Confidence does not originate by self-effort, but rather by reliance on God. The same of self-fulfillment!

The sense of identity, confidence and assurance that the psalmist and Bonhoeffer found is the kind we need. Perhaps we can then open better to others, relate better to others, experience true freedom from inner turmoil and tension, and in short, live lives of satisfaction and fulfillment — ever moving toward being a whole person.

Charles Grandison Finney: A Devotional

Editor's Note: In my study I find an abridged copy of Finney's autobiography that Pastor Knox encouraged me to obtain and read sometime in the spring of 1982. His interest in Finney never waned.

You will seek me and find me when you seek me with all your heart (Jeremiah 29:13, NIV).

I pastored in Rochester, New York, and before going there, during, and since, I've been interested in a man for whom this was his personal biblical text: Charles G. Finney. Rochester and the East was the scene of many of his activities.

But let us go back to a young lawyer at age 26 — a lawyer from head to toe. His law book, strangely, made him finally a Christian. In quite a different sense, the law was his schoolmaster to lead him to Christ — different, that is, from the rabbi, Paul!

When at age 26 Finney began practice with a prominent attorney in Jefferson County, New York, he admits he was as ignorant of religion as a heathen. He hadn't heard a half dozen sermons. He had no interest in matters preachers talked about.

However, in studying law, he found old authors quoting frequently from the Bible, especially Mosaic enactments as authority for many principles of common law. This excited his curiosity. He bought a Bible, the first he had ever owned. So when authors cited Scripture passages, he looked them up and reviewed the context. This led to great interest in the Bible.

From then on Finney lived in law books and the Bible. At first the Bible was treated like any other reference book. It never occurred to him to be ashamed of it. *But*, when the Bible began to get to him at a deeper, personal, spiritual level, he became sensitive about it and kept it out of sight. If someone entered his office and the Bible was out on top, he quickly covered it with law books.

However, in the end the Bible won over the law books. It became his supreme court, the final court of appeal, the one solemn tribunal to which all questions were submitted. He said, "I felt myself shut up to my Bible."

Yet, he was a lawyer to the end. He thought as a lawyer, pleaded as a lawyer. He said that he had accepted a retainer from the Lord Jesus Christ to plead His cause.

Vigorous of personality, acute in intellect, persuasive in oratory, Finney was destined for the highest places in his profession. One described his preaching as "logic on fire." So he was effective with members of his profession. He said that lawyers took a more intelligent view of the plan of salvation "than any other class with whom I have had to do."

He believed the gospel was preeminently reasonable, that unbelief was intellectual absurdity and hindrance to man's greatest powers. But he saw a greater logic in Calvary than Sinai. It appealed to his intelligence and conscience. His preaching on two continents usually got the verdict he sought.

No preacher had a part in the conversion of Charles G. Finney. The Bible did it, and one verse in particular: *"You will seek me and find me when you seek me with all your heart"* (Jeremiah 29:13, NIV).

So when the Bible began getting to him, he took it home and read it in secret. It was no longer a book of *reference*, but of *revelation.* He suddenly saw the reality and fulness of the atonement, the work of Christ as full and complete — and for him. He said, "On my part I was to consent to give up my sins and accept the Savior." "Wanting in Him — *nothing!* Wanting in me — *my own consent!"*

On October 10, 1821 the issue became just that clear and narrow. He had been reading before going to his office. He resolved to settle the issue. He went to a thick wooded area outside the village. He had often gone there. He sought the quietest, the most remote spot. Discovering where fallen logs made a sort of sanctuary, he resolved to make this *the* place. He vowed not to leave until assured of salvation.

Finney knelt in prayer. There was no answer to his frantic supplication. Then he heard the rustling of leaves and arose in embarrassed confusion. No one was near. Then, ashamed of his shame, he shouted at the top of his voice. He declared he'd not leave until forgiven "though all men on earth and devils in hell should stare at him. ... To think that I should have been ashamed of being caught in the act of making my peace with my offended God! ... The wickedness of it appeared awful, infinite. It broke me down!"

Like a bolt out of the blue, the passage from Jeremiah shot into his heart. He felt it was surely the Word of God. He said that at that moment he was as conscious of trusting the veracity of God as of his own existence. He said, "Lord, I take Thee at Thy word! Thou knowest that I do search for Thee *with all my heart.* I have come to this place for that very purpose, and Thou has promised that I shall find Thee!" That settled it. He had sought! He had found!

He walked back to the village. It was noon. He spent the afternoon in his office and then went home. These are his words: "There was no fire and no light in the room, yet it appeared to be perfectly light. As I went in and shut the door, it seemed as if I met the Lord Jesus Christ face to face. He said nothing, but simply stood before me; and I fell down at His feet and poured out my soul to Him." And there, in the evening, the work of the morning was consummated and crowned.

"With all thine heart" stood out for him. That he found to be the stipulation of *love.* The one unpardonable sin for Love is apathy. Love wants courting with ardor, persistence, intensity. These were the qualities which were to characterize Finney. With all his heart he believed — labored — preached.

Through his long life he stated his case as an advocate — with penetrating, pitiless, overwhelming logic. But logic on fire. He reasoned with all his heart, *but his heart was hot.* When he preached, wrongs were made right all over town. A Rochester attorney told Finney, "I have been examining the record of our criminal courts and I find that, whereas our city has increased threefold since your visit, there are not one-third as many prosecutions as there had been up to that time."

His preaching with fire stung. There was reaction — angry mobs, plots on his life. Because of friendship with William Lloyd Garrison, the pioneer abolitionist, and his sympathy with the cause of slaves, his church was burned. Firemen refused to extinguish the flames.

Finney was firey, and fire spreads. It was the contagion of the preacher's joy which drew crowds and made profound impressions. This produced a spiritual awakening and ethical reformation.

Dr. Charles Bush said that one year there was an increase of 1,200 new Presbyterian ministers in Rochester as a result of his ministry. Finney's books were read avidly at English and American firesides.

As Professor of Pastoral Theology at Oberlin College, he impressed character upon all his students and infected them with his intense and ardent spirit.

And with all his heart he worked to the end — to age 83! He still stood erect, a fine figure that inspired universal reverence. On a beautiful Sunday evening in the summer of 1875 he didn't go to church. At sunset he walked his wife to the gate to hear music wafted toward them from open windows of the sanctuary. To bed — to sleep. He awoke in the presence of Jesus.

He had sought Him and found Him, for he had searched with all his heart!

Chickens and Humans

"Chickens have a very low capacity for avoidance learning." Carl Sagan, in *The Dragons of Eden*, bases his conclusion from watching two chimpanzees mistreating a chicken. One chimp extended food to the chicken. When the chicken got near the food, the other chimp would thrust at it with a piece of wire it had concealed behind its back. The chicken would beat a hasty retreat. But when the food was offered again, it would try to get the food, only to be beaten once more.

Sagan also concludes something about chimps. They behave much like humans. They cooperate, plan a future course of action, deception, and cruelty.

Well, if chimps are much like us, it also appears we are much like chickens.

We humans seem to have "a ... low capacity of avoidance learning." Shall I translate that? Quite simply we are slow to learn how to avoid a beating. We are so intent on getting what we want that the beatings incurred do not seem to deter us.

Our great-great-great-great- ... grandmother was (shall we admit it?) very much like the chicken. Eve wanted what she wanted despite reliable, expert advice. Her Creator's advice was rejected. A beating resulted.

The Bible is filled with stories of human chickens. It seems we are slow to learn how to avoid beatings in life.

Have you read newspapers and magazines lately? If so, you have witnessed a long parade of human chickens. What is it the Dutch say — "get so quick old and so late smart"?

Does a bad experience with alcohol or drugs keep some humans from chicken behavior? No, indeed.

Do earthquakes keep humans from rebuilding on top of known earth faults? No, sir!

Some human chickens seem to get beaten and burned repeatedly. Why?

Well, the reason can't be found in the comparative size of the brains. Old Aristotle knew enough — and that was a long time ago — to tell us that "of all animals, man has the largest brain in proportion to his size." The chicken's brain is hardly noticeable by comparison. So we could offer excuses on behalf of the chicken — small brain, many beatings!

And we are learning a bit about how marvelous the human brain really is. There are in it more identifiable bits and parts than in that great universe we try to pierce with telescopes. Truly, man is fearfully and wonderfully made.

An updated computer would need to be ten thousand times larger than the human brain in order to process the information packed in the brain. The brain is a densely packed information and retrieval instrument — about ten billion bits per cubic centimeter. Nothing like a chicken!

If the brain does not account for our injuries — injuries which could have been avoided — then why? Why?

There seems to be beyond the brain, a choosing self — something that can either use the magnificent brain or can choose to ignore it.

Something is haywire with that self. It all goes back to Eden. It stems from wrong choices, not from low brain capacity.

Our central problem is one of choice. We choose self-enthronement over placing God at the center of all things. This is the risk the Creator took in endowing us so amply. It is the wrong choice(s) about the use of those endowments which causes human suffering, sorrow, alienation, and trouble of every sort imaginable.

The good news is that God has undertaken to bring us back to Him, which is the same as "coming to ourselves" again. God visited us in Jesus. Jesus died and rose again to stab us awake. God plans to help us to so love Him again that we will use rather than abuse our brains — so that we'll be human, not chicken.

Christ! At the Door or Table?

Behold, I stand at the door and knock; if any one hears my voice and opens the door, I will come in to him and eat with him, and he with me (Revelation 3:20, RSV).

See, I stand knocking at the door. If any one listens to my voice and opens the door, I will go into his house and dine with him, and he with me (Phillips).

Here I am! I stand at the door and knock. If anyone hears my voice and opens the door, I will go in and eat with him, and he with me (NIV).

What graphic, pictorial language! So suggestive! May reflection on the words hang several pictures on your mind. Let it grip your heart and mind.

These picturesque words were originally directed to a group of unworthy Christians in Asia Minor, the Laodiceans — and on behalf of the Lord Himself.

It is the "anyone" of the words that sets it free of time or country. Its plain truth is this: wherever a human heart is closed to God, Christ is just outside gently entreating.

Let us visualize three scenes in these reported words of Jesus:

1. The Shut Door
2. The Door that Opens
3. The Table that Is Set

1. The Shut Door

You may be familiar with the great painting of that genius, Holman Hunt, "The Light of the World." He paints part of the scene from Jesus' words. I saw it in St. Paul's in London, the cathedral which is the creation of Sir Christopher Wren. Recall the scene.

Hunt paints the fast shut door — rusted hinges — rank poisonous weeds overgrowing the door. How well it tells the story of long closure, of retreat from Christ. But our eyes fasten on the Figure standing amid night dews and darkness! It is the patient Son of Man!

Look again. One hand is on the door. The other bears a light. The Hand! The Light! How meaningful! Grace and Gospel are thus illustrated powerfully. He reaches toward us. He lights the way. Everything about the scene seems to wait for light to break through to the outside.

Now look at His face — on it is the look of love repelled, of pity that is all but wasted. Look again at His hand — see the touch of both gentleness and authority, but an authority and a gentleness that can be ignored.

Hunt's "The Light of the World" is the portrait of infinite tenderness, but also of divine and human tragedy. The story of love spurned, of opportunity missed, of rich fellowship rejected.

It is the ultimate in the many stories of "might have been" — the saddest story in any of our lives. And it should remind us of the many "little" but life-determining hinges along the journey of life. Have you ever thought of those little hinges and how differently life might have been had different decisions been made?

Hunt's painting is true to life. It needs painting. It needs re-seeing. The great spiritual fact of our text is that just now Christ is either at your door *or* at your table! Which is it?

Pascal said that we have a God-shaped vacuum in our hearts. There is a significant little prayer chorus, "Lift up Jesus! He's the only One who can fill the void in me." And it is this vacuum, this void that Christ wants to fill.

Christ is what Francis Thompson called the "Hound of Heaven," ever seeking us. Paul says that *"God was in Christ, reconciling the world unto himself"* (2 Corinthians 5:19, KJV).

Christ at our door is a two-fold revelation:

First, it is revelation of His yearning love to each of us. What else can we call that desire to be let into the heart of another? What higher tribute can be paid anyone? Every time we take Communion we should be reminded that He wants us so He can give us Himself.

Second, it is revelation of Christ's infinite long-suffering and patience. Remember again Hunt's portrait. The weeds overgrowing the door speak eloquently of the long closure, the careless indifference.

But despite both rejection or failure to respond, He waits

just outside — the patient, wooing, courting Lord, as though you were too precious to be lost, too valuable to be given up. As indeed you are!

And as long as there is a ghost of a chance — He waits. How long has He been seeking, tapping, wooing? Mercy alone makes the offer of Himself, over and over. Even *now* you do hear His voice.

You may have steeled yourself against knowledge of His love. You may have become deafened by the rush of passion, whispers of self, scurry of business, academic pursuit, absorption in things, lost in social competition.

But He's still there. Hoping some light may get through cracks in the door — the door to your very soul. He's still there speaking. He says, *"I ask you ... open ... let Me in, I want to bless you."*

Have you ever thought that the strange turns and bends in your pilgrimage to eternity may be His calling you? Has nothing happened in your life to cause you to ask, "Does He want me?" He calls each of us to Himself.

Christ says, *"Behold, look, see! If you'll let me into your life I can help you toward joy, fulfillment, self-regard. I can help you where you cannot help yourself."*

Paul says the very mercies of God, His blessings poured into our lives, are *"beseeching us,"* that we should *"yield ourselves to Him as living sacrifices."* It's the way life works best. Oh, that just now we'd join Samuel of old and say, *"Speak, Lord; for thy servant hears you."*

Just outside the door, so near and yet so far!

2. The Door that Opens

We need very much to be reminded that the One outside is not simply a messenger. He comes with the offer of Himself. This is so much more than words, commands, advice. It is the offer of Personal Presence — Love — Life — Himself! Isn't this always best? Letter writing, phone calls, telegraph versus the presence of our Lover!

Again, remember a detail of Hunt's portrait which is a great visual truth — the handle is on the inside! *"If* any man open the door" — exactly, there is the big "If." There is the truth of our personal responsibility for accepting or rejecting. It's entirely ours. Life's important doors are always opened either by our action or response!

You can respond. Nothing can hinder — but you. No one

keeps the door shut but you. You bear total responsibility for its shutness or its opening. You decide to take or reject Him as Saviour and Lord. And you decide even when you say you will not, for the decision not to decide is in fact to decide.

I expect that most try to face the issue by not deciding. But that is the most effective way of keeping the door shut. Very few consciously, openly, rationally, deliberately reject Him. Most *ignore* Him out of their lives. They just sit tight behind the doors or barricades until they can no longer hear the knocking. We are so like the original pair, Adam and Eve, who did not care enough about God to do His will!

And God in Christ is gentlemanly in behavior toward us. He respects our freedom, even when He knows it means our doom — we are men, not machines.

To do nothing is to do the most dreadful of things — for so you keep the door shut in His face. No passionate antagonism is necessary, no violent rejection. If we wish to ruin the potential of our lives, we can — and by simply doing nothing. Bill Sands, in *My Shadow Ran Fast,* declares, "The opposite of love is not hate; it is indifference."

Would you like to open the door? Let me tell you how. It's very simple. But like many simple things, we find them difficult. Trust Him who died on the Cross for you. That implies, requires, a renunciation of self. You cannot let your weight down on Him and trust self at the same time.

Trust Him for the fulfillment of your life, for your sins, for your future, for eternity!

Take by faith, keep by an obedient walk, relationship. Trust Him as the only Saviour, only Lord! Open comes the door — in comes sunshine, purity, cleansing, life — *Life* itself marches in because we receive Him — His presence. He comes as invited by trusting faith. He is shut out by the lack of responding faith. And so we come to ...

3. The Table that Is Set

The coming of Christ to Mansoul is reality beyond metaphor to express! It is the center of Gospel reality. The fact of a living, loving, present Lord becomes our new experience through union and communion with Him — this is all decisive.

Recall Paul's favorite phrase, *"Christ in us."* Indeed He dwells in us so that ...

Into our emptiness — His fullness
Into our sinfulness — His cleansing, forgiveness, righteousness
Into our death — His life
Into our weakness — His strength
Into our ignorance — His wisdom
Into our awkwardness — His grace

Jesus makes a promise, *"I ... will sup with him."* That suggests the desire for close, happy, familiar communication. And recall that it is John recording. He is likely remembering the Upper Room and the loving fellowship, repose and satisfaction experienced there.

But for some there is a problem in setting the table for Christ. We may be ashamed of what we have to offer. The house is a mess, dishes are anything but china, sink is full of dirty pots and pans, furniture is shabby, the linen tattered. Pictures — well, we would not want Christ to see them. And the food? Well, it is meager and of poor quality.

Ah, but that is just where He wants to go. Nothing is so coarse, poor, unworthy but He will receive and transform and use, if love be in it. Oh, how He will transform!

They said of Jesus, *"He has gone to be a guest of sinners."* Thank God! If He was not constantly, presently doing that, where would I be ... and you? What a glorious criticism!

Now we need a word of caution. Be careful who you set a place for in life: Satan, World, Flesh? Expect *consequences.* Set for Christ — expect *results.* Something always happens in either case.

J. C. Furnas wrote on the life of Robert Louis Stevenson. He and his wife trailed over Great Britain, Europe, America, the South Seas to gather material. He wrote, "It has amounted, strangely, to living with the man. As we returned from Edinburgh, talking of nothing but Stevenson during a long ten-day voyage, my wife warned me, 'We will probably be setting a place for him at dinner when we get home.'" A dramatic picture of a dominating interest and how it can affect one.

Emil Ludwig, famous biographer of many, wrote, "If you are to write a real biography of a man, you must eat with him, think with him, live with him." Question! Is Jesus your dominating interest? Does He enter all your life? "Be present at our table Lord. Be here and everywhere adored!"

Do set a place for Him: heart, home, church, work, play — in the councils of men, etc. Will it make a difference? You answer — and indeed you must!

Hear Jesus: *"If any man love me he will keep my commands, and my Father will love him and we will come and make our home with him."*

Now for a kind of fourth act!

This Jesus turns out, strangely, to be — and wants to be — both *guest* and *host*. But He must be guest first in order to be host. Note text: *"I will sup with him, and he with me."*

Recall the post-resurrection scene on the road to Emmaus? Christ is invited in for a simple meal. Then it was *He* who broke the bread. In that act He was known. It is still just like that. We really know Him when He takes over as host in our lives and breaks to each of us exactly what we need.

He brings the feast and furnishes the dwelling. Changes pictures on the wall. Recarpets the floors. Moves in new furniture, new linen, new dishes. You name it, He does it. He does it out of the riches of His grace.

Finally, remember that wonderful first miracle He ever performed. It becomes a marvelous metaphor of what happens when Christ takes over. We hear about it at most weddings, for it was the wedding at Cana in Galilee. He came to the wedding as guest. The wine ran out. That too is a metaphor of so many of our lives. He came as *guest.* He became the *host.* And that is the metaphor — the picture of a reality beyond metaphor.

So the best of the wine was at the last of the feast. Ah, it is true! Reality! The best of life is when He takes over. When Jesus Christ is Lord indeed.

The appeal of the Lord Jesus Himself is coming to you right now, and He is saying, *"Do not keep Me just outside — so near and yet so far, so very far, an eternity of farness. Let Me in! Set a place for Me."*

Where is Christ just now? At your *door* or *table?* It makes a world of difference. It makes an Eternity of difference!

Christian Healing: Miracle and Mystery

As Peter traveled about the country, he went to visit the saints at Lydda. There he found a man named Aeneas, a paralytic who had been bedridden for eight years. "Aeneas," Peter said to him, "Jesus Christ heals you. Get up and arrange your things." Immediately Aeneas got up. All those who live in Lydda and Sharon saw him and turned to the Lord.

In Joppa there was a disciple named Tabitha (which, when translated, is Dorcas), who was always doing good and helping the poor. About that time she became sick and died, and her body was washed and placed in an upstairs room. Lydda was near Joppa; so when the disciples heard that Peter was in Lydda, they sent two men to him and urged him, "Please come at once!"

Peter went with them, and when he arrived he was taken upstairs to the room. All the widows stood around him crying, and showing him the robes and other clothing that Dorcas had made while she was still with them.

Peter sent them all out of the room; then he got down on his knees and prayed. Turning toward the dead woman, he said, "Tabitha, get up." She opened her eyes and seeing Peter she sat up. He took her by the hand and helped her to her feet. Then he called the believers and the widows and presented her to them alive.

This became known all over Joppa, and many people believed in the Lord (Acts 9:32-42, NIV).

Last evening I addressed the subject, "Christian Holistic Healing." This evening I will speak briefly on "James' Ritual for Healing." But we now take an important step in consideration of this important subject. Please note:

Healing as Biblical-Historical Fact

1. Healings are part of the Judeo-Christian tradition. That

many healings have occurred and are recorded in the Old and the New Testaments is a simple matter of fact.

2. But special attention must be given to Jesus' holistic mission on this earth. He healed frequently. These acts were acts of both war and compassion. They were acts of war on all that is unredeemed in human life. They were also acts of compassion. This compassion's ultimate expression was a cross where Christ did something real about our basic human dilemma.

We must not only see His holistic mission. We must see His mission holistically. We have to gain perspective. A thoughtful approach to the record of Jesus' mission can provide that needed perspective.

Jesus did not see Himself as a miracle-worker turning water into wine, loaves and fishes into a super-abundance of food, or healing the blind, or a hundred other disabilities. His primary mission was to redeem us at the core of our personhood, thereby starting the process of total well-being or wholeness or complete health.

His purpose is found in a kind of relational healing. Jesus would continue to impart health and wholeness to us by living in us and extending His health-giving presence to our very neurons. He starts with releasing us from sin and by putting us into the way of right relationships (righteousness).

Ultimately, there is no real health or valid healing apart from the deeper redemptive transformation.

Let us now note several things regarding Jesus' ministry.

A. *The Decreasing Emphasis on Healing* in Jesus' ministry as He moved steadily toward the cross and its ultimate redemptive act. The significance we can attach to healings also diminishes. As conflict with religious authorities increased and as misunderstandings of His mission multiplied, He performed fewer acts of physical healing. John's gospel makes this very clear. In fact, Jesus condemned sign-seeking Jews. He emphasized the redemptive objective of a relationship with Himself and He accented the ethical results.

You can hear Jesus saying that some will not believe even though one returned from the dead. That would certainly satisfy the desire for the spectacular which always exists among humans. But Jesus denies that it would have transforming influence or necessarily be faith producing. After all, Jesus *was* from another world and was rejected by those who should have been more prepared for His appearance among them.

B. *Jesus Rejected Spectacular Means* as a Kingdom way. Jesus' wilderness experience with its rejected temptations is enough to make that forever clear.

Now let us view:

Healing as a Gift of the Holy Spirit

This has two aspects: the individual and the corporate or the healing-gifted person and the healing-gifted church as the body of Christ (dealt with previously in "Christian Holistic Healing"). We are obligated to both recognize and cherish this gift. We have clear biblical teaching regarding the gifts of the Spirit. Note a few items: Each gift is to be exercised under the lordship of Christ and is, therefore, subject to Him. Each gift is intended to contribute to the common good. Each gift is to flow out of divine love as the *controlling* grace over every gift.

The gifts have twin controls: the *love* of Christ; the *lordship* of Christ!

It appears that some gifts may be present at one time and not at another. Healing is certainly one such gift especially as exercised by the individual Christian. The testimony of centuries makes this clear.

This then provides us with a caution: beware of showy or prideful behavior on the part of supposed healing practitioners. There is no place for pride in any gift since *it is a gift!* A gift is never ours in any inherent sense. So when pride enters the Christian character, genuineness, authenticity, spirituality depart. Whatever we have is *given*. Of course there is a sense of contentment and satisfaction when God chooses and is able to work through us, but not pride.

I fear that healing movements are to be seriously faulted with their elaborate, glamorized, man-praising, man-exalting campaigns. My experience and observation over several decades of these exercises in manipulation lead me to see little but spiritual disaster.

Now we turn to observe a variety of understandings of this subject:

Various Interpretations

First, I note that John Calvin and many others since him saw the gift of healing as granted for a short and special period in the history of the church and not intended as a permanent part of the ministry of the church through the ages.

John Wesley, on the other hand, believed that healing was designed to remain in the church and is only forfeited by unbelief. He believed that if the church remained fully alive to her privileges within the grace of God and alive to her potentialities, she would still be able to exercise the ministry of spiritual healing, but not as a substitute for cures possible through medical science and practice. Wesley wrote books on health and medicine. While they were very primitive from a current perspective they reflected the knowledge of his day. He peddled books to his people because he wanted them to be at their best and he did not expect everything handed out by special acts of divine intervention.

We should note that there is current longing in old line denominations for recovery of an earlier faith which permitted an effective healing ministry through the church.

We need also to note that there is a variety of movements which make healing central, if not dominant, in their interpretation of the gospel.

The feature common to this wing of the church is the teaching that healing is in the atonement of Christ in the same fashion as forgiveness and cleansing from sin. But starting with that fine-sounding thesis or assumption one reaches some undesirable ends. In this view, if you are a Christian and are *not* healed it is your own fault. Hence, guilt is added to the burden of illness. In other words, you are equally responsible for receiving healing as you are for forgiveness and cleansing.

I know a former conference superintendent's widow who was fanatically berated when her husband died. It was her fault. She either lacked faith or something was askew in her Christian experience. How cruel! How unchristian! How much a caricature of the Christian's God!

When I pastored in Rochester, New York, we were visited by relatives, a Canadian couple whom we knew but slightly. They stayed for two or three days. The wife confided to my wife that she felt terrible. She said, "I'm sick."

"Why don't you go to a doctor?"

"Oh, I would not dare. My husband would have fits. I don't dare tell him how I feel."

"Why?"

"Because I've been prayed for. I'm supposed to be healed, and I don't dare be honest and tell him how I feel."

The believers this couple were identified with emphasized that illness is the result of demons at work in us or of sin in the individual life or a lack of faith. Jesus made it clear that this is a fallacy. What He taught was far different from saying that sickness is part of the demonic which He opposes and will finally put out of business. Sickness is part of our lot in an unredeemed environment.

Certainly we may with joy speak of healing as the *privilege* of believers within the general scope of the atonement. But certainly not as *responsibility*. We are, indeed, responsible for receiving the benefits of the atonement of Christ in forgiveness and cleansing from sin. And having done so we are usually on the way to physical and emotional benefits. We cannot place such healing, however, on a par with the moral remaking of man.

Another variation on the above approach is found nearer to our own circle, our family of denominations. The teaching goes that it is God's will that we be made whole, that provisions have been made for this so we need never pray, "Thy will be done," and to pray thus cuts the nerve of faith. Again it turns out that if one is not healed the guilt of responsibility is our added burden. So we come full circle. To seek healing is always to seek God's will.

Such interpretations ignore the realistic tensions and paradoxes we face as we look squarely at the Bible and at life.

1. We are in an environment which is both good and bad. Glib and poorly based theories do not banish the realities of evil, sin, death, suffering, sorrow, accident, disaster or a virus-infested environment. We live in an environment damaged by evil and which awaits a final redemption, a time when every atom shall be brought into relationship with Jesus Christ as the center of a new environment: heaven and earth.

God created a good environment. But something having cosmic dimensions happened, so now for us there is labor, sweat, pain in child-bearing, weeds, disease and death. Something is awry in the physical as well as the moral universe. So here we are, surrounded with both a wonderful and good environment and one which is flawed. That is fact.

There is another important relevant factor to be considered. We must remember the picture. God made an assignment to man. It was to have dominion in this environment. We've loused it up! God gave us responsibility to manage the planet for food and harvest, to search for herbs and medicines and on and on. It is part of God's design and assignment of responsibility.

Simplistic approaches fail in full biblical treatment of our dilemma. They fail to say why Paul got "no" for an answer from God not once, but three times. Why is it that the holiest of people have not been healed? Their faith we dare not question. Nor do we dare to make God out as capricious, unreasonable, and in the end an enemy of true faith and trust.

2. Next, we face what appears to be antithetical portraits of God: power versus holy-love. And what of Omniscience and Wisdom?

3. We face the realities of a law-laced universe designed by a Good God. We face the fact that we are not released from these realities because we have become Christian. Heat still burns. Gravity can kill. Cold can freeze. Yes, Christians can be and are victims.

So there are tensions and paradoxes to live with. There is tension between the concept of a God of power and the laws of environment. Why does God permit auto and plane accidents? Why tornadoes and war and tidal waves? Why does He not heal the young who seem to have extraordinary natural and acquired abilities for forwarding the gospel and the good? Why does God heal some and not others? Why are not usefulness and piety always God's criteria for healing? To some these are real, crushing, and often defeating questions.

I came across a bit of anonymous verse that says it for me.

I Don't Need a Why!

I lay my "whys" before Your Cross, in worship kneeling,
My mind too numb for thought, my heart beyond all feeling:
And *worshipping,* realize that I, in knowing YOU, don't need a "why"!

For me, the helpful resolution of questions and paradoxes lies in the acceptance of both *miracle* and *mystery.* I accept both. Yes, God is powerful. It is more important to know that He is Holy Love! He always acts out of holy love plus a total knowledge and ultimate wisdom. That tells me that in every situation God is TRUSTABLE!

He may not perform by standards I can grasp in my finiteness and ignorance. Hence, the basic question for the Christian is not what God can DO, but whether He is trustable.

There is a fascinating Indonesian Creed by the Huria Kristan Batak Protestant Church. Its doctrine of God reads, "We believe and we confess: God is one, without beginning and without end, almighty, unchangeable, trustworthy, omniscient, inscrutable, a righteous Judge, gracious, all bountiful. He fills heaven and earth. He is true, perfect in holiness, full of love."

Then the creed says, "We ... reject with this doctrine the teaching that God's power is greater than his holiness and his love." Well said!

Rest and resolution of tension for the Christian comes as it did with Job with an acceptance of the trust-ability of God and in a meeting with God. In His presence questions fade and perspective is given.

When I trust, I am freed from the uptight, judgmental approach that accuses, "If you pray 'Thy will be done' you really do not believe." I rather fear the assertion of self-will and unbelief which is the cry of the first Adam rather than the second. The first Adam sought his own will. I choose, rather, to follow the Second Adam to Gethsemane and with Him pray, "Nevertheless, not my will but thine by done." There is my model of trust.

When God intervenes I have a *miracle;* when He does not I have *mystery.* Both I accept in trust. It is for me the mystery of inscrutable holy love, of a Father who cares. It is a mystery because my finite mind does not understand. But neither do young children understand parents. However, they learn to trust what must at times seem contradictory behavior. They come to believe a good parent while they may not understand. They do not believe the parent to be simply capricious. God's power provides us with *possibility,* not with the necessity of miracle. And we most certainly should accent the fact that God's power is displayed every moment in our ever-restoring health and in an orderly universe.

The Christian learns to trust the wisdom and goodness of God in the details of life. Trust provides joyous confidence in the design of God for us. See Romans 8:28 and 35-39. We face the world cured of pessimism on the one hand and false optimism on the other.

The Christian Rejoices When Man Exercises Good Judgment

For example:

1. We rejoice when new insight is gained regarding the complexity of our human structure so that more intelligent action can be taken to help and heal;

2. We rejoice when new knowledge is gained regarding health habits including diet, rest, recreation and sanitation;

3. We rejoice when new knowledge is gained regarding diseases in search for cures, i.e., polio, cancer. Or when better treatment is devised for our mental, emotional and physical problems.

4. Or we also rejoice when God acts in His own special ways to heal our attitudes, like resentment, hate, jealousy, and ill memories, or diseases of body or disorders of mind;

5. We certainly rejoice when we consider the promise of newness beyond time and space in what we call glorification. We rejoice that the day is coming when the environment will be redeemed and sin, death, sorrow and pain will end.

But to deny the nature of our present environment makes us appear irrational and cop-outs!

So, what if there is mystery rather than miracle in our own experience of life? When we've gone as far as Bible and reason will take us and haunting questions remain and the journey ends in mystery — what then?

It is, I affirm, a warm and reassuring kind of mystery, not a cold or terrifying mystery. For that mystery lies within the heart of Him who spared not His own Son but sent Him to Calvary for me, for you. The coldness of the universe is gone for the Christian because of Christ. Faced with mystery, we do not merely acquiesce in fatalistic sense or stance. Rather, we accept what we cannot penetrate, resting joyfully and assuredly in the confidence that God's will is best even though we can't pierce it or understand the reasons.

Lastly, let us address the matter of our attitude in the face of mystery rather than miracle.

A Lutheran Sunday school superintendent, a farmer-salesman, sat in my publisher's office at Winona Lake. I do not recall what he was selling. I know that he lived near Angola, Indiana. He told me how some months before he had backed a vehicle over his own small daughter, crushing her to death. I could not even imagine the father's anguish. He talked about it and about his Christian witness. We wept together. He said, "I finally could look into the face of my heavenly Father and ask, "What can I, O God, learn from this?"

This man was not, and nor am I, suggesting that God sent this tragedy as some sort of learning experience. My Christian view of God forbids any such conclusion. But the question is, "Since faced with tragedy, how can I respond so that God can make me a bit taller, stronger, richer in His grace? How can this be used to mature me in my movement to Christ-likeness?"

I rest the case.

The God I know is trustable.

O Jesus of the scars, we give You our wounds for You alone of the gods have scars and wounds. You alone know how to heal our wounds, our scars. We give them to You. Thank You. We trust You.

The Christian Paradox: Eternity Now!

Editor's Note: Given at Light and Life Biblical Seminary, Commencement, April 1965 and at Spring Arbor College, Baccalaureate, May 1965.

Long before our dramatic invasion of space, God the Eternal invaded earth and time. God has not only visited man. He has entered into man himself and added another dimension to life. The values and virtues of the eons to come are manifest in this age. God's future with its judgment and its order has become a renovating force in "the now."

Love, light, life, justice, and holiness, as interpreted in the New Testament, are not the products of man's aspirations. Neither are they abstractions. They are concrete manifestations of eternity in time.

So we face action rather than abstraction, the concrete rather than the general, when we face the Christian paradox: eternity now! The incarnation of God in Christ is the concrete historical act upon which the experience of "eternity now" rests.

My life is given meaning and purpose when the Christ of Eternity comes savingly to my "now." The impact of the eternal, that which is beyond us, is what gives us vision, hope, and drive. God in my life and in the Church is the operating base of eternity in time.

1. Let us look at the way the Christian Paradox operates in the individual.

Florencia Gomez received her Th.B. degree from Light and Life Biblical Seminary in Butuan City, Philippines, after I had delivered the commencement address. She is from a killer tribe in the remotest interior of the Philippines. Her father had three wives and was the area witch doctor.

The people worshipped the devil and were filled with superstition and ignorance. Florencia was in training to succeed her father as witch doctor. She was his eldest and seemed to possess the necessary talents.

In the providence of God, Florencia finally came to Butuan City for a public school education. Invited to a Christian home, she was so impressed by the way they lived and in particular by their returning thanks for meals, that she wanted to become a Christian. She says of her friends, "They led me to Christ so carefully. I found Jesus as my Lord, which was the greatest discovery I had experienced in life."

Her people could not understand what had happened to her and were fearful. Then her father learned he had cancer and had only six months to live. Our missionary, John Schlosser, told me how, with Superintendent Felix Canete, they answered Florencia's call for help and made the difficult journey to talk with Mr. Gomez about Jesus.

They told him the story of Jesus and gave him a pre-tuned radio used by the Far East Broadcasting Company. With good care it might last six months. In fact, both Mr. Gomez and the radio lasted about thirteen months, a remarkable thing in itself. During this time Christ made a great change in him, his home, and his friends.

Florencia has translated two Bible books into her own tongue. They are published by the Philippine Bible House. She is one of their best translators. This June, Florencia goes for advanced training to Union Biblical Seminary at Yeotmal, India, so she can more effectively minister to her own people.

It was a thrill to see her receive her degree. It is a great joy to know that other members of the family are coming to the seminary at Butuan City. Florencia stood before me on commencement morning, April 26, 1965, as concrete evidence of "eternity now." She is not an isolated miracle. She is typical of the results of the Eternal manifest on earth.

2. In History.

About twenty centuries ago this new life began to manifest itself in Palestine and then spread throughout the Roman Empire. It not only changed the lives of men; it changed or created new institutions; it transformed the social climate by giving dignity to the dispossessed and the disinherited. It improved the condition of slaves, women, and children. It set a new course for history and brought a breeze right out of another world into this one which was smothering in its own evil.

People talked about the kingdom of God, the church of Jesus Christ, eternal life, redemption, salvation, love, judgment and justice, holiness and mercy. They not only talked; they lived so that they were called "people of the Way." The ancient and pagan virtues were reversed. A new order was introduced into a decaying world. Men without hope found hope. Meaning and purpose suddenly appeared where there had been boredom and nothingness. The world was turned upside down. This is the way the paradox operates.

I have tried to describe the Christian paradox which is "etenity now." Description demands definition. A new and radical way of life demands explanation. Hence, much of the New Testament is concerned with explaining the paradox. Eternity manifested itself in the lives of people, in historical events, and in institutions. It still does.

3. A Paradox.

A Christian soon learns that paradox — seeming contradiction which in reality is no contradiction — is at the heart of his life, his basic beliefs, and his Book. The Bible poses insurmountable problems to any mind which cannot entertain a paradox, and this inability has created theological division. A good example is the paradox of the sovereignty of God and the freedom of man. The Bible simply asserts both truths.

There are many biblical paradoxes. But the ultimate paradox may very well be the concept and reality of our topic — eternity now! Yet it may be argued that it is the outgrowth of the paradox of God's sovereignty and man's freedom. Because God is sovereign, He invades time. This is His decision and act. But because man is free he may limit or forward the purpose of the invasion. He may receive or rebel.

But I speak of "eternity now" as *the* Christian paradox because it is the nearest, the most practical, and most meaningful paradox for us at the level of daily life. There is a sense in which the entire New Testament was written to explain, extend, and make real this unique experience.

4. Incarnation is central.

Jesus is at the center of the paradox, even as He is at the center of the Bible and life. He is the supreme reality and symbol of the paradox. God in the flesh is the full expression of a new dimension within time. In fact, He is the Paradox. He has brought into time, a new dimension, a new quality and action. The destiny of the universe is set on a different course. It is precisely that important.

5. The Paradox is social.

The Incarnation is more than a theological or philosophical concept. It is the *act* of a personal God relating himself to time and people so neither can ever be the same again. So we must never separate the words Jesus spoke from the paradox. We keep this in mind when He speaks of the kingdom of God.

Jesus provides many verbal angle shots of the kingdom. Each begins with the words, *"The kingdom of God is like."* By the series of pictures He gives, we get a fuller portrait of the kingdom. The kingdom is the age which is to come made present.

The kingdom is the term used for the social aspects of the paradox. Jesus in the Sermon on the Mount asks you to plead for and expect "eternity now" by praying, *"Our Father in heaven, hallowed be your name, your kingdom come, your will be done on earth as it is in heaven"* (Matthew 6:9-10, NIV).

Extreme dispensationalists like C. I. Scofield, editor of the well-known Bible bearing his name, declare the Sermon on the Mount does not concern the church in time, but gives the laws that will apply in the future millennial reign of Christ on earth. He writes, "It gives the Divine constitution for righteous government of the earth, whenever the Kingdom of Heaven is established ... the Sermon on the Mount gives neither the privilege nor the duty of the Church."

If Dr. Scofield was right, then Jesus was wrong in teaching us the disciples' prayer. I believe Jesus meant His words to be taken seriously.

6. The Paradox is personal.

Jesus spoke in personal as well as social terms. He talked of *"eternal life,"* and He said, *"The kingdom of heaven is within you."* The Apostle John says that Jesus came that we might not perish but that we might have eternal life. He records Peter's great affirmation regarding Jesus, *"You have the words of eternal life"* (John 6:68, NIV).

Jesus states categorically that He gives *"eternal life"* to those who become vitally related to Him. In His high priestly prayer Jesus observes that the Father gave Him power for the purpose of giving eternal life. He says, *"Now this is eternal life: that they may know you, the only true God, and Jesus Christ, whom you have sent"* (John 17:3, NIV). It must be noted that in the New Testament, *knowing* God is more than knowing *about* God. Its primary meaning is that in *knowing* God we are *united* to Him.

The terms "Kingdom of God" and "eternal life" concern neither the extension nor duration of time; nor is the primary concern the future. They *do* speak of a dramatic *new* thing in time — a *new* quality, a *new* dimension, a *new* relationship, and a *new* activity.

7. The Paradox in the New Testament.

The Christian paradox, "eternity now," pulsates through the New Testament. John in his Gospel deals with the great themes of light, life, love, resurrection, and judgment. He gives contemporary meaning and application to these eschatological themes. He makes it clear that the absoluteness and finality which are part of the great last day belong also to time in Jesus' earthly ministry and now in the Church.

The light, life, and love of the age to come is the gift of Christ through Himself who is Light, Life, and Love. These are exotic qualities, even as Christ is an exotic Person. Eternal qualities do not grow here — not in any New Testament understanding of the terms — nor are they in us naturally. Paul, for example, wrote that the love of God was shed abroad in our hearts by the Holy Spirit.

John relates light to judgment. Christ revealed that men love darkness rather than light. He stated plainly, *"For judgment I have come into this world, so that the blind will see and those who see will become blind"* (John 9:39, NIV) — and there is another of Jesus' paradoxes.

The great fact is that the judgment of the last day and of the Man who shall judge is brought now to bear on us, on society, and on the race. Christ is now Judge. The world, not Christ, is on trial. Even His Church comes under the searching, reviving light of the Lord.

John relates life to resurrection. While the raising of Lazarus was symbolic, the resurrection of Christ is the ultimate sign of life through Christ in the present and forever. These are relevant, contemporary though eternal truths.

The tragic human drama and the divine intention toward man required that features of the age to come be transferred to this world. Nothing less than such an act of grace and mercy could reverse the prevailing order of darkness and death. A new fresh breeze — the very Spirit of God — blew across our death valley. New and exotic seeds were planted on our earth planet. The new breeze, seed, and life is from the age to come.

The future has suddenly become present without doing away with a yet fuller future. And this is the message which was able to dispel the gloom of the ancients in their overwhelming concern with death, and of the Greek Hellenistic society haunted by the spectacle of "a process by which all things pass into nothingness."

The paradox is expressed in other ways in the New Testament. All the expressions add up the same. The very qualities of the "age to come" are effective now. Christians are not conformed to this age but are transformed by the invasion of the eternal which renews their minds. And indeed they are nothing if not new men.

8. The Paradox creates tension – difference produces tension.

The insertion of eternity into time creates tension, struggle, opposition. Adjustment and accommodation are not Christian terms. We are not called to a tensionless life. A recent *Time* essay on "The Worldwide Status of Democracy" said, "Perhaps the biggest single obstacle to the spread of democracy is that at its core lies a paradox — the tension between freedom and order, between the individual and society" (*Time*, April 23, 1965).

Christians must learn to accept the fact of tension created by the introduction of the foreign "eternal" into the native "time." We are not called to a tensionless existence, to adjustment and accommodation. We are called to be redemptive rebels, life and order changing persons.

9. Jesus accepted and used tension.

The current emphasis on "peace of mind" can end in spineless living. Jesus was most poised when much opposed. He did not accept "life adjustment" as a criterion for success. Remember, He said: *"Do not suppose that I have come to bring peace to the earth. I did not come to bring peace, but a sword"* (Matthew 10:34, NIV).

He also said: *"Anyone who loves his father or mother more than me is not worthy of me"* (Matthew 10:37, NIV). And this is set in the context of Matthew 10:38-39 (NIV): *"And anyone who does not take his cross and follow me is not worthy of me. Whoever finds his life will lose it, and whoever loses his life for my sake will find it."*

Christians have frequently accepted a false picture of a Jesus meek and mild. Remember, Jesus was tried as an insurrectionist, and died a death reserved for the worst of criminals. He was regarded as a threat to vested interests. He was too dangerous to be allowed to live.

He was a menace to civil and religious order. All He was and all He taught were recognized by selfish men as a protest and threat to the evils that blight and degrade. Remember, He drove money changers out of the Temple, violated a current code by healing on the Sabbath, and placed persons above institutions. So He had to go! Indeed, Jesus was involved in the life of His age so much so that it cost Him his life.

10. There is tension in involvement.

We are not called to a life of non-involvement. People write us at the Publishing House and ask, "Why talk about the race problem or sex?" We are advised to stick to the gospel, stay clear of problem areas and remain postureless. This monastic attitude is a denial of all that Christ lived and taught. When we touch any live issue or sin of our day, immediately we get letters branding us as "communists."

The spirit that killed Jesus is still alive in the world. And as in Jesus' day, it is found among the respectable of society and religion. Incarnation means involvement, and both mean tension. And I assert that tension is both healthy and necessary in a world like ours.

11. A search for concrete answers makes tension.

Tension comes from an attempt to resolve the question, "How can Christians bring eternity to bear on the present?" Some time ago I wrote an article entitled "A City Troubles Me!" I was encouraged to discover that others were haunted by the needs of the metropolis. Today I can say another thing with new personal meaning, "A World Troubles Me." I packed what seemed a year of living into fifty days as I completed a round-the-world swing. The Christian task, I confess, looks more formidable than before.

I can see the multitude of Egyptians walking on the highway between Asyut and Cairo as they make their annual pilgrimage to graves of relatives; the Holy Week pilgrims in Jerusalem kissing holy places, rubbing handkerchiefs over them and wailing at the thought of Jesus' suffering.

I can see the poverty and filth of Egypt, India, and Arab refugee camps. I am amazed at the moving masses in railway stations in Tokyo and Osaka. Once again I see the "H" blocks of high rise apartments in Hong Kong where a minimum of five people occupy a space 10 by 12. Again, I hear throngs moving day and night, night and day.

How do we make eternity relevant in a complex world of many cultures, customs, beliefs, institutions, and practices? Can we reach, not masses, but the individuals who make up the masses of people? Think of the babel of languages. Face the superstitions, cynicisms, and varieties of materialism.

Perhaps the concern of most people in the world is not communism, democracy, civilization, or Christ, but how to get a meal and a place to sleep, or how to provide for a family. The mind reels from the task of imagining even an approximate answer. Easy answers will not do.

12. Greatness declines in the absence of the Paradox.

A look at past glories provides no clue. There is abundant evidence of past greatness. Start in Luxor at the temples of Karnak and Thebes and across the Nile at the tombs of the ancient kings. For me, here is the evidence of grandeur and skill surpassing that of Athens and Rome.

Note the ingenuity, skill, artistry, organization, and heroic adventure that have preceded us by millenniums. But their glory is gone. Heroic deeds have given way to museums. Civilizations have come and gone. There is no hope for the recovery of ancient splendors, magnificence, or dominance.

The decay is pitiful. Why does greatness wane? A number of years ago I made extensive research into the supposed causes of the decline of the Roman Empire. The causes were multiple. But I suspect that underlying the lost glory is the fact that the efforts and the vision of each civilization were encased in time. There was no eternal dimension.

I wholeheartedly applaud and appreciate the products of man's genius in art, sculpture, education, science, government, industry, and other creative efforts. In fact, I bow in reverence before God because these products clearly mark man as belonging in a special way to the Creator. Man is clearly endowed with special equipment to contemplate himself in relation to the world, to others, and to deity.

Man is endowed with creativity like unto his Creator. Indeed, he is made in God's image. The reach for the Eternal is, I believe, evident, though in different forms, in both the ancient and modern worlds. But that reach, unaided from outside, falls short, and decline is inevitable.

Our civilization can decline. Cities with great universities can disappear. Science can retreat to a new dark age. Our standard of living is perhaps the most fragile thing in our hands. So to save whatever is worth saving we must have a concern and vision that go beyond culture and civilization.

Our biggest job is to improve man rather than to add to a growing list of space accomplishments. That job is impossible without tension between the eternal and the present. This tension is creative and revolutionary. It is the only hope for that which is basically new, progressive, and revolutionary.

The Incarnation is then the only sure clue to the present or the future. It is both the symbol and the reality of our indispensable help. In fact, our paradox is the only way to an understanding of past, present, and future. Under this reality it is clear God has a cosmic purpose which He is in the process of fulfilling through Christ and His Church.

But no civilization has hope without relating its every feature to Christ. No person has hope apart from Him. For in Him all things "consist" or hold together. Apart from Him everything falls apart.

13. The Church and the World live in tension.

Paul in the Ephesian letter says that God has placed all things under Christ's feet, and has appointed Him *"to be head over every-*

thing for the church, which is his body, the fulness of him who fills everything in every way" (Ephesians 1:22-23, NIV).

So Christ shares with us the Paradox and its destiny — a very sobering truth. Christ and Paul said it in many ways: You are the light of the world; you are the salt of the world; you hold in your hands the very word of life.

You, the class of 1965, can move out into the world as part of the answer if God has moved into your life. However, this is no easy thing. It requires the intelligent and dedicated devotion of minds and bodies. It means a critical and constant evaluation of concepts.

Good and pious people can be so terribly wrong and short-sighted that they fix their entire attention and energies on ants, while elephants tramp over them. Some can see the anachronisms in other cultures, religions, and practices (for example, in Moslem lands and India) but fail to see their own crippling concepts.

Our heritage can be our bondage unless we go back to our roots in the New Testament. But even then we must be reminded that the New Testament finds its source in the encounter of men with the Eternal. The same sources are there for us to touch.

There is some pride for the Arab that the language of radio and press is still the pure, divine, and unchanging language of the Koran. But it is quite impractical, for language cannot be frozen. The ordinary Arab speaks the vernacular and finds the classical difficult. This we recognize as a barrier to progress.

There is a beauty in the maneuvers of the colorfully robed guards and well-groomed horses on Whitehall just off Trafalgar Square, London, as they go through the ritual of guarding a palace long gone. And every tourist wants to see the changing of the guard at Buckingham Palace, but the pomp reminds one of a vanishing empire.

There is expectation as one steps into Wesley's Chapel (the Westminster Abbey of Methodism), stands in his pulpit, kneels in his prayer room, and visits the bedroom where he died. But the power is gone. Many regretfully report that British Methodism is now considered more liberal theologically than most of the Church of England.

Remember, God is always in the act of doing a new thing. We need an anchor to the past, but we also need an expectation of the fresh winds of God constantly wafting eternity into time. God is always making new wine that cannot be kept in old wineskins.

Dr. Paul S. Rees said, "The beginnings of great movements, whether political, social, or spiritual, are never the same as their on-going. If they are to live on, they must return again and again to the sources from which they sprang, and adapt themselves to the new circumstances and fresh challenges which they will inevitably face."

There is tension between that which has become customary and that which is necessary at the moment. Very often we succumb to the familiar, the cozy, and the comfortable. Anything else may simply be too painful.

Many Christians live with a pitifully limited, narrow, and inhibiting view of the life of Christ. They are bogged down with trivia. They remind one of a person spending all his waking hours absorbed in contemplation of his big toe. He is unable any longer to relate himself to his environment.

This is a day for concern with how to become involved and articulate in bringing eternity into time. No lesser concern is worth our energies. Satan is happy if he can sidetrack us into false piety and false holiness.

Dag Hammarskjold found a faith that held him in probably one of the world's most difficult jobs. He found a balance between action and piety. He stated the secret for any generation when he wrote, "In our era, the road to holiness necessarily passes through the world of action." Nothing monastic in that! You are called to live in two worlds, and tension is part of the price and the privilege.

14. The call of the Christian Paradox.

Finally, what is the call of the Christian paradox, "eternity now"?

A. The Christian Paradox calls you to be committed.

It calls for an unconditional surrender to Christ who is the Paradox. This commitment involves every area of life. It involves your past in forgiveness, your present in cleansing, and your future in service.

B. The Christian Paradox calls you to be conditioned.

You must be willing to be conditioned by the Eternal. You must resist being squeezed into the mold of our own age. You must be sensitive to the breezes of God, to the Holy Spirit himself.

C. The Christian Paradox calls you to be creative.

God is not through with his creative task, but is even now expressing himself in redemptive creativity. The challenge is for you to be partner in this creativity. The new spiritual frontiers loom in never-ending vistas. Be open to the voice of God through Scripture, by the Holy Spirit, and in the temporal events. Be ready to respond to the new under the leadership of the Holy Spirit.

D. The Christian Paradox calls you to be courageous.

If you will make eternity relevant in time it will take courage. It may require your very physical life. It could mean for some the surrender of an ecclesiastical head, of an educational career, or of acceptance in a community. It takes courage to be relevant. Anyone can decry sins of which none are guilty.

I was jarred by a book title I saw on display in a little bookshop window on Trafalgar Square in London. It read, *Contraception and Holiness.* I do not know what the writer had to say, but I do know that the title was a symbol of the attempt to relate eternity or holiness to life as it is lived now, and this is essential.

E. The Christian Paradox calls you to be involved.

Christians are an involved people. This, again I say, is the message of Incarnation. We are involved with the world in its sufferings, not only as fellow-sufferers but as physicians.

A friend said this of Dietrich Bonhoeffer's involvement in the life of his country, Germany, under the Nazis. Despite pacifistic leanings, he realized that "the sin of respectable people reveals itself in flight from responsibility." So he could not avoid involvement. It cost him his life.

Our very faith requires our involvement. Someone wrote:

"Faith is an affirmation and an act
Which bids Eternal truth be present fact."

For those caught up in the paradox of "eternity now," there is no escape from involvement and no desire for escape. Courage is not the lack of fear; it is the pursuit of the right despite shaking knees. We are called to shape the world, not escape the world. The future can be a better one because *you* have answered the call.

The Christian's Realistic Hope

The Bible presents the kingdom of God as a reality which is present and future, individual and corporate, actual and ideal, internal and objective. It is a comprehensive kind of concept. Its many-sidedness at first glance is confusing, but if one continues to search for meaning the significance finally emerges in all its multi-dimensional splendor.

Thy kingdom come!

Our prayers, "Thy kingdom come," must not shut out any of the magnificent scope intended. Let the prayers begin with me. Let God have full command over life. Let His rule be *the* rule. For the Christian, this prayer is a request for the lordship of Christ to be extended and deepened within the pray-er. In this there is an underlying priority — a kind of unspoken understanding that the external world is changed by first changing our internal world.

How the world is changed

There is no biblical endorsement of those who would change the order — those who seem to believe that by changing the external world you make men new. Indeed, the world — the external world — needs changing, and desperately. But we must remember that in the temptation battles of Jesus, the short route was rejected.

The world is not changed for the better by the resources and forces of man. The world is changed by what must first be an inner revolution. Attitudes, priorities, values, motivations must first be changed. It is impossible to change these and not have that change reflected in the outer world. But to change men by changing the social order is a pipe dream. And we are hurting because this kind of reality has fled so many churches and church leaders.

But let no one find too much comfort in these words believing they can retreat into quietism, into a religion that is consumed for private edification. We must translate our own Christ-transformed inner world into the realities of the outer world. That is a hard, rational, thinking task to be powered by the love of God shed abroad in our hearts by the Holy Spirit.

The church's opportunity

The church appears to have a greater opportunity than it has had in a long time to bring hope, meaning, and significance to the lives of frustrated, angry, depressed, hopeless persons. We must intersect them at the points of these needs. They are not interested in our second-rate sociology, economics, or politics. They need a hand that reaches within and touches and heals deeply so that life is never the same again.

The church is sure to suffer if it fails the needy questing crowds. Christ wants to set up a new kingdom now and within each person. In this is hope for the individual, for society, and for the future.

Realistic and total

Ours is a realistic hope because it refuses the rope of sand offered by humanism and materialism. Rather, our hope is based on the victory of Calvary and Resurrection. Calvary is God's method; Resurrection is God's result. The church's power will be the power of that Resurrection, or its weakness will be evident to observers if not to communicants.

Our hope is cosmic — total. God has undertaken to put Humpty-Dumpty together again. He has taken on a cosmic and racial task. He will not fail.

The Christian's Three-Fold Knowledge

W*e* ***know*** *that any one born of God does not sin, but He who was born of God keeps him, and the evil one does not touch him.* ***We know*** *that we are of God, and the whole world is in the power of the evil one. And* ***we know*** *that the Son of God has come and has given us understanding, to know him who is true; and we are in him who is true, in his Son Jesus Christ. This is the true God and eternal life* (1 John 5:18-20, RSV).

John comes here to a kind of summary. He tells us of the wonderful things we know. They are:

1. The certainty of our security
2. The certainty of the most important of our relationships
3. The certainty of the Incarnation and its significance for us.

John is writing with the Gnostics in mind who denied the Incarnation and claimed special mystical knowledge. Gnosticism developed into a rather elaborate way of thinking and was heretical. So this provides the clue to John's use of "**know**" and the accent on the incarnation of God in Jesus of Nazareth.

1. We know the certainty of our security (v. 18)

"We know that anyone born of God does not continue to sin; the One who was born of God keeps him safe, and the evil one cannot harm him." So we know (by experience) our security against sin, against the evil one. This is all because the Incarnate One, *"the One who was born of God keeps him safe."* Our security is based on the significance, the reality of God's Only One, His only Son.

Our birth is from above. It is therefore not natural that we should sin willfully or knowingly or continually. It is not our habit to sin. Since our spiritual birth is of God, it should be made easier to have the victory and to be "overcomers." We live **above** the world, the flesh and the devil. *"You have been born anew, not of per-*

ishable seed but of imperishable, through the living and abiding word of God ..." (1 Peter 1:23, RSV).

The next word sounds like we keep ourselves, but that is not the meaning. The meaning is that God's Son, born to be our Savior, keeps us. Of course there is a sense in which we keep ourselves unspotted from the world.

We enter into a life-long partnership with the Son of God, which keeps us secure. We cease to conform to the world. We begin to be transformed by the renewing of our minds. So we live lives that prove that *"good and acceptable and perfect will of God."*

The evil one cannot touch him or cannot harm him. Literally, it means "cannot lay hold of us." He may touch us but he cannot take hold of us and keep us in his grip. He can't harm us. We are principled and prepared against the fatal touches, the sting, of the wicked one.

This whole verse is not a mere narration of the duty or practice of the regenerate. Rather, it is an indication of our power by virtue of our regeneration. So what wonderful security is ours: Victors over the flesh or self; victors over the Devil, the wicked one. All of this is not by our virtue but by the virtue of our being born of God.

2. We know the certainty of our relationships (v. 19)

"We know that we are (children) of God, and that the whole world is under the control of the evil one." In this we find ourselves in two relationships — to God, and to the world.

These may be simple statements. But they should be taken seriously. It is a wonderful thing to know we have had a second birth. We are God's by creation, but we are now His by a special grace that makes us His own dear children, being molded into His image.

Our first and foremost relationship is vertical. How many of us try to navigate without constant reflection on our vertical relationship, our upward relationship? Our relationship is alive, real, joyous, profitable, necessary and commanded. What a blessed certainty!

But that is not all we know. It is not all we need to know. We need to be world-wise, as in street-wise — a kind of sixth sense that guards us from attack. We need to know the nature of our spiritual environment. So John says that we know the whole world is under control of *"the evil one."*

In other biblical language there are two kingdoms: of God and of Satan. Only God's is enduring. Satan's is doomed. Fallen Babylon has within it the seeds of its own destruction. Wickedness is opposed to God, and so are the values, the systems of this world. We can have no accommodation with this world.

The Scripture says that Christ *"... gave himself for our sins to deliver us from the present evil age, according to the will of our God and Father; to whom be the glory for ever and ever. Amen"* (Galatians 1:4-5, NIV). Those who have not been translated out of darkness — the world — dwell wholly within the sphere of Satan's dominion and, what is more, they lie there in evident helplessness.

3. We know the certainty of Incarnation (v. 20)

"We know also that the Son of God has come and has given us understanding, so that we may know him who is true. And we are in him who is true even in his Son Jesus Christ. He is the true God and eternal life"(NIV).

This is, as mentioned, John's reply to Gnosticism. It affirms that God's Son became incarnate, enfleshed. The Incarnation is absolutely basic to our faith and practice. Because Christ came, we have understanding. We have a disclosure of God — his mind, heart, intentions. And He reaches to us very personally.

So our knowing of God is not a speculative exercise but a living experience. We know because we have encountered Him, received Him and allowed Him in our lives. It is far more than to know about Him.

The experiential nature of this knowledge is further accented by the words, *"we are in him."* So close and vital is our relationship that only such a mystical expression of intimate relationship can describe it.

We are in him *"who is true,"* who is reality above all realities. He is God above all other clamoring gods. And He is eternal life. So the way to eternal life is by union with the Christ. Not only is He the living God, but He **is** life itself — the Source and the Giver of it!

"... keep yourselves from idols" (1 John 5:21, NIV). Let God be God! Keep Him and Him alone on the throne of personhood!

Christmas Meditation

I've been to the land of our Lord three times. First at Easter time, next in June, and the last time in January. And at this time of year it is but natural that scenes of that land flash on my mind — present day Israel and most of all thinking of it in terms of what it was when Jesus was born in Bethlehem, grew up in Nazareth, and ministered in Judea and in Galilee.

I shall never forget the full moon of Easter, the Catholic mass just outside the walls of the Old City at about the southeast corner. It was truly a night of spiritual reverie, of thoughtful communion. There was a combination of mood and meaning that shall never be forgotten.

I was there in January 1979 with my wife who was advancing through the stages of Alzheimer's disease and who most of the time hardly knew where we were. But every once in awhile she would take my arm and say with a sense of awe, "This is where Jesus was." If the trip did nothing more than that for her I have no regrets for the difficulties encountered on the way.

And I wish we could all close our eyes and see that land now with its slopes, hills, grass and plains. I wish we could envision Bethlehem's dirty streets and then the barren stretches — or so they seemed to me — where the shepherds dwell. How do they ever make it? They do, and they have for centuries.

What I hope is that we can in our busy modern swirl of events stop, get quiet, and meditate. Make these days ones in which we experience a rebirth of **wonder**. **Wonder** as we ponder the heavens. Step outside. Take time. Drink it in. Think of the Great God of space and planets and solar systems, of universe or universes. God of the macrocosm and God of the microcosm. God of the infinite and infinitesimal and God of Bethlehem.

We deal so constantly with hard facts, with computers and math and science and political matters. We face unrest and tragedy. Every time we open the paper or tune in the TV news we face another dose of an earthly, and often sordid, sort of reality.

Let us take time to consider **mystery**. Life is composed not only of hard facts but of mystery. The mysteries and the wonders of life are many. We need time to think about them.

And most of all, we need to take time to think of the **wonder** and **mystery** of the Christ Event. There is so much that is extraordinarily ordinary that should catch our attention in these days.

Who but the God of the Cosmos, the God who is Father could have designed the method whereby He would take on Himself human flesh and experience all human experience? How, if we were God, would we have done it? With hoopla, fanfare? Would we bypass palaces and the pomp and circumstances of the great and mighty?

BUT what did He do? He came through a virgin mother and a helpless babe. He came to simple shepherds on Judean hillsides. He directed others with a star. That and the singing heavenly hosts were rather spectacular, weren't they? But it was all really mostly unspectacular!

Why make announcement to shepherds? Why go rural? Why not a city center? Why not Jerusalem? What clues about Himself was God giving? Was He trying to tell us that He loves us, however ordinary we may consider ourselves or our tasks in life?

Why a manger, and that borrowed? *"Foxes have holes, birds have nests, but the Son of Man is without a place to lay his head"* (Matthew 8:20, paraphrase). That is another scriptural portrait of the God who came to live among us in Jesus Christ.

We know the stories well. Let them ignite afresh our imagination, our **wonder**, our **awe**, and finally our **love, adoration,** and **worship**. Let Incarnation speak to you this Christmas Season!

Communion Service

(Free Methodist Church, Greenville, Illinois)

Lord's Prayer for Disciples

Our Father

What joy we share as we call You, O God, Our Father. As we look at Your Son's cross we see into Your heart.

Thank You for loving us.

Thank You for wanting us as Your sons and daughters.

Thank You for hanging in there with us when we have not deserved it.

Thank You for all the promises You have spoken to us, especially the one made precious by your Son —

"Behold, I am with you always to the end of time."

We turn our will in submission to You: Teach us; guide us; help us to grow tall and straight and useful (pause).

Our Father Who Art In Heaven

We see heaven as that upward pulling atmosphere of love and joy and peace that You create, Father, for us as our special environment.

The environment which makes our earthly living livable.

Yours, we believe, is a heaven that "comes down our souls to greet, while glory crowns the mercy seat."

And we thank You for enveloping us — if we will have it — in a heaven to go to heaven in.

Thank You for the upward pull — Your pull on our persons, on our lives.

Keep pulling us upward and onward.

Forbid that we'd let the earth-drag exceed the heaven-pull!

Hallowed Be Your Name

We want our lives to holify Your name, to lift it up.

We do not want a thing in us to bring Your name down in the eyes of any observer.

We want Your Name to be the Name above all names.

We want You to be the number one Person in our love, our aspirations, in our hopes.

We want to help make You the star of earth's human/divine drama — the leading Actor on the scene.

We even dare to pray that it may be so.

Your Kingdom Come

We know, Father, Your Kingdom comes only as Your Name is hallowed.

We do not want to postpone the coming of Your Kingdom to a far off, distant year.

We want to help Your Kingdom to come now.

We want the rule in life You intend to begin now in our boys, our girls, our youth, in our homes, in our businesses, in our socializing, in our church assembling. Let it begin in me!

Father, we see much where Your Kingdom holds no sway.

We are saddened.

We are grieved.

We want to change all that.

We want to know how to hook on to a partnership with You in extending Your Kingdom in the here and the now.

Your Will Be Done

This, Father, may be one of the tougher lines You've given us.

We too often find *our will* preventing Your will.

Father, we are looking at Your Son's Cross and we know Your will is best.

Keep us from self-deception.

We see Your Son kneeling in Gethsemane. We hear the words of our great Second Adam.

We *are* listening, Father.

Yes, we hear those words: "Let this cup pass — nevertheless not my will but Yours be done."

Make us followers of Your Son, our Second Adam, so that we can say and mean His words.

Forbid our falling into the first Adam's words, "My will be done!"

Take a new hitch on our will right now, Father, make them more nearly Yours than they've been before. *Thanks!*

Your Will Be Done In Earth, As It Is In Heaven

O God! Help us to mean it.

Let me hear it as "on" earth and "in" earth.

In society. In me.

We seek the actualizing of Your will, Your kingdom in history and in personal experience.

Give Us This Day Our Daily Bread

Father! We have so much. We are tempted to see this as the unessential prayer.

Remind us of those who have neither bread for body, nor food for soul.

Continue Your earthly and spiritual blessings in their daily flow to us.

We acknowledge with gratitude our dependence on You.

We would not have it different. Accept our profound gratitude.

What a Provider You are, Father.

Thank You for food for the physical.

Thank You for food for our inner being.

We don't want to take this for granted, a matter of course.

We rejoice in our dependence.

Forgive Us Our Debts

Father, they are so many!

We don't even want to think about them.

We'd rather push them down and away from us.

But give us the honesty to acknowledge them.

And the humility to seek Your forgiveness.

You died for this. With our heads we know it.

Help us now to feel it.

And help us to feel also the assurance of Your forgiveness.

Joyfully we seek this, but not in our own name.

For we are bankrupt.
We plead, rather, Your Son's Name.
Thank you!

Forgive Us Our Debts, As We Forgive Our Debtors

But we protest, Lord.
You've now made forgiveness conditional.
You are saying that You can't forgive unless we do.
That, dear God, is a tough word.

You'll have to give us grace that we don't have, to accept this word and to do it.

We know, we are now looking at the cross of Jesus.
I know, we know what He said from there:
"Father, forgive them for they know not what they do."
Father, that seems very generous. They did know, Father.

We need You to help us see and accept the profounder truth that Jesus spoke.

You'll need to give us a very special grace if we are to measure up.

You know how tough this one is You've handed us.
So help us forgive so we can be forgiven.

And Lead Us Not Into Temptation

We know that you never do.
We know that life tests us.
May we know Your help to cope and win.

Deliver Us From Evil

Evil is our environment. We need Your deliverance.
Evil is all around us in persons and in institutions.

Make us partners with You in defeating Evil wherever and whenever it appears.

For Yours Is The Kingdom, And The Power And The Glory, Forever. Amen.

It is Your Kingdom.
It is Your Power.
It is Your Glory.
We are glad it is all Yours and that we are Yours.

Lead on, O King Eternal!
"Your cross is lifted o'er us;
We journey in its light:
The crown awaits the conquest;
Lead on, O God of might. Amen."

Creedless Christianity?

We gladly went with our hosts to their Baptist church in Iowa. "What association does your congregation fellowship with?"

"I think they are General — no, they are Baptist General —"

Since he was not certain, I asked, "Where is denominational headquarters, Chicago or Evanston, or — ?"

"No, I don't think so. Really, I guess I don't know. You see (and he smiled), I'm just a Christian; not too much a Baptist."

Many — maybe most — churchgoers would resonate to this approach.

Does it matter?

I just read in a book presenting the creeds of the church through the centuries that Christianity was *never* creedless. The attempt to be creedless has always ended in failure. Virile Christianity is creedal. It is certainly not enough to recite the creed together or to know our articles of religion. But if the things we believe — or should believe — ever reach our nerve endings, it must begin with knowing and understanding.

Creeds are what we confess, what we believe. It's what we say and how we say that which is essential to our Christian faith. But our creed is never really ours until it is incarnate, enfleshed. So our creed is not only what we say. It is what we live. It is what we'd die for.

So through the centuries, the church has exercised great care in how it has stated its belief. Those of us who work often with words are made aware of how tricky they can be. How often we have not been understood in the same way we understood our words!

Some people complain that historical struggles over the creeds have been too technical. But if one is ever involved in an attempt to put the creed into words for himself and others, sympathy for those who went before us in the task develops rapidly.

The care with words in the creeds was and is necessary. Perhaps one of the greatest threats facing Christianity now is its creedlessness. What you believe about God, man, sin, and salvation makes a difference — often an eternal difference.

Head and heart are more closely related than some persons seem to believe. Ultimately, the heart will not follow a fuzzy head. Normally, the heart ignites by what the head feeds it. In turn, the heart drives the mind. When mind and heart get their act together, then effective action is next on the agenda.

If the Free Methodist Church is to be alive, well, and moving, it must know and practice its creed. I recommend frequent reading of our Articles of Religion. They get quickly to the heart of our commitment.

Doing Good

Jesus, the greatest of teachers, taught by modeling. He said, "I am among you as He who serves."

One of the most dramatic moments in the life of Jesus and His disciples occurred at supper time. I think He feared that a central teaching had not been fully understood. And He was near the end of life on this planet. What He would do must be done quickly. So He washed their feet.

He wanted them to understand the symbolic act. "Do you understand what I've done to you?"

We may well wonder how well they or any of us understand, accept, and practice what Jesus deliberately modeled. Jesus *accented* service. He *dramatized* service. He *lived* an entire life of service. He *died* a death of service. Jesus modeled and Jesus taught.

Matthew records Jesus' picture of the judgment for us. It's a strange and fascinating drama. The Judge sends some persons to the right, others to the left. Each group registers surprise. Perhaps there would have been no surprise if they had been congratulated or condemned for what they did about law observance, or membership in the Jewish race, or temple devotion, or generous contributions to the temple programs.

Rather, the focus is on simple acts of charity. It's on humane, thoughtful, caring behavior. Behavior reflects attitudes and values. But behavior is observable and measurable. True, God sees the heart and must certainly judge motivation. But again, our acts are reliable indicators of what's inside us.

The behavior, blest and blasted, is open to most of us. See how simple and demanding are the services commended at the Judgment:

Need	**Service**
Hunger, Thirst	Food, Drink
Stranger, Naked	Took in, Clothed
Sick, Prisoner	Looked after, Visited

It requires awareness, sensitivity, and willingness to respond to needs. Behavior is a measure of the response. It indicates respect for persons.

The drama recited by Jesus had familiar elements for His Jewish hearers. The "Son of man" is the language of Daniel's prophecy (7:13-15). The simile of judgment (sheep — goats) is as old as Ezekiel (34:17). The white sheep symbolize the pure apparel of the righteous; the black goats, the dark deeds of the wicked.

But with the familiar elements, Jesus does one thing which would be strange to His hearers. He emphasized "my brethren," which in the New Testament is equivalent to "Christians." Eternal life is promised to those who show kindness. But compassionate kindness among the Christian fraternity is an essential symbol for the viewing world. If men are to be won to Christ and the church, they need to see the benefits demonstrated in the community which bears Christ's name.

Of Jesus it is recorded, "He went about doing good." Blessed are those who follow in His train.

A man was severely handicapped as a result of a farm accident. Relatives did little to care for his needs. Except Jenny. Even though she lived farther away than the others, she came and cared for him. Often he mistreated her. He even removed her from his will. Still she loved him and served him.

Death finally came, and the unattentive kin callously collected the estate. Jenny got nothing. It didn't matter.

The years have passed and Jenny still goes about like Jesus — "doing good" for anyone she finds who needs help. Her smile is contagious, her spirit cheery. She feels very small (she said so) in the presence of most other Christians or leaders. But in reality she is one of Jesus' pure, white sheep. She may not get public attention, but there is yet the Great Judgment. She'll probably be surprised and honored.

I know other people who think and act for others. They are outgoing and giving persons. They don't have much time to develop neurosis. So they do have a present blessing. And the best is yet to be.

Each of us may well ask, "Whom do I model?" Or, "How will I fare in the Great Judgment?"

Emotional Stress and Spiritual Development

(Summary and steps to emotional well-being and spiritual maturity.)

Self-concept and self-image indicate the thought, attitudes, and feelings we have about ourselves.

Self-esteem is the evaluation one has of his own worth, competence and significance. The first is description, the second is evaluation. What is first and second? Actually, in our mind, they overlap. They can change with experience. They can be hung onto in spite of evidence that we have in fact changed. Self-concept-image-esteem have great influence on how we think, act, or feel despite a conversion experience with Christ.

A biblical view: sins and failures dot our human landscape, but while the Bible acknowledges this fact, it does not demean our profound personal significance in God's view. Both creation and redemption assure us we are of great worth, significance and value. Would God spend Himself on us if this were not true?

We are loved of God. We are made in His image and even though that image is marred, He respects the damaged product and does everything He can to remake us. This remaking is by both spiritual crisis and maturing process.

By grace-faith we find a new life and new relationship with God in Christ. This forms the base for reprogramming which is a process and may take longer for some than others. The rate of reprogramming likely depends on how deep our hurts and infirmities are and how responsive we are to the process of reprogramming.

Sin is the result of disruption of relationship both vertical and horizonal. Sin, in fact, is the violation of those relationships. The consequences are found in *guilt, anxiety, fear, anger,* and *frustration;* and in turn these can lead to depression.

Let us now differentiate between pride and self-esteem. Pride is arrogant. It assumes it is superior and hence disregards others in their opinions and desires. It has an exaggerated desire for notice and praise.

Self-esteem seeks always for an accurate self-understanding and appraisal. It is considerate of the opinion of others. It can acknowledge imperfections, frailties, realities, weaknesses, while at the same time recognizing gifts, potential, abilities and achievements. The person with high self-esteem recognizes that all the good which he claims is God-given. The humility of self-esteem gratefully acknowledges dependence on God, but does not indulge in self-negation or dismissal of God-given strengths and abilities.

The Bible teaches proper self-love. Jesus calls for it in His three Commands and Paul echoes it in Ephesians 5:28-29.

Feelings of Inferiority: The sources are faulty theology, sin, past poor experiences, poor parent-child relationships, unrealistic expectations, faulty thinking and community influences.

Things We Can Do

1. *Be honest with and about yourself.* Remember, you may not wish to disclose your strengths, even to yourself, for that will create a higher demand upon yourself. Some prefer to wallow in their weaknesses, shortcomings, and inferiorities.

   A. *Make a list of your weaknesses, inabilities, less desirable characteristics.* Ask yourself, "Is this what others think about me? Have my experiences shown this list to be accurate?" Write these down and keep them available in a notebook or elsewhere.

   B. *Make a list of assets, gifts, strengths, good traits, commendable behavior patterns.* Ask the same question as above.

   C. *Start writing how you can take steps to strengthen your strengths,* use your talents, and reduce your negative features.

   D. *Honestly assess those areas where it seems you need reprogramming.*

2. *Re-examine your expectations, goals and priorities.* Consider long-term/short-term goals and priorities. Write these down. You'll need to refer to these to help you evaluate progress. Determine that you shall become a better person, more satisfying and acceptable to

yourself when you look in the mirror, regardless of how another may view you. Break goals down into manageable units so you can measure your success. Be sure in this process to consider the worthiness of your *motives*. Self-esteem is improved by having goals and by having praiseworthy motives.

3. *Seek self-understanding.* Do you understand yourself better than when you started this odyssey? Will you continue to read and reread to strengthen and expand your self-understanding? Beware of allowing introspection to damage your self-concept. Don't indulge in self-flagellation!

4. *Find honest supporters, encouragers.* This may not be easy. Do not select those who tell you only what you want to hear. A real support person(s) will help you to be honest with yourself and at the same time give you the support you need. Do not permit yourself to make negative statements about yourself, expecting your friends to deny your negativism. Check yourself against seeking this false sort of comfort.

5. *Avoid the tendency to negative thoughts and statements regarding yourself and others.* Accent the positive.

6. *Practice specifics which help you respect others.* Pay honest compliments, give encouragement, give respect in all the ways you can to others, who are made in God's image. Others have as great a need for encouragement as you.

7. *Practice real listening, genuine communication.* This is not as easy as you may have supposed, but once you increase your capacity for listening and communication you will discover that it smooths and supports interpersonal relationships.

8. *Use the Bible in specifically supportive ways.* Hunt out those positive, supportive scriptures. Organize them to be available for special times and specific instances of need. The help is there. Dig it out. Use it. You may locate little booklets with verses arranged for this purpose. Ask for such aids at your Christian bookstore.

9. *Stop exposing yourself to destructive influences* — i.e., sin which generates guilt and leads to depression and loss of self-esteem, negative talk, critical spouting parties, and unforgiving influences. Maurice Wagner in *Sensation of Being Somebody* identifies destructive tendencies which alienate us from people, prevent spiritual development, and lower our self-esteem.

Some tendencies are manipulating others, which means that

you treat them as objects; resenting painful and unpleasant circumstances; being angry when control of a situation is lost; resenting humiliating happenings; giving up when proven wrong; being paralyzed and unwilling to act when afraid; dreading problems instead of accepting them as challenges. Which of the above do you need to deal with in utter honesty?

10. *Give thanks for the Christian perspective on what it means to be human.* Secular humanism sees man as little more than a highly developed animal. The Christian sees man as of worth in the eyes of God. God has been actively demonstrating His love and care. He has invested heavily in us. Dismiss those well-intentioned but erroneous accents in the church which build inferiorities and lead to depression.

11. *Cultivate a positive perspective in the following areas:*

A. *The world and life experiences.* Look for the good, the positive in the world about you. Accent the beautiful, the good that is happening around you, what is good in people.

B. *Yourself.* Think of all the good aspects of your person, capabilities, etc. Learn to appreciate and thank God for the good in yourself and the good you can share.

C. *Cultivate hope!* The Bible is a tremendous "hope" source. Look on today and tomorrow as opportunity, adventure, possibility, rather than frustration or despair. Remember that pessimism is a child of depression; depression fosters pessimism, so it goes around and around. Let *hope* fill your mind.

D. *Changed thinking produces changed feelings.* If you want to feel differently, start thinking differently. You CAN!

E. *Cultivate trust in God.* Check out every anti-trust urge that comes your way. Get rid of it by affirming your trust until it wears a groove in your thinking pattern.

12. *Practice praise* especially to God, but to others also. Most of us are short on praise. Praise works when we have unhappy feelings. Praise is called for by James when we are feeling happy (5:13). Use scripture to express praise. Use the hymnbook to assist in praising.

13. *Practice prayer.* Again James admonishes us to pray when we are in trouble (5:13), when illness comes our way, when we

experience sharp mood swings. Pray the prayers written by others. Look for those which express your feelings and meet your needs. Write your own.

14. *Employ confrontation.* You have the right and the responsibility to let your feelings be known in interpersonal relationships. Nothing is solved by enduring in silence and nursing hurts. Each party should learn to handle honest confrontations of feelings. Feelings that get buried and which lie unexpressed become an increasing supply of dynamite waiting for an explosion. The expression of feelings should come when the parties involved are rested and rational.

Ejection from Eden

Ejection from Eden is a vivid, ancient story. Some have understood it symbolically. Others understand it as a real event on a given day in our human saga. Either way, it is powerful. What gives it power?

It is a convincing picture of our *racial disaster.* Somehow, we gather a very personal feeling of being the sad inheritors of that event. Almost instinctively, we get a sense of being this side of Eden and that, somehow, that is to our distinct disadvantage. We may very well feel saddled with a handicap — a handicap for which we do not bear responsibility, but nevertheless a handicap with which we must cope or make some kind of accommodation.

There may be another reason for its power. Do we not get a feeling that in some sense we are reruns of the story? While not being at all sure of what that primeval paradise experience was, we get a sense of also being ejected from Eden. So Eden becomes *symbolic* in a true and powerful fashion. We are inwardly torn by the loss of Eden — an Eden we really never had — a kind of racial ghost.

The sense of ejection is perhaps strongest when we face reality, when we come closest to knowing ourselves. Do we really want reality? Do we really care to know ourselves?

If ever we do, we are thrust from the comfort of make-believe, of self-deceit, of false security and into the dilemma of ambiguity.

What's that?

We know ourselves as neither gods nor animals; as neither autonomous nor automatons (neither free nor coerced). We leap for the stars; we sink beneath the animals below us on the creative scale. We have the saint wish and the sinner bent. That's ambiguity — and it hurts. And we retreat from what hurts.

Paul felt ejected from Eden.

Paul got a true glimpse of himself. He didn't like the reality he saw. He saw his tornness. There was the good, the bad. When he thought he'd chosen the good, he discovered there was another dimension: power, self — what was it? — that thwarted performance. Indeed, it seemed almost like a "sub-self" or other self, which fouled up the computer. It was like an inward static which erased the good input on the computer. It was like an imbalance in heat and humidity that played the same trick! But the trick is finally and embarrassingly discovered. You then wonder if you can trust the computer!

Paul faced reality: the ambiguity of his situation. But not with despair.

Ernest Becke (*The Denial of Death*) says that "to be born again ... means for the first time to be subjected to the terrifying paradox of the human condition." Certainly that is part of it. But there is more. In the midst of the "terrifying paradox" which Paul describes even more graphically as "the dead body attached to me and bringing me to death" — in the midst of that! — there is a vision of vertical intervention. Into the human paradox, the horrible ambiguity, comes the wonderful, marvelous grace of God. To the cry of Paul and each of us — *"Who will deliver me from this body of death?"* (Romans 7:24, RSV) — comes a shout, the shout of the new born: *"Thanks be to God through Jesus Christ our Lord!"* (Romans 7:25, RSV).

Ejection from Eden! All its mystery is personally resolved, for *"There is therefore now no condemnation for those who are in Christ Jesus"* (Romans 8:1, RSV).

Ah, that is the therapy of the grace of God which every mortal needs. But even when we have experienced the therapy, we are like members of Alcoholics Anonymous: We can take nothing for granted. Living back in Eden requires the moment-by-moment experience of the grace of God in the fellowship of our beloved Therapist, Jesus Christ our Lord! Again, thanks be to God!

Free Methodists: Reformers as Reflectors and Reactors

(Prepared at the request of the World Methodist Historical Society.)

Historians are expected to evaluate and portray persons and movements within the matrix of their own historical period. Harsh judgment regarding Calvin's role in the Servetus affair must be tempered, for example, by understanding that "tolerance" was an attitude as yet unborn. And we should not sneer (smile perhaps) at Wesley's small book on medicine. I found in it a good source for healthy laughter.

I recall that my mother had a large medical book, *The Perfect Woman*, written by a woman M.D. around the turn of the century. Our family found it immensely interesting and amusing. But it was full of insight regarding the state of medicine in that period and the attitudes of women. I found it helpful in my attempt to understand my mother's fear of pregnancy and things sexual.

We may, returning to Wesley, discard the outdated medical notions which he reflects. We cannot as readily dismiss his practical concern for his world parish. He wanted to help the poor and hence condensed for easy reading and wide distribution the medical wisdom of his day.

Any branch of the Methodist family may discover and discard quaintness found in the family tree. But we are enriched by the historical "search and separate" process if we will have it so.

I recall assigning a clergyman the task of making selections from the writings of our leading founding figure. I wished to publish the best of B. T. Roberts' ideas.

My clergy friend was appalled at some things he discovered and said, "Some things he wrote ought not to be repeated now." That may have been so, but each generation has not only the right but the obligation to evaluate and learn from their own roots.

Free Methodism began as a reforming movement hoping never to leave its mother. But it can readily be noted that history bears witness to the tendency among reform movements to reform too much. Some are surprised, certainly most Free Methodists, to find that Calvin, as well as early Free Methodists, banned musical instruments from worship. In this respect, Geneva must have resembled worship as I first experienced it. Free Methodists got around to reforming that part of their early reform by first permitting the use of one instrument and only one and finally opening the door to anything from Jew's harp to violin to organ.

Parenthetically, some of us who have lived through these changes may be permitted to observe that we now take less personal responsibility for singing in the congregation. I no longer hear the exhortations to sing with both the "spirit and the understanding," nor am I treated to the leader lining a hymn, that is, reading it line by line for thoughtful consideration.

Happily, our founding leaders understood the ongoing need for change and renewal. They deliberately provided the means in the original constitution. They did not make it easy; they did make it possible. We may too easily join those who can find the faults of our predecessors. But the failures viewed from the vantage point of the lately come 20/20 vision should be fully considered in their historical context. Furthermore, we should appreciate the motive and what has enduring value.

A Free Church

The reforming motif, I believe, dominated our founding. To understand the nature of the reform envisioned, it is necessary to see the founders as reflectors and as reactors. First, they reflected rather accurately social and political ideas which were gaining currency.

Second, they reacted to change which they identified as decline in the parent body. So these early Free Methodists provided a mixed portrait. They were conservative in doctrinal concerns. They wished to maintain Methodism in what they viewed as the true Wesleyan pattern. In ecclesiastical policy they were seeking revolutionary change.

Faced with this seemingly contradictory reform movement,

the designation "Free" comes to have overriding significance.

In the years of my pastoral experience I moved from Southern Michigan to the old Genesee Conference to be pastor of its downtown Rochester First Church. Here I was in the area where controversy, conflict, and finally organizational separation began. I heard my members speaking of us as "The Free Church." "Methodist" was not used.

It had been a long-standing custom in that area. I became newly aware of just how significant "Free" was in our denominational name. Indeed, the designation can only be understood, in its full meaning, in the light of social, political, economic, and ecclesiastical conditions and ideas of the time.

The founders, following in the train of Wesley but motivated and molded by things American, were keenly sensitive to the wide range of concerns gripping the minds of churchmen and citizens. They were socially and politically alert and sensitive. But there existed an equal concern and sensitivity about the perpetuation of the essence of Wesleyan doctrine. They were therefore bound to resist what they saw as signs of slackened commitment to the theological emphases of John Wesley from whom they took their cues. Coupled with doctrinal concern and part of the conservative mix was alarm regarding the shift in lifestyle to what was deemed "worldly" involvements, dress, and amusements.

Free Persons: Slavery and Masonry

Unless persons were free, institutions were in danger. A lack of personal freedom could only result in injustice and coercion. Slavery was an assault on the dignity of the individual for the benefit of the privileged. Masonry's invasion of church politics was dangerous because it found its members in secrecy. They were no longer free. And that very lack of freedom led to secret rather than open politics in the affairs of the church. It was essential that all persons be free if there was to be health in society, politics, or ecclesiastical matters. It was this logic, which the founders believed to be expressions both of a biblical theology and the growing concern for fully representative government, that gave impetus to the name "Free."

The advocacy of freedom was no mere ideology. The principal founder, B. T. Roberts, actively assisted in raising money in order to buy the freedom of slaves.[1] For a brief period he belonged to the Know-Nothing Party. He was attracted by its strong anti-slavery position along with its call for free and liberal educational institutions for all classes and sects. He saw the party as a means to assist in the struggle for human freedom, but he finally came to the conviction that this involvement was hindering his spiritual development.[2]

However, he continued in his ministry of speaking and writing to advocate in strongest terms freedom for all persons. Zahniser, in *Earnest Christian: Life and Works of Benjamin Titus Roberts, 1824-1893*, notes that Roberts' editorials in *The Earnest Christian* gave encouragement to Lincoln to make "emancipation" an issue on a level with "union."

In the May 1862 issue of the magazine, he wrote, "Leaving slavery still in the body politic, is like emollient plasters over an eating cancer in the human body; they may hide something of deformity, and for a moment diminish acuteness of suffering; but the policy will only leave time for the cancer to deepen its roots, extend its area, and bring in increased suffering, with inevitable death. The only safe course is to cut out the cancer, dry up the thing."[3]

It seems clear that Lincoln was much more devoted to union than to freedom. However, when in the judgment of Lincoln the military situation made it possible to express a political view on the issue of freedom, he did so. That movement arrived in the summer of 1862, in the same year that Roberts had made his appeal, when Lincoln issued the Emancipation Proclamation document. Roberts greeted the announcement with enthusiasm.

Roberts' writings consistently echo Wesley who wrote, "Give liberty to whom liberty is due, that is, to every child of man, to every partaker of human nature. Let none serve you but by his own act and deed, by his own voluntary choice."[4]

Only six days before Wesley died, he wrote to William Wilberforce urging him on in his reform activities, "Go on, in the name of God, and in the power of His might, till even American slavery (the vilest that ever saw the sun) shall vanish away before it."[5]

The church was agreed in its posture. An excerpt from the 1866 *Discipline* is convincing. "The Golden Rule, Free Methodists hold, applies equally to the colored as to the white race. The first Free

Methodist Church ever organized was in St. Louis, a slave-holding city, and at a time when slaveholders were freely admitted to the churches generally. (Organized early spring 1859, more than a year before the formation of the denomination.) Yet they made non-slaveholding a test of membership, prohibiting, as they ever have done, 'the buying, selling, or holding a human being as a slave.'"

In sharp contrast, the Northern Methodist General Conferences of 1836 and 1840 took position against abolitionism and defined their churchly task as that of "spreading scriptural holiness" rather than to "divert Methodism ... to questions of temporal import involving the rights of Caesar." The latter conference declared that owning slaves should not bar admission to any level of ministry. It refused to hear a minority report on abolition.

The northern church placed institution above human freedom, even as the politicians usually placed union of the states above emancipation. Biographer R. D. Clark says of Bishop Matthew Simpson, "He approved abolishing slavery so long as it did not injure the institution of Methodism."[6]

Methodist churches both North and South had slaveholding members until the Civil War. Not until 1864 did the northern church vote in General Conference to "restore to its General Rules a clear-cut prohibition of slaveholding, and refer the same for ratification to the annual conferences."[7]

Leslie R. Marston, author of an interpretive history of our denomination, has documented the dominant concern of Methodist leadership in this period for the preservation of the great institution of Methodism and its fear of abolition sentiment as the destroyer of unity. He notes that despite the cautious and pragmatic approach to the slavery issue, disunity resulted. The Wesleyan Methodist Church was formed in 1843 as an abolitionist secession. This was quickly followed in 1845 by the organization of the Methodist Episcopal Church South. The policy of compromise was also a factor in the 1860 formation of the Free Methodist Church.[8]

The Earnest Christian (August 1860) carried a call for an organizing convention to be convened at Pekin, New York, on the 23rd of August. It was a call for a "Free Church." Three items were identified as the basis for possible organization. Number three stated simply and directly read, "No slaveholding, and no connection with secret and oath-bound societies."

The responding lay delegates were three times the number of clergy delegates. This convention did in fact formally organize the new denomination. Given the delegate distribution, it is no wonder that item two in the call read, "An equal representation of ministers and members in all the councils of the Church."

The founders embraced a holiness teaching free of pious passivity when faced with personal or social expressions of wrong and evil. They did not agree with those noted holiness leaders who promoted holiness of heart and life but deliberately restrained followers from bringing the slavery issue into their religious pursuits and gatherings.

Phoebe Palmer is a notable example of holy passivity. Dr. Nathan Bangs, president of the Ministers' and Laymen's Union of the Methodist Episcopal Church, was another opponent of abolitionism and advocate of moderation regarding the slavery issue. A reporter for the *Northern Independent* (June 13, 1861) observed that even at that late date, "Methodist D.D.'s are tender of the feelings of slave-holders."

Roberts labeled such holiness as "spurious." There were no prayers for the liberation of slaves nor testimonies against this "sum of all villainies" in the meetings of these promoters of holiness passivity. "Holiness," he wrote, "is not indifference. One who is truly holy does not feel that he has done his duty by simply abstaining from sin."

Marston in a special appendix to his volume of history provides examples of the intense and continuing social and political concerns in the early story of the "Free" church. The annual session of the Illinois Conference, September 1865, following the Civil War, laments the assassination of Lincoln. A fascinating paragraph summarizes the course and end of slavery. "At first in the history of our country it was simply *tolerated,* but like every other sin it speedily claimed the *right* to exist, then it stood at the baptismal font, witnessed a good confession and was taken into the church; then it assumed the control of national affairs, and attempted the foul usurpation of power at the expense of right. Its power, its religious character, its right to exist are gone, and its presence is no longer tolerated in our land. We recognize the hand of God in our delivery and attribute all the glory and success to Him."[9]

The same conference demanded the vote for the freed slaves.

It called for a constitutional amendment to guarantee to every person civil rights regardless of "his creed, condition or color." It called for a program to educate the freedmen "morally, socially, religiously" to make amends for degrading acts of the past. It called for the removal of "the remaining spirit of slavery" by denying offices of power to those retaining that spirit.

The other issue affecting the freedom of persons and hence endangering institutions was oath-bound secret societies. Of primary concern was the Masons, since the founding leaders of Free Methodism felt they suffered at their hands, particularly in the Genesee Conference of Methodism. Those who took the required oaths, it was believed, were more loyal to each other than to Methodism and its basic principles. Masonry, they believed, played a large role in the expulsion of both laymen and clergy which made necessary a new denomination.

Free Seats

To freedom from slavery and secret oath-bound commitments taking priority over commitment to Christ and the church was added concern for the dignity of persons. The church withdrew that sense of dignity through the "pewed system."

Roberts' experience in evangelism in tough city areas led him to write in *The Earnest Christian* (January 1863), "It is an insult to God and humanity. God's house should be as free as his grace." The pewed system, he contended, was unscriptural. There should be "free" churches for the poor. Paupers' seats were often provided, but this drew attention to one's poverty and hardly enticed one to church or salvation. Pewed churches were referred to as "stock churches."

In a letter to his father, Roberts said, "Till our exclusive church system is abolished in this city we cannot do much towards infusing the Spirit of Christianity among the masses."[10]

The call issued for the organizing convention identified "free seats" as one of the bases for organization. Discrimination on the basis of wealth was deplored. In some cases churches had been built by purchase of pews. In other instances rental became a means of financing the operation of the church. In either case the practice of purchasing or renting became a symbol of growing affluence.

Complaints against the system were often coupled with expressions of dismay at an accompanying ostentation in dress. It may be parenthetically noted that a pewed system was a violation of an early Methodist rule which divided the seating of men and women. The historical course of the pewed church in American Methodism is irregular. But, by 1852, it had been legalized.

Marston writes, "The Christian principle of freedom of rich and poor alike to gospel privileges, and as well the slave's claim to civil and political freedom, were soon to play an important part in the formation of the Free Methodist Church and would principally determine its name."[11]

Ecclesiastical Freedom

Marston states that the founders sought freedom from "ecclesiastical domination." They reacted to the extraordinary power of bishops; they reflected the current desire for representation in government. They felt they had suffered, both clergy and laity, at the hands of bishop- and clergy-dominated assemblies. The laity had lent support to the leaders of reform. They had been read-out of membership. It was logical that in any new organization these pious churchmen should be treated as equal partners in the enterprise of the church.

Experience had convinced the founders that it was an ecclesiastical disadvantage to promote lay representation. A speaker at the 1847 Methodist Conference at Philadelphia said, "I had as lief travel with the devil as with a lay delegation man."[12]

The year of the founding of the Free Methodist Church, the Methodist bishops at the General Conference recommended lay delegation but in the form of "a separate house," according to Methodist historian Abel Stevens. Lay representation in all the councils of the church was part of the call to organize.

Roberts wrote in *The Earnest Christian* (September 1860), "The deep interest and close scrutiny of the intelligent laymen who were present as delegates must have convinced anyone that that church is a great loser which excludes them from her counsels."

Before this, the only protection for the interests of laymen was the withholding of financial support. This was an approved practice within the Methodist system. However, it was hardly designed to secure justice for all parties and concerns. The Methodist Episcopal Church had denied representation privilege and responsibility from its inception in 1784. Twelve years after the founding of the Free Methodist Church, laymen were seated in a General Conference but not in equal numbers. Only two members were permitted from each conference. Limited lay representation in the Annual Conference came later, and only many more years later would full and equal representation be made possible.

The "Free Church," under its restrictive rules, made any change in lay representation as difficult as changing anything pertaining to doctrine, standards, itinerant ministry, and free seats.

Steps were taken in reaction to what was perceived as oppressive dominance to restrict or check clerical control at all levels of church administration. Bishops were not to be elected for indefinite periods. They did not assign clergy to pastorates. Their powers resided principally in their persuasive ability and the general respect accorded them as elected leaders. The title "Bishop" was denied to Roberts though later applied to the general superintendents.

It seems clear that the new denomination *reflected* the democratic mood prevailing in the country while it *reacted* against concentration of administrative power in leadership. The reaction stemmed also from the fact that the leadership was exclusively clerical.

Free Worship

Marston in *From Age to Age a Living Witness* includes in "Appendix A. New School Methodism," the entire article on the subject written by Roberts and published in the *Northern Independent* in 1857. The article did much to precipitate the crisis which ultimately led to the formation of the Free Methodist Church in 1860.

The article was a response to articles carried in *The Advocate* which had previously been called *The Buffalo Christian Advocate*, a change which Roberts noted as appropriate. It appears that this magazine carried the liberal views of a party in the Genesee Conference labeled "New School Methodists."

They had written, "Christianity is not, characteristically, a system of devotion. It has *none of those features* which must distinguish a religion grounded on the idea that to adore the Divine character is the most imperative obligation resting upon human beings. It enjoins the observance of but very few sacred rites; nor does it prescribe any *particular mode* for paying homage to the Deity. It eschews all exterior forms, and teaches that they who worship God must worship Him in spirit and in truth."

Roberts answered that the Old School Methodists hold that, "'to adore the Divine character' is the most imperative obligation resting on human beings — that Christianity has *all* of those features that must distinguish a religion grounded on this idea. That he who worships God rightly will, as a necessary consequence, possess all social and moral virtues; that the Gospel does not leave its votaries to choose, if they please, the degrading rites of heathenism, or the superstitious abominations of Popery; but prescribes prayer and praise and the observance of the sacraments of baptism and the Lord's Supper, 'as particular modes for paying homage to the Deity'; that there is no necessity for antagonism, as Infidels and Universalists are wont to affirm, between spiritual worship and the forms of worship instituted by Christ."

"Free" did not mean a lack of order in worship. The founders did, however, seek to be free from mere ritualistic formality, free from performance as an end rather than a means and open to spontaneity and sharing. Testimonies could punctuate any service along with the voiced "amen" or other verbal expression of praise and joy. Nevertheless, leaders could and did, as occasion required, call a halt to individualistic excesses.

It appears that the "peril of the pendulum" is always present in religious as well as social, economic, and political affairs. On one hand there is the peril of disorder and induced emotional response. On the other hand is the stultifying effect of elaborate, unyielding order along with the emotional appeal inherent in the liturgical which induces a desired mood rather than the outgoing of genuine feeling or passion. Neither whipped up emotions in a "free" setting nor induced moods in a "controlled" order points the worshipper to the proper source of emotional response. A sense of God's presence and comprehension of gospel truth providing ever new visions of grace should be sufficient to stimulate the emotions of the Christian worshipper.

That order and freedom of worship were the twin foci of the new church is shown by the full page given to the concern in the 1910 *Free Methodist Hymnal*. It is the first page.

Order of Worship

The following order is chiefly based on directions in the *Free Methodist Discipline:*

(Let all our services begin exactly at the time appointed, and let all our people kneel in silent prayer on entering the sanctuary.)

I. Singing from *The Free Methodist Hymnal,* the people standing.
II. Prayer, concluding with the Lord's Prayer, repeated audibly by all, both minister and people kneeling.
III. Scripture Lessons from both the Old and New Testaments.
IV. Singing from *The Free Methodist Hymnal,* the people standing.
V. Notices, followed by Collection.
VI. The Sermon.
VII. Prayer, both minister and people kneeling.
VIII. Singing from *The Free Methodist Hymnal,* the people standing.
IX. Doxology and the Apostolic Benediction (2 Corinthians 13:14).

Note: The foregoing may be abridged for afternoon or evening by omitting one of the Scripture lessons; also by the omission of singing from the Hymnal after the final prayer.

The proper context for true worship, as advanced by the founders, included buildings designed for both simplicity and comfort, kneeling for public prayer, bowing the head in reverence as one entered the pew, and a general attitude of worship in God's house.

Marston in his interpretive history, timed to coincide with our centennial, felt his church held a strategic position in the area of worship. He writes, "It maintains simplicity and earnestness, with restraint against an undue liberty that sacrifices true devotion by exalting the flesh on the one hand, and maintains a vitality that resists the creeping death of ritualistic formalism on the other.

"There seems to be little danger now that the church will veer from its course into the extravagances of the former, but may it guard against the subtle pull of the liturgical current, and refuse to take on forms and symbols to induce the mood of worship while allowing the fire of devotion to die down on the altar of the heart.

Only thus can it minister to the inner experience of cleansing and power in the individual, and insure simplicity of worship in the freedom of the Spirit in the congregation."[13]

In the matter of worship the Reformers were "reactors." They were reacting against the creeping formalism of the parent body.

Free Society

The Free Methodist movement represented a cluster of religious, social, economic, and political attitudes and concerns. In *First Lessons on Money*, Roberts aimed at economic reform. He had a front page quote from William Penn reading, "A man should make it a part of his religion to see that his country is well governed."

Roberts, with a master's degree and training in law, could hardly be expected to confine his concerns to things purely ecclesiastical. He did not believe that ignorance was bliss. He did not subscribe to religious passivity where the needs of persons were denied. He rejected the kind of spiritual commitment that closed eyes and mind to the world of daily life. He was utterly committed to education, believing both church and society needed enlightened, trained minds as well as evangelical hearts.

Much of his energy went into the institutions of education launched by the young church, but especially the one which now bears his name, Roberts Wesleyan College. It began as Chili Seminary and then became Chesbrough Seminary before taking its present name. Roberts would have read with approval the words of W. W. Sweet, authority on religious sects in America, when he wrote that "there is a very close relationship between the history of higher education in America and revivalism."[14]

The pious and the practical combined in Roberts as it did in Wesley. The intertwining of the practical, the devotional, the social, the economic, and political found one institutional expression in the founding of Chili Seminary. Roberts and his wife Ellen were personally and deeply involved here in the development of a "work-study program."[15]

Roberts was concerned that America be a free society — free from slavery and secrecy bound by oath. He stood for other freedoms. Marston observes that it was a "gilded age" of materialism and huge capitalist empires which failed to share with the poor.[16]

Roberts believed a single gold standard played into the

hands of capitalists and against the poor and debtors. He worked for the passage of laws in the interest of the people and which would not "favor the moneyed class and rich corporations." He was a bimetalist. He was active in organizing help for the farmers. He vigorously opposed monopolies and trusts. He echoed Wesley in his strong advocacy of social betterment. His ideas, as Zahniser has noted, are advanced in social and economic matters yet "are combined with an extreme conservatism in the field of religion."[17]

But, Roberts was no narrow religionist. He prided himself on his own farming ability and often managed the Seminary farm. He was active in organizing the Farmers' Alliance in New York, argued against tariffs which were harmful to farmers, while at the same time they protected those business and industry segments which were "organized." He was critical of the franchises giving special privilege to banks and railroads. He worked vigorously to remove unfair railroad rates imposed on farmers. He saw the problem of the farmers lay in their lack of organization. He saw the "organized" segments of the economy constantly able to secure economic advantage.

He opposed tight money policies and high interest, advocated free coinage of silver, believed the two great parties of the country were largely controlled by bankers and bondholders. The control was the result of effective organization. He concluded that effective organization was essential to secure justice to each segment of society. In *The Free Methodist* of December 22, 1886, he declared that Wall Street was "directly in conflict with the interests of the great body of American citizens."

He offered an opinion regarding the causes of economic depression: overproduction (the seven-day workweek), extravagance of the rich and the laborers, and pricing conspiracies. He contended all money should be issued by the national government and not by national banks.

In the same issue of the magazine noted he wrote, "The farmers, unorganized and undisciplined, are overpowered by money-lenders though they greatly outnumber them." In the March 1889 issue he described farmers as the goose which lays "the golden egg for the nation" and the monopolists as "the masters who appropriate the golden egg." He thought the farmer was being "picked to death" by excessive taxes. He contended that the farmers should have income matching that of the manufacturing enterprises. He went so far as to advocate fighting back with boycott and the private use of the spinning wheel and the making of their own clothes. He persistently inveighed against the monopolists since they "operate against the welfare of the community at large."[18]

In his book *Pungent Truths*, Roberts wrote, "Our nation needs a Cromwell" who would apply the words of Dunbar written at the time of his last victory over the royalists: "Relieve the oppressed, hear the groans of poor prisoners. Be pleased to reform the abuses of all professions. If there be anyone that makes many poor to make a few rich, that suits not a Commonwealth."[19]

It may be noted that Roberts advocated the ordination of women to the clergy, a clear indication of his opposition to discrimination in social and ecclesiastical affairs. It was some years before deacons' orders were voted for women and still more before elders' orders were available to women.

His notable book, *Ordaining Women*, finally bore fruit. In the quest for a free society it would appear the founders were reflecting the currents of their day and their prophetic-like understanding of society. They were likewise reacting against injustice and the lack of concern characterizing the mother church.

Free from Sin

Doctrine and lifestyle were important to the founders. The envisioned free society and free church depended on free persons. Persons were not genuinely free until free from the slavery of sin. A gospel of full deliverance was the essential doctrinal element in the holistic concern for human beings.

The founders were convinced that the parent church had drifted both doctrinally and in matters of lifestyle. They gave clear expression to their doctrinal concern by adding two Articles to the twenty-five Articles of Religion of the Methodist Episcopal Church. The first was a statement on "Entire Sanctification"; the second was entitled "Future Rewards and Punishment." The latter was a response to the current trend toward Universalism.

It is the first Article that is pertinent to our discussion. It intended to convey a distinction between sanctification as the entire process from beginning to end of the Christian life and "entire sanctification" as crisis within the process. It held to two things important to the founders. First, that "entire" sanctification was God's work *subsequent* to justification, and second, that it was *instantaneous* since it was the response of faith to grace.

The freedom envisioned did not remove the human element from the everyday life of believers. It pointed more clearly to the purification of motive, intention, and desire, leaving one still subject to the frailties of humanity in their physical, psychological, and social aspects. It was freedom to be truly human. It did not indicate a stop, a period, an end of sanctification as process, growth, and development. Rather, it was the beginning of more rapid and better development. The entirely sanctified were on the way to holistic wholeness with joy and singleness of heart and mind.

The question Paul raised about himself and for all of us, "Who will deliver me?" was also answered by Paul for all of us, "Thanks be to God through Jesus Christ our Lord!" "The old vicious circle of sin and death," as Phillips translates, has been ended by the "Spirit of life in Christ Jesus" (RSV).

Conclusion

The founding Free Methodists were primarily reformers. The first priority was the church itself. The focus was on the perpetuation of deep piety, simple lifestyle, free worship, and Wesleyan doctrine, with a special emphasis on "entire" sanctification and freedom from sin.

The next priority focused on concern for persons evidenced by advocacy of free persons, free pews, free society, a free economic system, and an open ecclesiastical system — open to the laity and free from excessive leadership control.

These "Free" reformers were *reflectors* and *reactors.* They reflected democratic contemporary currents which were manifest in social, political, and economic issues. They also reacted against the decline of doctrinal integrity and behavioral standards in the parent church. They reacted against formalizing tendencies prevalent in worship. They reacted against depersonalizing institutions of the day.

Notes

1 C. H. Zahniser, *Earnest Christian: Life and Works of Benjamin Titus Roberts,* Circleville, Ohio, Advocate Publishing House, 1957, p. 65.

2 Ibid., pp. 97-98.

[3] Ibid., p. 202.

[4] John Wesley, *Works* (Emory ed. 1853), Carlton and Phillips, N.Y.; v. 6, 286 et seq.

[5] Wesley, *Letters,* Epworth Press, London; v. 8, 265.

[6] R. D. Clark, *Life of Matthew Simpson,* The Macmillan Co., New York, p. 56.

[7] L. R. Marston, *From Age to Age a Living Witness,* Light and Life Press, Winona Lake, IN, p. 157.

[8] Ibid., p. 160.

[9] Ibid., p. 581.

[10] B. H. Roberts, *Benjamin Titus Roberts, a Biography,* The Earnest Christian Office, North Chili, N.Y., p. 78.

[11] Marston, *From Age to Age a Living Witness,* p. 167.

[12] Zahniser, *Earnest Christian: Life and Works of Benjamin Titus Roberts,* p. 132.

[13] Marston, *From Age to Age a Living Witness,* p. 358.

[14] W. W. Sweet, *Revivalism in America,* Charles Scribner's Sons, N.Y., p. 181.

[15] Marston, *From Age to Age a Living Witness.*

[16] Marston, *From Age to Age a Living Witness.*

[17] Zahniser, *Earnest Christian: Life and Works of Benjamin Titus Roberts.*

[18] B.T. Roberts, *The Free Methodist.*

[19] B.T. Roberts, *Pungent Truths.*

The Fruit of the Spirit Is Love

Love is patient, love is kind. It does not envy, it does not boast, it is not proud. It is not rude, it is not self-seeking, it is not easily angered, it keeps no record of wrongs. Love does not delight in evil but rejoices with the truth. It always protects, always trusts, always hopes, always perseveres (1 Corinthians 13:4-7, NIV).

But the fruit of the Spirit is love, joy, peace, patience, kindness, goodness, faithfulness, gentleness, self-control. Against such things there is no law (Galatians 5:22-23, NIV).

Joy is Love's **Celebration**
Peace is Love's **Security**
Patience is Love's **Endurance**
Kindness is Love's **Conduct**
Goodness is Love's **Character**
Fidelity/Faithfulness is Love's **Strength**
Gentleness/Meekness is Love's **Style**
Self-control is Love's **Mastery**

Love, as we see in Galatians and 1 Corinthians, has components, expressions, faces, and aspects, and there is a correlation between these two passages. But look briefly at the Galatians aspects of love.

Joy is Love's Celebration: This is love's high. Love knows nothing of a dour, long-faced religion. It celebrates life. It celebrates life's relationships. It is contagious. Joy needs others with whom it shares if it is to be maximized.

Peace is Love's Security: Here is love's confidence in God, self, and others. It is secure and content. It is not competitive, though it pursues excellence. The excellence it pursues is related to knowing one's own gifts, potentials, worth. It can therefore rejoice in the achievements made and laurels won by others. It is not jealous, boastful, or arrogant — it is at peace.

Patience is Love's Endurance: Love has lasting power. It hangs in there. It holds on! It bears all — endures all. Love can last because it is first secure in a Father's love and next because its hope lies beyond self-resources. Its anchor is within the veil — that is, it is in Eternity and is fastened to the Father's throne.

Kindness is Love's Conduct: This is how love behaves — not rudely or in irritation. It is not boastful. It is courteous in church or small group meetings (1 Corinthians 14). It treats others with the sort of kindness one wants to receive. It does not perform to get even or pay back. It is never mean.

Goodness is Love's Character: Love is holy. Holy love is goodness. God is good because He does what is right, and He does what is right because He is right(eous). Love knows nothing but goodness in attitude or act.

Fidelity/Faithfulness is Love's Strength: Love is not flashy, but it is strong. It bends without breaking. Its strength derives from its commitment. Love is utterly committed to God and to others. Love's strength is known in the quality of its relationships. Love keeps on keeping on in both the vertical and horizontal relationships of life. It is faithful.

Gentleness/Meekness is Love's Style: Love is never arrogant. It does not insist on having its own way. It understands its own limits. It respects what others can do and can offer. It rejoices in the right. Love is no "bull in a china shop."

Self-Control is Love's Mastery: Love is disciplined. It is no mere emotion. It is a life posture. It is goal-oriented. The goal is maturity in Christlikeness. Love is sensitive to guidance. Love has the will to use the brakes as well as the accelerator.

No wonder *"Love never ends; ... So faith, hope, love abide, these three; but the greatest of these is love"* (1 Corinthians 13:8, 13, RSV).

Funeral Service – Esther Sittig

(Pearce Memorial Church, North Chili, New York, May 28, 1976.)

The morning of April 23rd, Harriet and I had the privilege of moments together with Esther, Bill and Bob — moments we shall never forget. Hallowed moments. Moments tinged with sadness but dominated by awareness of a heaven that for awhile swung low to minister to each of us. I only wish that Penny and John had been present.

You see, the older one becomes and the more mature in Christ, I believe that our relationships with each other become more important. That is one thing that can make the role of a pastor such a rich one. And these are moments of memory for each of us. Each different. Each rich in its own way and with its own texture. These are moments when we have a new awareness not only of the brevity of life but of the utmost values of what we may mean to each other.

It was my great privilege to officiate as Bill and Esther united their lives to each other. It was my privilege to cradle Penny, John and Bob as their parents presented them for infant baptism. Our lives have crossed and re-crossed since then — not frequently, but with great meaning for us.

Let me tell you about that morning just over a month ago. Esther was weak. I felt we had visited as long as was good for her. That morning I felt led to read a portion of Romans 8, beginning, I believe, with verse 18. So when I reached for their large Bible and told her my "leading," she raised her hand and tears flowed down her cheeks and she said, "That is my favorite chapter. I want that used at my funeral." And so it shall be.

Well, I could wish you each had your Bible open to this great chapter. I especially recommend reading from the Phillips translation. Romans 8 is, of course, one of the grand peaks of the New Testament.

It begins, *"There is therefore now ..."* and *"therefore"* immediately takes us to the end of the previous chapter and the vivid words of Paul as he describes the inner division and warfare that he had experienced. He in fact uses the very ugly practice of binding a criminal face to face with a dead body until death came to the criminal.

With that brutal picture in mind Paul cries, *"Who will deliver me from the body that is bringing me to death?"* And immediately he answers for himself and for us, *"Thanks be to God through Jesus Christ our Lord!"* And then he declares that *"the law of the Spirit of life in Christ Jesus has set me free from the law of sin and death."* Or as Phillips has it, *"in"* Christ Jesus we are lifted *"out of the old vicious circle of sin and death."*

So Paul triumphantly points to the genesis of a life that can be everlasting because it is — to use Jesus' phrase, *"eternal life"* — a new kind of life. A life of such quality full of such potential that only eternity is appropriate for its unfolding development. Now this is a magnificent Christian conviction and the basis of our hope today and every day.

Let us observe highlights of this great chapter which meant so much to Esther. I certainly do not know all of the reasons, the flood of insight over a period of time that made this chapter so dear to her. But we can, I think, do better than guess at some of the reasons. That day only a month ago I began reading at about verse 18 and moved leisurely to the end. Those ancient, vivid words impacted on me as never before.

I said, "Esther, have you ever noticed that chapter eight begins with *"no condemnation"* and ends with *"no separation"*? That really says it **all** regarding the life which is lived *"in Christ"* and *"by the Spirit."* ... No condemnation ... No separation!

And so it is that right now we know that Esther has begun her experience of a new and wonderful dimension, to what Paul meant when at the end of the chapter he exults, *"For I am sure that neither death, nor life, nor angels, nor principalities, nor things present, nor things to come, nor powers, nor height, nor depth, nor anything else in all creation, will be able to separate us from the love of God in Christ Jesus our Lord"* (Romans 8:38-39, RSV).

Separation from loved ones. Separation from family and friends. Separation from a life on this planet that has had meaning and purpose — yes! But not separation from the love of God. No separation from *"Christ Jesus our Lord."*

And I believe that because there is no separation for the life lived in Christ Jesus our Lord, there is also a blossoming of the meaning and purpose Christ has given to the life begun and matured here. What that future holds, enveloped in the love of God in Christ, must be exciting to the Christian who has begun to tingle to the truth of Romans 8.

What are some of the things that vibrate Paul in this chapter and which in turn have communicated vibrations to fellow Christians down the centuries?

NO CONDEMNATION — but freedom from the law, or from the circle of sin and death.

NO MORE DOMINATION BY OUR SINFUL NATURE — but new life as we are prompted and led by the Spirit, a new life which Paul sees related to the power which raised Christ from among the dead ones. A new life made possible because, as Phillips translates, *"God sent his own Son Jesus Christ to live in that human nature which causes the trouble."*

NO MORE SLAVISH FEAR — but such a happy trusting relationship to God that one cries out quite naturally, *"Father, my Father."* Or as I heard Chaim Potok say, *"Daddy, Daddy."* God has in Christ become the first intimate in our relationships.

NO MORE PESSIMISMS ABOUT THE PRESENT AND FUTURE — rather, realistic optimism, based not on humanism but upon the past and the contemplated acts of God. Let us look at Paul's marvelous cosmic view in verses 18-25 (Phillips):

In my opinion whatever we may have to go through now is less than nothing compared with the magnificent future God has in store for us. The whole creation is on tiptoe to see the wonderful sight of the sons of God coming into their own.

The world of creation cannot as yet see reality, not because it chooses to be blind, but because in God's purpose it has been so limited — yet it has been given hope. And the hope is that in the end the whole of created life will be rescued from the tyranny of change and decay, and have its share in this magnificent liberty which can only belong to the children of God!

It is plain to anyone with eyes to see that at the present time all created life groans in a sort of universal travail. And it is plain, too, that we who have a foretaste of the Spirit are in a state of painful tension, while we wait for that redemption of our bodies, which will mean that we have realized our full sonship in him. We were saved by this hope, and let us remember that hope always means waiting for something that we do not yet see. For whoever hopes when he can see? But if we hope for something we cannot see, then we must settle down to wait for it in patience.

Now I am impressed that Paul always had a firm grip on reality. But it was a reality bigger than time and space — and now it was a reality that took in a cosmos, a universe or universes. Whatever he visioned made place for all we may discover of the growing hugeness of the whole, of which our planet is but a tiny part.

Paul saw an end of the *"tyranny of change and decay."* For Paul, reality included a redeemed cosmos. Reality embraced time and eternity. Even in the matter of our relationship, reality was changed because of what Christ had effected for us. So in Ephesians 3:14-15, he says, *"I bow my knees before the Father, from whom every family in heaven and on earth is named,"* (RSV) or as the KJV has it, *"the whole family in heaven and earth is named."* There is good reason for the ancient creeds affirming that the communion of saints is a communion of those here and those there.

"I believe in the Holy Ghost, the holy catholic church, the communion of saints, the forgiveness of sins, the resurrection of the body and the life everlasting."

There is a thin veil between the two realities, the two locations of one family. Esther was keenly aware of this as she mentioned one after another who in a few days would be greeting her on the other side of that thin veil.

NO FEAR, BUT CONFIDENT HOPE. Hope that has more than a tinge of reality. Hope that transforms the present as the Spirit of God dwelling in us actually does our praying for us *"in agonizing longings"* which are nevertheless wordless. Hope that is daily being translated into reality as God lifts His own children *"to the splendor of life as his own sons."*

Then the final paragraph beginning with verse 31 (Phillips):

In face of all this, what is there left to say? If God is for us, who can be against us? He who did not grudge his own Son but gave him up for us all — can we not trust such a God to give us, with him, everything else that we can need?

Who would dare to accuse us, whom God has chosen? God himself has declared us free from sin. Who is in a position to condemn? Only Christ Jesus, and Christ died for us, Christ also rose for us. Christ reigns in power for us, Christ prays for us!

Who can separate us from the love of Christ? Can trouble, pain or persecution? Can lack of clothes and food, danger to life and limb, the threat of force of arms? Indeed some of us know the truth of that ancient text: For thy sake we are killed all the day long; We were accounted as sheep for the slaughter.

No in all these things we win an overwhelming victory through Him who has proved his love for us.

I have become absolutely convinced that neither death nor life, neither messenger of Heaven nor monarch of earth, neither what happens today nor what may happen tomorrow, neither a power from on high nor a power from below, nor anything else in God's whole world has any power to separate us from the love of God in Christ Jesus our Lord!

NO DEFEATING ADVERSARY — rather, a risen and interceding Christ. Paul in typical manner raises a rhetorical question anticipating a resounding and positive answer. The question, *"If God is for us, who is against us?"* The answer is NO THING, NO ONE can prevail against us to separate us from the love of Christ. Tribulation? Distress? Persecution? Famine? Yes. Nakedness, Peril, or Sword? Yes, all of these may be a part of the Christian's life. The promise is not one of escape but of triumph!

"No, in all these things we are more than conquerors through him who loved us" (Romans 8:37, NIV).

THEN THE FINALE:

"For I am sure that neither death, nor life, nor angels, nor principalities, nor things present, nor things to come, nor powers, nor height, nor depth, nor anything else in all creation, will be able to separate us from the love of God in Christ Jesus our Lord" (Romans 8:38, NIV).

Paul, we want to join in your shout of affirmation!

We rejoice in Esther's coronation!

We ask for the grace to join the Apostle in declaring, *"I am ready for anything through the strength of the one who lives within me"* (Philippians 4:13, Phillips).

These are words that Bill, Penny, Bob and John all need. May the God of all comfort — comfort!

The God We Can Trust

Our working portrait of God is important. It has a direct effect on our whole range of beliefs, values, attitudes, and behavior.

The Holiness of God

Holy God: A word used to describe the essence of God. It represents a fundamental reality regarding the God of Israel and the faith of Israel. It is one of the few predicate adjectives used of God. (Predicate: the word or words which make a statement about the subject. Adjective: words used to limit or qualify, such as "good," "every.") God is holy and all holiness comes ultimately from Him — it belongs to the very being or essence of God.

Primary Use: God's difference, separateness from all else that exists. It is the term which sets God apart from creation and in contrast with gods, earth, and rebellious persons. It speaks of His complete otherness.

Secondary Use: God's purity — the utmost in moral quality. Speaks of a God who does the right thing. Righteous.

The Holiness of Man

Holy (man): Holiness which people, places, times, things may have comes from God. *"You shall be holy for I the Lord your God am holy"* (Leviticus 11:44, paraphrase).

Primary Use: To designate set-apartness. By implication it involves otherness, difference, separateness, unlikeness, which come from the same features of God. Holiness for man is relational, but not in any mechanical or abstract sense. Rather, holiness for man is relational within a personal context. So in the Old Testament the Covenant becomes the thing, because it is the instrument of commitment of a people to Jehovah. It is the Covenant relationship which requires acts and symbols of devotion to God. We are set apart to God for His use. In this light, Romans 12:1-3 becomes significant; the primary use of "holy" is particularly relevant: *"Therefore, I urge you, brothers, in view of God's mercy, to offer yourselves as living sacrifices, holy and pleasing to God — which is your spiritual worship. Do not conform any longer to the pattern of this world, but be transformed by the renewing of your mind. Then you will be able to test and approve what God's will is — his good, pleasing and perfect will"* (NIV).

Secondary Use: As with God it is purity, moral quality. Above, see verses 2-3 of Romans 12. But the purity is the result of being set apart in a new relationship with Deity. Commitment to God involves surrender to God's intention to cleanse us in the dynamic of our relationship. The process involved in commitment, devotement to God, is one of cleansing and conforming. Cleansing from all barriers to fellowship — conformity to the likeness of the One receiving our commitment. In New Testament terms, the merits of Christ's atonement are ministered to us by the Holy Spirit in a moment-by-moment cleansing. And the relationship effected by the indwelling of the Holy Spirit remolds us within, shapes us into likeness of the Son, our Redeemer.

Love (God): Unconditioned givingness, care, and respect for persons. Romans 5:8 (RSV): *"But God shows his love for us in that while we were yet sinners Christ died for us."* It is the attitude and act of concern demanding no reciprocity.

Holy Love is the highest designation it is possible to give to either God or man. In personality, holiness and love unite as the very essence of God and of Christians. Neither God or Christian is holy without love, or loving without being holy. Each attitude and act is the blend we have designated as holy love. Any attempt to separate holiness from love, or love from holiness has undesirable results.

To emphasize holiness alone tends to a distorted view of God as harsh, judging, unaccepting, and demanding in legal aloofness. To emphasize love alone tends to a distorted view of God as a kindly grandfather who never says no, never deals in penalties, and never expresses wrath. Both God's judgments and redemptive acts are expressions of holy love. Likewise, with an exclusive emphasis on holiness or love comes distortion in terms of Christian attitudes and acts. Holiness alone tends to legalism; love alone tends to libertinism. Each is a necessary limitation on the other.

Other Features of God

In addition we must observe that God is a Person not an abstraction. He is a Person of Holy Love! No wonder then that He is portrayed as our Heavenly Father, which also means He is trustable, wise, and good.

God is also Spirit. God is Presence and Power. He is near and active. The Holy Spirit ministers to us the presence of our Lord. *"Lo, I am with you always."*

"... I shall be in you." The Holy Spirit is "God in Action." God acts in power, that is, with energy and effectiveness. But His acts are controlled by His essence: Holy Love. And His nearness is the nearness of Holy Love.

Our Environment

Now another fact needs emphasis. God created and it was good. But there is also the story of the Fall. Since the Fall something is awry in our physical environment. We are surrounded with the reality of a wonderful and good environment which is also infected with disease, mortality, sin, pain, sorrow, and death. Consequently, Christians often have problems reconciling the **power** of God with harsh and painful realities of life.

Before we move forward logically, we must observe that in the fallen world God gave a command. It was to have dominion. This is an important factor as we shall see later.

Perhaps now we can put our elements together in a meaningful picture. When we do we can understand better why we experience both miracle and mystery. The Christian lives in a kind of tension between the concept of a God of power and the realities of death, disease, sorrow, and sin. And there is another reality. It is the reality of an orderly, law-laced universe designed by a good God.

Early experience teaches that heat can burn and gravity can hurt. The fact that we are related to Christ does not release us from the laws of our environment. So the tension between a God of power and our environment raises questions:

Why does God permit auto and plane accidents to happen to Christians? Why does He allow war? Why does God not heal persons who are young, or who seem extraordinarily important to the forwarding of the gospel? Why does God heal some and not others? Why are not usefulness or piety always God's criteria for healing? Why does God permit tragedy of all sorts to the redeemed? These are real, crushing, and too often defeating questions for the uninformed Christian.

Trust Resolves Tension

The beneficial resolution of the tension lies in the acceptance of both miracle and mystery. I can arrive at this solution by seeing that God, while powerful, is above and beyond, that He is HOLY LOVE and therefore trustable. He is omniscient, all-knowing, therefore in Holy Love He may not perform by standards acceptable to our finiteness or ignorance. The basic question for the Christian is not "What can God do?" but "Is God trustable?"

The rest and resolution of tension for the Christian come in acceptance of the trust-ability of God. When I trust I am freed from the uptight, judgmental approach which declares, "If you pray 'Thy will be done' you really do not believe, or you thereby cut the nerve of faith." In fact, that declaration is the real assertion of self-will and unbelief. It is the prayer of the first garden (Eden). It cries, "My will be done." It is a denial of the validity of our Lord's life and attitude which finds consummate expression in another garden (Gethsemane) when He prays, "Nevertheless, not my will but thine be done." There we have the model of trust.

Emphasis on the **power** of God, rather than on the **essence** of His character, leads inevitably to distortion and false expectations. But a balanced concept of God leads to a ready, tensionless, trusting response to God in the midst of disaster of any kind. Miracle and mystery are both facts with which we can live and in the strength of Christ rejoice. I trust Holy Love to do what in wisdom He wills.

I observe that sometimes He intervenes in the ordinary operation of the laws of His universe. But I also recognize that if He always intervened it would no longer be miracle. And if He did it for Christians only, everyone would be a Christian to secure a foolproof insurance policy. When He does not intervene I am left with mystery. But it is the mystery of Holy Love. It is mystery because I do not understand the criteria for His actions. But neither do young children understand parents. However, they may learn to trust our apparently contradictory behavior. True faith trusts! How can anyone find joy in tribulation when he places the power of God before the character of God?

In fact, Christians who make demands on God focus on their own wishes and wisdom and deny the priority of Christ's lordship. The demands are akin to pagan practices born of improper concepts of the deity and are a denial of God's holy love and trust-ability. Often the tragedy does not end there. It reaches the relation of Christian with Christian. It condemns the unhealed as unbelieving. It becomes judgmental, censorious, and superior in attitude. It is thus wrong and damaging to the Body of Christ.

God uses His power consistent with His character of Holy Love and His unlimited wisdom.

God's power is not to be directed by the private desires of humans, even though they are Christians. A Christian does not have relationship with God to make God a servant. Rather, our relationship with God requires the lordship of Christ.

God's power provides the possibility, not the necessity, of miracles.

God's power is displayed every moment in the functioning of an orderly universe. This is true even though our planet is sin and corruption infected. Even then it is a world of cause and effect. There is a kind of orderliness even in the seemingly ruthless features of the environment.

The Christian learns to trust the wisdom and goodness of God in the details of his life. In fact, he learns to trust when he cannot understand, trace, or explain. Trust provides joyous confidence in the design of God for us. Romans 8:28; 35-39 (NIV):

And we know that in all things God works for the good of those who love him, who have been called according to his purpose. ...

Who shall separate us from the love of Christ? Shall trouble or hardship or persecution or famine or nakedness or danger or sword? As it is written:

"For your sake we face death all day long; we are considered as sheep to be slaughtered."

No, in all these things we are more than conquerors through him who loved us. For I am convinced that neither death nor life, neither angels nor demons, neither the present nor the future, nor any powers, neither height nor depth, nor anything else in all creation, will be able to separate us from the love of God that is in Christ Jesus our Lord.

As we face the world, trust saves from pessimism on the one hand and false optimism on the other hand.

The Christian rejoices in every evidence of man exercising dominion in compliance with the command of God. He rejoices when:

1. New insight is gained regarding the complexity of our human structure so more intelligent action can be taken to help one another.
2. New knowledge is gained regarding healthy habits, such as rest, food, recreation, sanitation.
3. Medical science secures breakthroughs in search for cures of disease, such as polio and cancer. Or when better treatment is devised for our mental, emotional, and physical needs.
4. God acts in special ways to heal attitudes (resentment, hate, jealousy), disease of body, or disorder of mind.
5. He considers the promises for newness beyond time and space: glorification. We rejoice that the day is coming when the environment will be redeemed and sin, death, sorrow, pain will end.

To deny the nature of our present environment makes cop-outs of men. In religion it drives men to storm cellars of cultism, i.e., Christian Science. Ascribes to demons what is inherent in the environment.

A Christian is glad to recognize and applaud the progress of science, knowledge, technical advance which give us greater control over the environment for the good of mankind. He also recognizes that knowledge and skill can be used to destroy. This he deplores and offers the gospel of Christ as the only effective value system capable of directing the genius of man for good.

There are current trends which are in effect a retreat from reality. They tend to reject knowledge and science. These trends have invaded segments of the church. Some Christians think that to truly practice their faith means to refuse help other than divine intervention. This is folly that flies in the face of revelation. Some deny the place of medical doctors, hospitals, or other forms of human assistance, asserting that our only need is dependence on God and faith. This stance is the mark of false religion. It is not the faith of our fathers, the faith of the Bible. God is trustable! A

Christian's primary response to a God who is Holy Love is that of unreserved trust.

Good Friday – The Birth of Hope

Called "Great Friday" in Orthodox Church

(Kiwanis Club Meditation, Warsaw, Indiana.)

Returning from Israel aboard a 747 with a large group of Christians, most of whom I knew, I was talking with a pastor friend from Florida when someone gently tapped my shoulder from the seat behind. It was a Jewish woman who wanted to know who we were. "You seem so happy," she said. I told her we'd been to Jerusalem to a prophecy conference.

She immediately expressed deep feelings of guilt. She had travelled over much of Europe. Spent lots of money. Had done it before. But had never made a pilgrimage to Jerusalem. "And here you Gentiles have been to Israel and to Jerusalem." She was in near despair with herself.

As the conversation continued, she turned to the treatment Jews had received at the hands of Christians through the centuries, and of course she thought this all stemmed from the fact that we Christians blamed the Jews for the killing of Jesus.

It was my turn to express guilt over portions of our so-called Christian past. But I pointed out that historically it seems clear that a majority of the religious leaders of the Jews (the Sanhedrin) were convinced that the elimination of Jesus was the only security for their faith, and their position within Jewry, and in relationship to Roman authority.

I noted that while the Sanhedrin took the lead, it demanded the partnership of Rome to put Jesus to death. So historically, there was cause for the position taken by many Christians blaming the Jews.

"But," I said, "there is a more profound view about the crucifixion of Jesus that you may never have heard. It is something many, and I would hope most, Christians hold to be true. It goes something like this:

"While Jew and Roman were the incidental agents in the death of Jesus, the more profound truth is that we all were there. The entire human race helped nail Jesus to the cross. There is a sort of cosmic or racial sense in which time collapses and we are all present at the cross. And we are all by our own sins consenting to His death.

"Still, His goodness shames us. His purity condemns us. His demand for the good above the right, for the moral above the legal, for the person above the institution makes us recoil. We look bad by comparison with all that He is. We are therefore uncomfortable." (May I make the aside comment that it is for these reasons that we all stand in need of divine forgiveness.)

I said to my new friend, "You see, we feel guilt for His death. We stand in need of His forgiveness, the very forgiveness He prayed we might receive as He was dying on His cross."

And then I remembered an experience I'd had only a little while before. By chance I tuned my TV onto a satellite exchange between important persons located in the U.S., in Europe, and in Israel. The exchange concerned the then notorious Auschwitz. The discussion was fascinating, penetrating, compelling.

But only one feature remained clear and vivid in my memory. And so I told my Jewish friend of the experience. I said, "One of the European participants spoke to the Israeli member of the panel and asked, 'Could there ever, in your judgment, be a Jewish Eichman?'

"I shall never forget his unhesitating response. He said, 'Yes, indeed, there could be, for you see there is an Eichman in each of us.' There," I said, "is in essence the same sort of thing I've been saying about the attitude some of us hold toward the crucifixion of Jesus of Nazareth."

I listened with friends Sunday night to the last section of *Jesus of Nazareth,* to me a deeply moving and exceptionally well done movie of an exceedingly difficult subject matter. In our discussion following the film we discovered that each of us had had the question raised in our own mind: Just how would we have responded in the situations presented so skillfully, so true to life?

Perhaps with the accumulation of years and the gathering of insight regarding ourselves we are not so confident of our pristine purity, our nobility, our ability to see through conflicting logic and conflicting realities.

Where would we have stood? With Peter, with Judas, with Joseph and Nicodemus of the Sanhedrin, with Pilate, or with John, Mary, etc.? I felt the logic of Rome; the logic of the Zealots (Barabbas); the logic of the Sanhedrin; the logic of evil; the logic of "that is the way life is."

It is all so compelling! And love seems so unrealistic! And yet that is why He died! In fact, the logic of the Sanhedrin, "Is it not better that one should die than that a whole nation should suffer?" is the curiously twisted reason Jesus offered Himself. For He gave Himself in the place of, in the room of many, as a ransom. Not just for Jews, but for all of us to the end of time.

It was during World War II that I was pastoring in Ferndale, Michigan. At dusk I was returning to the parsonage. A soldier stood by the side of the road looking for a lift. It had just been widely broadcast that there was a flurry of robberies committed by persons dressed in Army uniform and not to pick up hitchhikers.

Nevertheless, I did with some nervousness. He did not help my feelings by keeping his face averted from mine. And he did not respond to conversation. And I got more nervous. Finally I got a bit of talk out of him and inadvertently, I believe, he turned his face enough that I could see the most horribly scarred face I'd ever seen.

Immediately I had a normal feeling of recoil, of revulsion. It was that terrible. But that was quickly followed by another feeling. It dawned on me that he had been to the Front. He was wounded brutally. And indeed what he had suffered was for me personally, and for every other American. Compassion and gratitude replaced my feelings of revulsion.

The Old Testament, looking toward the Christ, says, *"He was as one from whom men turn their eyes. He was despised. He had no beauty that we should desire him."* But it also says, *"He was wounded for our transgressions, and by his stripes we are healed"* (Isaiah 53:2-3, 5, paraphrase).

There is still great fascination with Calvary by visitors to Jerusalem — whether Gordon's or the site now within city walls. Calvary is time and earth's ultimate symbol of the worst human beings can be and do. It symbolizes our weak and futile attempts to unseat God and goodness.

Calvary is history's darkest moment. It is our clearest, deepest look into ourselves. It marks the nadir — not the zenith — of our attitudes and behavior. Auschwitz, the Holocaust, they are but reruns, rehash of Calvary in miniature. And we are part of Calvary, of the Holocaust. We tried to kill God. Calvary was the ultimate expression of our deep intent, albeit unconscious, to dethrone God — and consequently to kill goodness.

But what we Christians celebrate each year at this time is our failure and God's success. And we have reason to give thanks for each. Thank God we did not succeed!

Yes — we can forget, as far as placing blame is concerned — the historical and incidental figures, Jewish or Roman. We were there. The Negro spiritual — as is often the case — gets at the profound and plaintive truth when in a kind of questioning lament we sing, "Were you there when they crucified my Lord? Were you there? Sometimes it causes me to tremble, tremble — were you there ...?"

But Good Friday is symbol not only of the worst mankind can be and do. It is symbol of the best God does. It is ultimately the symbol, not of despair but of hope. Here is how a good God behaves. This is what Goodness incarnate does.

Good Friday is indeed the birth, the beginning of HOPE. The worst we could do, did not, does not dethrone God. Go to the end of the biblical record and we get a beautiful portrait and comforting words: *"He that sat upon the throne said, Behold I make all things new"* (Revelation 21:5, KJV).

It is of more than passing interest to me that Luke records that once when the disciples came back from a particularly satisfying mission they reported to Jesus, *"Lord, even the demons submit to us in your name."* The fascinating reply of Jesus was, *"I saw Satan fall like lightning from heaven"* (Luke 10:17-18, NIV).

It was Calvary that sealed the doom of Satan and the satanic. Calvary spells out the deepest and ultimate badness we are capable of. It should serve always to shatter our confidence in our autonomy. Our boot-strap operations have been disasters. We need a God who is still there when in our proud autonomy we run amuck, when our self-rule ends in failure.

Good Friday tells me that God and goodness survive my ridiculous efforts at autonomy. When we come to the end of our arrogant ways, the God who made it past Good Friday to Easter morning waits for us at the end of our self-defeating wanderings to rescue us, to deliver us from our urges to autonomy, and to bring us to the glorious moment when we willingly, joyfully crown Him Lord of everything and of all.

Today we are again reminded that the initiative rests not with us but with the God of Good Friday. That initiative is called, in biblical terminology, "grace."

Every time we pick up a newspaper, magazine, or tune in TV to "and that's the way it is" syndrome, we have pictures of man's continuing urge to willful autonomy. Good Friday tells us we will never make it alone — either individually or corporately. And the God who will yet make all things new would in characteristic fashion begin with me. That is the birth of hope for me! Multiplied, it becomes our corporate birth of hope!

There are little crosses to be found scattered by the roadsides of Europe. Upon examination they are found to carry these words: *"Is it nothing to you all ye that pass by. Behold and see if there be any sorrow like unto my sorrow."*

The sorrow of God is intended to lead to our joy. Good Friday is the birth of hope!

Holy Love

— two words distill the essence of what God is and what Christians are to be and become!

God is holy!
But what does that mean to you?
Do you stutter and grope for a response?
What flashes instantly on your private TV screen — a kind of abstract aura, "clean" or "moral" in the absolute and likely abstract sense? Do you get a feeling of vagueness? Does the picture fade with no clear and concrete outline left? If it is any comfort, there are many who have the same kind of reception difficulty.

The Bible helps!

The Bible does help to clear the picture. It removes the abstract about both "God" and "holy." It gives us the kind of reality we can get hold of. We need a very personal and concrete understanding about God and what it is for a personal God to be "holy." Some may not wish to have the "abstract," the mystery, the magic, and the shibboleth elements removed from the use of these two best of words. But neither word increases in value because someone shouts it!

Holy says two things

First. Holy means that God is different, other, and separate from all that exists. He is not to be equated with what He created — that is animism. It means that God exists and performs in contrast with the gods, the earth, and rebellious persons. It is the complete otherness of God. This meaning has priority.

Second. Holy is the word that tells us that God is a person who is the utmost in moral character. He is the One who in an absolute sense does the right thing, the good thing. God is goodness and does good.

God is love!

And what does that mean?

How's your TV screen on this one? Do you get a flabby God, a kind of Father Christmas — benevolent but doddering, who winks at evil?

Unconditional moral caring!

Love is used in the Bible to say something warm and wonderful about God. If "holy" emphasizes the "otherness" of God, "love" emphasizes the nearness of God! If "holy" accents the moral nature of God, "love" accents the *moral caring* nature of God. God, who is the ultimate in what is moral, also cares and without condition! He cares, gives, and respects unconditionally! In this is the defenselessness, the vulnerability of God. The Apostle Paul puts it with incomparable beauty. First he says that it is difficult to find someone who will die for a "righteous" or a "good" man. *"But God shows his love for us in that while we were yet sinners Christ died for us"* (Romans 5:8, RSV). Paul continues to draw the picture of a love so set on reconciliation that its vulnerability takes it to the cross — the most ignoble of deaths.

He will love us to hell

Love is the unchanged and unchanging posture and practice of God toward us. It hopes for our free and spontaneous response, but it does not demand our love. God will love us even without our response. He will in fact love us to hell! There we may leave Him, but He does not leave us!

Steadfast love

The Revised Standard Version uses a beautiful and meaningful phrase again and again in translating Old Testament passages. It is "steadfast love." Jeremiah quotes God. And God says that a man should not glory in riches, *"but let him who glories glory in this, that he understands and knows me, that I am the Lord who practices steadfast love, justice, and righteousness in the earth; for in these things I delight, says the Lord"* (Jeremiah 9:24, RSV).

There is the moral unconditional caring of God. Joel declares God is "*abounding in steadfast love.*" The psalmists talk much about this love. *"Many are the pangs of the wicked; but steadfast love surrounds him who trusts in the Lord."* He exults in the fact that *"steadfast love endures for ever"* (Psalm 136:1, RSV).

So God is holy love

Because of His "otherness" He can lift us. He is moral and good and does the right and the good. That is His holiness. But His holiness is paired with an unconditioned caring and respect for all persons in His universe. That is His love. And this is the kind of God who created us and our environment and gave us freedom to be, choose, and do right or wrong. Wrong cannot exist without hurt to ourselves or others, and not without pain to God.

Whatever else theology and the Bible may tell us about God, these are the words — holy love — which unveil for us His essence. Here we know what God is. It is more important to know this than to understand such words as *omnipotence* and *omniscience*. God has all the power He needs to act effectively, but His acts are controlled by His essence: holy love! In knowing God as holy love, I know enough to predict and to trust His attitudes and acts in His relationship with me and my fellow humans. What can be more important?

Don't separate the words!

Holy love is the highest designation we can give to either God or man. In personality, holy and love unite as the very essence of both God and Christian. God is not holy without love; He does not love without being holy. Each attitude and act becomes a blend of holy love. As in God, so in Christian.

There is no mere exercise in semantics. Words stand for realities. And whenever in thought and practice these two words — *holy* and *love* — get separated, we are in trouble about both God and Christian. Separate the two, and the accent tends to fall toward opposite poles. At one pole the harsh, judgmental, unaccepting, demanding, and legal; at the other pole acceptance without moral quality, the rejection of anger, wrath, and judgment as expressions of love in situations where relationships are deliberately violated. Both judgment and redemption are legitimate expressions of holy love. One more thing. Holy and love place necessary limitations on each other. Keep them together in thought and in life.

Holy Christians?

And who are saints? (*Saints* derives from the same root word as *holy.)*

Saints are "holy ones."

First Peter 1:15-16 (RSV) says, *"As he who called you is holy, be holy yourselves in all your conduct; since it is written, 'You shall be holy, for I am holy.'"* But what does that mean? In the Bible, people, places, times, and things are called "holy" when they are set apart unto God. The holiness of a person must relate to what makes God holy — *otherness* and *moral character*.

(1) I am holy when I am set apart and given to God in a personal relationship with Jesus Christ as Savior and Lord.

(2) I am holy as the new relationship and commitment purifies my life.

A revolutionary process

This means a revolutionary process has begun in my life. I am being changed from center to circumference. At the center is the change in loyalty from self to God. At the heart of holiness is a constant giving of self. The *dynamic* for this change is located in the death and resurrection of Jesus. The *reality* is by the work of the Holy Spirit who establishes the lordship of Jesus Christ within me.

This is an intensely personal and relational business. And here we may discover the significance of the biblical covenants which required acts and symbols of devotion to and relationship with God. And since in this new relationship we are set apart unto God we can be used by God. (Read Romans 12:1-3. Verse 1 is especially relevant.)

Commitment/consecration involves surrender. The new relationship is costly. We find that the process involved in commitment, in devotement to God is one of *cleansing* and *conforming*: cleansing from barriers to fellowship, conformity to Christ.

Christian love!?

But what is love? The answer is found in re-noting what love is in God. It is *unconditional, responsible moral caring*. But that sort of Godlike and Christlike love is just what we do not have. It comes from the age to come and lasts into eternity. And it comes to us by the infusing of the Holy Spirit. He sheds it abroad in the very center of self ("our hearts"). Only then can we also cultivate such caring. It is this un-asking, defenseless, vulnerable love that alone can save us from Spot No. 1 on the endangered species list!

Be good at loving

"Make love your aim" (1 Corinthians 14:1, RSV). Christians may fail in many things, lack many skills, show few social graces. But let Christians be good at loving, at caring for and believing in persons, at relieving fears and tensions, at lifting hopes, at creating an atmosphere of acceptance, and inciting the pursuit of excellence!

Don't just stand there

To love is to act — to do something — not just to stand there passively! It is affirming one another. It is understanding, respecting. It is looking at one another until you learn something that heightens your appreciation, deepens your compassion, stimulates your action. It is suffering with and for another. It is full of faith and hope which are really strands in the rope of love, giving it tensile strength and unbreakable resilience.

Reach out

Love is when we reach out, not in dramatic, news-making acts, but in quick and quiet moments of touching another in assurance, appreciation, and self-giving. These are life-giving moments for the one who touches and the one who is touched.

Holy love – the business of the church

Love is the business of the church — the creating of an environment in which its members can *grow* up in holy love and achieve the maturity open to those committed to responsible attitudes and acts. Holy love acts in no Pollyanna fashion. It is realistic. It faces differences, tensions, and misunderstanding honestly, straightforwardly, constructively, and with tenderness and concern, all the time seeking to create a situation in which holy love may *continue to grow.*

Holy love is good news

Holy love is good news. The fact that holy love was incarnate in Jesus is still mankind's headline good news. The fact that holy love is incarnate — though at times falteringly and imperfectly — in human persons is our continuing good news.

Words for Christians

Holy love — the two most important biblical-theological words for Christians! What they mean is what the Christian life must mean. To seek anything other than holy love is to seek amiss (with apologies to Wesley!). And the pursuit of holy love is the pursuit of a growing relationship with Jesus as both Savior and Lord. Christ embodied holy love. Holy love is Christlike. To this we are called! Make holy love *your* aim!

I Believe in the Church

"I call you 'Brother' with some reluctance," an irate critic once wrote to me, "but if I miss you in Christ, I at least hit you in Adam."

Indeed, you and I and all men are related and united in Adam. That is our problem. Around the world man is united in one thing — sin. And for this reason we are constantly separated from one another. Unity in sin bars our achieving the other unities for which we strive, noble as the efforts may be. And more profoundly, it is this sin deep within that not only separates men from each other but produces the torn, divided personality; we are at war with ourselves.

Symptoms

The communication media unite in the sad retelling of the news; man reaches for the answer to huge social, political, economic problems, but the solution always just eludes him. The dope addict, the alcoholic, the gambler, and the plain bored are only symptoms of deep and inward slavery. Watts, Berkeleys, and penal systems which do not rehabilitate point to our deep racial disease. Lonely and unloved people lead meaningless lives and kill the hours of hopeless days. Both the brilliant and the bums symbolize our lostness — neither can find the way.

Congenital Disease

Things are complicated because man is congenitally conditioned against true diagnosis. Only with outside help does he know the real problem. With that help he begins to see that basically the problem of the race is what man in selfishness has done with God and what man has done to himself. Self-will is seen for the fatal thing it is. Man has tried to dismiss God from his life. With God out of the way, as he supposes, he usurps God's place in the throne room of personality. This is our common racial situation. Not just one monstrous person has usurped God's place — nothing that simple. Rather, there is a world full of people who have mounted their prideful little thrones from which they declare and assert their sovereignty and rights. Strange, isn't it, that they should wonder why there are so many kinds of conflict in the world? It was all quite predictable, wasn't it?

Something Went Wrong

A peculiar thing happens. With God ignored or willed out of His universe and with himself firmly placed in the center of it, man nevertheless finds life is not to his liking. Something is wrong. By self-willed usurpation of God's place he loses wholeness, happiness, and harmony. He is disoriented and bewildered. He is aimless. The zest has gone. He is lost through broken relationships. He is unable to find his way back to either God or man. Man, says Olin Curtis, did not care enough about God to do His will. There is a deep sadness about that even as there is sadness about Calvary and about any son who turns his back to the Father's face.

The Church Is in the Center

God put Calvary in the center of the sad picture. He does more. He puts the church in the center as a continuing Calvary. Is the church being the church? Is it seeking shelter or solution? Is it running away in fear and inadequacy, or is it finding ways to be about the mission of its Lord? Is it serving or being served? Is it treating symptoms or healing at the center of corruption? Is it existing in legal purity or serving in redemptive, cross-bearing, sacrificial ways?

Answers must be both personal and organizational. We act out our answers daily. Our acted answers, not our words, tell what we really believe. What is it that we in the church believe so much that we will gamble all and lead others to gamble all on the validity of the belief?

My Confession

Looking candidly and clearly at the sin situation of man in God's world and at the successes and failures of the church viewed wholly from the human, I still confess, "I believe in the ... church." It is a borrowed confession; yet it is mine. The ancient words are a small part of the confession known as the Apostles' Creed. It is a personal and devotional expression of the Christian faith. Many thousands have drawn strength from it over many centuries, so I feel in good company. The creed reaches from eternity to eternity — from "I believe in God, the Father Almighty, Maker of heaven and earth" to "the life everlasting. Amen."

The Creed

"I believe in God, the Father Almighty, Maker of heaven and earth; and in Jesus Christ, His only Son our Lord; who was conceived by the Holy Spirit; born of the Virgin Mary, suffered under Pontius Pilate, was crucified, dead and buried; the third day He rose from the dead; He ascended into heaven, and sitteth at the right hand of God the Father Almighty; from thence He shall come to judge the quick and the dead. I believe in the Holy Spirit; the holy catholic church; the communion of saints; the forgiveness of sins; the resurrection of the body, and the life everlasting. Amen."

Our Confession

For centuries, this affirmation has reassured and reminded the Christian, whether in conflict or doubt, of his commitments. The language is in the first person. But the creed found use in the corporate worship of the early church. So before there were church buildings, people met in little house meetings and together voiced personal faith. In small crowded rooms elbow touched elbow, and the communion of faith was sensed as well as said. "I believe" became "we believe," and Christians were warmed by the knowledge that they were indeed the "Body of Christ."

Only the essentials of the faith were confessed, and the creed had the advantage of being notes on the unity rather than on the divisions of the church. Note also its trinitarian form: Father, Son, and Holy Spirit. The unity of the Trinity became a model and motive for the church.

The confession, "I believe in the holy catholic church," is of course conditioned by the entire creed. But what does it mean? I can only express in part what it means to me, for this is not an exhaustive treatise on the church. My confession of meaning is based on my understanding of the Bible as a whole, and of the New Testament in particular.

Chosen for Purpose

I. *I believe the church to be God-initiated and person-oriented.* The church is a special kind of community. It is the successor to Israel in this age. It is God's chosen community. This means it would not have existed had not God taken the initiative and brought it into being. It is *by* God, but *of* and *for* people. Israel often forgot it was "for" people — that it was chosen for *purpose* rather than for *privilege.*

Israel was a responsible community. Its purpose was to make known the holy love of God to the nations of the earth. Often it forgot it was God-initiated and person-oriented. Ultimately Israel failed. But the church must not fail. A denomination fails which forgets its origin, nature, and mission as related to the church of Jesus Christ. However, the church of Jesus Christ as a special, unique kind of community in the world will not fail!

The initiative of God we call "grace." This givingness of God is the natural expression of His holy love. In its love it becomes an extension of God's grace (givingness) to an outside community. It forever seeks to make members of the "outside community," members of the new race "in Christ."

Whenever in the church we see ourselves only as a company of the blessed or privileged, we are through. When we practice withdrawal from the world for the protection of either God's holiness or our own, or for any other reason, we are dead — waiting only history's undertaker.

Some may recall the quip of Bishop Gerald Kennedy of the Methodist Church, to the effect that if the church of Jesus Christ should disappear the Methodist Church would go right on. The quip reminds us that all our organized efforts must come under the constant searching of the Word and the Spirit. The mechanical can never substitute for the dynamic. While organization is inescapable and essential, we must never forget that the true church is an organism. It is indeed the "Body of Christ."

For the sake of my own Christian life, I must be reminded constantly that the church and the Christian life are not only God-initiated; they are also person-oriented rather than organization-oriented. This was one of the meanings of that historic community Israel, and it is a meaning of the community which is the Body of Christ. This is a saving thing for all of us.

Designed for People

The person-orientation of the church saves us from being program-oriented, organization-oriented, or competition-oriented. It saves us from sheer busy work. We are not here simply to "put something over." Our concern is for persons. We do not manipulate people. We do not use them for the sake of personal ambition, organizational prestige, or statistical advantage. The entire church enterprise must operate above the organizational and sales motivational level.

We serve. We are not lords or masters. We suffer with others in and out of Christ's community. I was delighted when a government agency declared to my son that a battery of tests he had taken showed: "You are incapable of using people for your own or government purposes." He was then reminded that a certain agency considering employing him was not a philanthropic organization!

When we really see the person-orientation of the church, we are seeing what Jesus saw. People consumed His life. When this happens, the meaning of goals is revolutionized. Statistics are no longer impersonal little marks on paper. They take on bones, flesh, and blood. Beyond the little marks on paper (statistics) I see faces — faces that remind me that people are in the image of God, however marred the image may be.

Faces remind me that God created and God suffered for all the faces — for everyone. Statistics are no longer ecclesiastical stripes of pride or shame; they are symbols of redemptive love. Denominational goals are not viewed as the imposition of materialistically minded ecclesiastics; but as intended, they are reminders that every Christian and every Christian group, under God, is committed to think, plan, and pray, and act redemptively and creatively in order to build the Body of Christ — to increase the number of the rescued, and to give the good news away and rob Satan of his slaves.

When the well-being of people in relationship with God and others becomes our only concern, then every act, every thought, every committee meeting will have a redemptive intent. Yes, even the committee meeting will be a means of grace and a launching pad from which missiles of love are directed to the unredeemed community. In this atmosphere, drudgery and tiredness depart, and the Holy Spirit is sensed as present and active.

A Biblical Image

II. *I believe the church is the Body of Christ. This is biblical.* The church is not a business, educational institution, club, lodge, or hospital, though it may exhibit characteristics of each. Hence, the executive, salesman, educator, or lawyer, for example, can be effective in translating ideas from his own speciality to the church *only* if he is well grounded in a biblical understanding of the nature and mission of the church. And the New Testament image, "Body of Christ," portrays both the nature and mission of the church.

The church is different from the world. It is the Body of Christ on earth. We have not always understood what makes the church of Jesus Christ different in and from the world. We are *against* some things because, first of all, we are *for* some things. We have negatives which derive from positives. So we are against all that retards the development of the true nature of the church in our congregations. We are against all that cripples the full expression of the redemptive mission of the church through our congregations. The church is made up of all sorts of redeemed persons who have, by the grace of God, become redemptive.

A Practical Mystery

The church is a mystery. The church partakes of the mysterious nature of Christ Himself, who was supremely redemptive because He was not only one of us but One above us. But for this mystery, the church would long since have disappeared. Since the church has Christ as its Head, it lives like Christ. Its servanthood is fulfilled in the world community, even though its life is drawn from above. It is human in its weakness, yet mighty in the power of the resurrected Christ.

Yes, the real church is different, and it is this difference that makes it so needed and relevant in a worldly community of which it is, and must ever be, a real part. In fact, I am so much a part of the world community that I can honestly join in praying, "Forgive us our trespasses." No effective man separates himself from his day, its people, events, and trends. We are part of the race, the world community, the nation — even its sins. This is inescapable. So in our redemptive mission it is not difficult to identify with the sinner. We do not feel superior to him. We do not look down on him. We stand beside him, with arm about him, and facing toward the cross we see One whom each of us needs every moment. As we stand there, we note that the ground is level and we are not taller than he. Through Christ's blood, and Christ's grace we share Christ's life, so we in turn can share.

It hits me, takes hold of me — the church is the Godlike, Christlike community on earth. Of all the New Testament images used to describe the church, the most comprehensive and meaningful one to me is "Body of Christ." I glow in the warmth of belonging to Him and to others. There can be no completely individualistic relationship to the risen Christ. When we are "in Christ," we are part of one another. The church I believe in is a fellowship. It is not held together by mutual attraction; it is united by common *relationship* to Jesus Christ. Nothing less can hold us together.

Continue Christ's Ministry

III. *I believe the church exists to fulfill the purposes of God in Christ.* The church that I believe in is God's means of continuing Christ's ministry on earth. This belief does something for me. It exhilarates and sobers me. It gives me wings so I am lifted above small considerations, monotonous motions, feelings of inferiority, and crippling fears. It causes me to perform for Jesus' sake, not for ecclesiastical or egoistic satisfactions, nor for man's approval. I am saved from the petty and swept along on the tides of God.

But I am also faced with sobering responsibility. I realize that the church is the world's ministering, suffering, redeeming community — and I am the church. This concept is devastating to minor, peripheral, and often destructive concepts which attach themselves to the church, falsely waving the banner of the holy. My pharisaical tendencies are rebuked. Harshness gives way to love. My inclination to withdraw from a dirty world meets a troubled Christian conscience. I know that in the name of Holy Love on a cross I must turn myself outward to contacts with that world.

The big issue is not whether the Free Methodist Church will survive; it is whether or not we are fulfilling our servanthood as the church of Jesus Christ. Are we in reality the Word's ministering community? Jesus my Lord was Servant. Am I?

Dr. Lamberta Voget, professor of sociology at Wheaton College, asks, "Have we (evangelicals) lost the capacity for making contact with people other than our own kind?" We cannot afford to be without sinner contacts. Jesus was a friend of sinners without talking down to them.

The church of Jesus Christ is the world's Good Samaritan. But is my church often a club of the clean, the uninvolved who are fearful of the real, live issues that families and individuals in and out of the church meet day by day? We — preachers, writers, editors, leaders — are told, "Don't preach, don't write, don't talk about these modern issues, like race and sex. Preach about the sins that do not disturb us — those that are non-controversial. Don't be realistic. Don't rock the boat. Don't make us suffer. Don't disturb our contentment. You see, our minds are made up. Don't confuse us with the facts — the biblical, theological, and human facts that threaten to dump us from our cozy little nests of complacency."

By contrast let us be like the minister who said to me, "I've just told my wife that it's a great day to be alive in the church. One day it seems on the brink of disaster, and the next day it is filled with hope — but it is an exciting, adventurous day to be in the church."

Indeed! What high responsibility and privileges are ours. Every Christian is not only his own priest and prophet; he is also his neighbor's. So he goes to God for his neighbor, and to his neighbor for God. He proclaims and exhibits in his life the wonderful redemptive acts of God. He fulfills D. T. Niles' description of evangelism: "one beggar telling another beggar where to get food."

Church – an Organism

IV. *The church I believe in is an organism — not an unchanging organization.* We often decry the monolithic structural aims of the hierarchy of the Roman church, forgetting that in a small way we too would like to achieve a static stance where all issues are forever settled. In that attitude we often differ none from Rome.

The book of Acts, according to the author, is a description of the continuation of *"all that Jesus began both to do and to teach ..."* (1:1, NIV). It is the description of a changing church — in beliefs, restrictions, attitudes, and actions. It is a dynamic church. It can be explained only in terms of the Head telling the Body how to react. Acts 28 did not end the history of the church as the Body of

Christ. The new wine of a risen Christ, alive in His community, could not be held within all wineskins, old concepts, old prejudices, old practices.

The enabling Holy Spirit is prominent in the story of Acts. His role is one of empowering and innovating. The words, "It seems good to the Holy Spirit and us," marked the turn of many a corner. And there were many who decried the changes but could not dispute the results.

"Change and decay in all around I see;
O Thou who changest not, abide with me."

These old lines are dear to all of us living in a sin-infested world. But change in the church is not always decay. One kind of change spells death; another means new life. Under the innovating leadership of the Holy Spirit, even John Wesley engaged in practices which violated his churchly sensibilities.

Churches Can Change for the Better

Even denominations can improve by change. The recognition of the need for change is seen in denominational provisions for legalizing change. We have heard that denominations seldom retain their original purity and power beyond a generation or two. But there are examples of change which help a denomination to more nearly reflect the New Testament church.

The Wesleyan Methodist Church organized principally on a social issue. It has come to higher ground doctrinally in the area of holiness. The Free Methodist Church took twenty-six years after its founding to come to its position on the use of tobacco. Today the questions for membership in our church, in keeping with the New Testament, are more demanding than when I joined. "Will you be a witness?" we are now asked. The utterances of the church in the *Discipline* and elsewhere give evidence that its sense of responsibility in the world is at a new, high level. Unfortunately, we seem to exhibit less of a social conscience in the matter of concern for the Negro* now than we did in 1860. Our vision of moral issues needs new breadth and depth.

***Editor's Note:** Given Dr. Knox's sensitivity to racial issues, a 1990s rewrite would certainly say "African American."

The church I believe in is a dynamic organism, and therefore creative. Several biblical writings point in this direction: (1) Christ is the Head of the church. Here is born all effective strategy. (2) Paul makes it clear that the very power which raised Christ from the dead is operative in the Christian and in the church, *"which is his body, the fullness of him that filleth all in all."* The resurrection dynamic is a resource of unlimited power. (3) Jesus is set forth as the world's creative agent, and it is not hard to believe that His creativity extends to new redemptive moves through His church. (4) The *Holy Spirit is seen as a prime mover* in the mission of the church. Hence, the surprising thing would be a static church. Like the wind the Spirit bloweth (moves) where He will (John 3:8). We should, under God, anticipate much that is new and creative — not to match our space age but to lead our fast-moving era by serving in life-changing ways.

Holy Church

V. *I believe in a holy church. This is a biblical belief.* Paul says that Christ loved the church. He gave Himself for it. The loving and giving were in order that He might set the church apart and cleanse it so it could be presented to Himself as a glorious church, beautiful and without flaw or wrinkle. It is to *"be holy and without blemish"* (Ephesians 5:27, KJV). This holiness consists in being Christlike; it immediately rejects pharisaic holiness and emphasizes the purity which can eat with sinners and gain no spot on the garments of holiness. It is separated unto God, but in Christ it is committed to reconciling contact with the world.

Inclusive Church

VI. *I believe in an inclusive rather than exclusive church.* The creed uses the term "catholic." Clearly this does not mean the Roman church. Both "catholic" and "ecumenical" have gathered bad connotations. They mean universal. And indeed the church of Jesus Christ is universal in that it is intended for all. Its proclamation is to all. Its fellowship is loving and redemptive, leaping all the artificial barriers erected by men. All may be saved, and all the saved are entitled to full membership in the Body of Christ.

I cannot believe in or belong to a club of the elite, the good, or the better, and call it a church. The church is composed of redeemed and reconciled sinners. Some of them may have been divorced, drunk, doped, duped, immoral, uncivilized, barbaric, mean, disturbed, sensual, or ugly sinners. Others may have been refined, sophisticated, cultivated, intelligent, educated, socially accepted, or self-sufficient sinners. The arms of the church like the arms of Calvary take us all in when we respond in trust to the givingness of God in Christ. The inclusive church measures its effectiveness in terms of redemptive love rather than by the letter of the law. Its mission is to lift those within and without its fellowship, because like God in Christ its nature is nothing less than Holy Love!

VII. *I believe in a paradoxical church. It is divine and human.* The Apostle Paul paints the portrait of the ideal church: holy, triumphant, self-sacrificing, and Christlike. But he also writes to churches which are divided, carnal, human, earthly, and very visible. We must not separate the churches in the paradox. They must continue in "creative tension." The ideal church remains the inspiration, reminder, and rebuke to all who strive to be Christ's church.

Perhaps we need to see that as our Lord Jesus Christ was both human and divine, and as our Judeo-Christian Bible is a human and divine instrument, even so the church of the Lord Jesus is both human and divine — it is "the Body of Christ" on earth. The treasure is in an earthen vessel.

The church must be in reality the continuing community of all Jesus *was* and *said* and *did.* Hence, all we are, say, and do must come under the constant critical exposure and informing presence of the biblical and theological.

The tendency to place our own opinion above the Bible is not confined to Rome. We need a better biblical, theological orientation. Great church renewals and evangelism find their origin here. And for the success of this critical procedure we must open ourselves to the Holy Spirit, who uses the biblical and theological to correct and empower the church of Jesus Christ.

We must remember that churches as organized congregations or denominations are purely functional. The justification for the continuance of the Roman church or the Free Methodist denomination is not found in ecclesiastical heredity. Whether we are apostolic or not is not determined by secular-type success. Our justification can only be sought in how faithfully we reflect the ministry of Jesus — what He did, what He taught, and what He was.

Our Common Task

Laity and clergy then must engage in a constant search for a full understanding of the nature and mission of the church in the Bible. What we find should inform and motivate the administration of the church in its worship, witness, and service.

Would this lead us to a greater emphasis upon the biblically revealed demands for membership in the Body of Christ, more than the demands of membership in a denomination? Would we, in fact, find this approach more demanding and effective? Would not the leverage, the motivation, be greater because it is based in Scripture? Could we not expect the results in our fellowship to be less legal, but more dynamic and redemptive? Must not our expectation of denominational loyalty derive directly from our loyalty to the Body of Christ, of which our Lord is Head?

Our Common Attitude

In the confession of the great creed — and I trust in mine and in yours — there is no trace of pride. Rather, there is joy at being redeemed and in belonging to Christ and to one another. Together we share the tearful joy of the forgiven woman washing Jesus' feet with her salty tears and drying them with her loosened hair. We confess our unworthiness. We reject pride of organization, pontifical pomp, ecclesiastical lordship, as we happily affirm our mutual servanthood in a hospitalized world.

The creed reminds us of our primary symbols: basin, towel, and cross. And it confesses a desire to be like our Lord.

The Only Hope

Despite its faults, the church is the world's only hope for sharing the reconciling, redemptive acts of God in Christ. Only thus can man recover his nature and destiny lost in the first Adam.

When the church is true to its nature and to fulfilling its mission, what it does is the most important thing happening in history. This truth is sobering. It should call us to new heights of holy love and redemptive suffering if we are to contribute effectively to the new race God is creating in Christ Jesus.

A Postscript

At the National Art Gallery in Washington, D. C., I stood before the stimulating painting of "The Sacrament of the Last Supper" by Salvador Dali. It had something to say to me about the church of my Lord. It became more significant to me since it was done by the artist after a revolutionary change in his personal life. Dali turned away from surrealism as an art of revolution, and from the writings of Marx and the Nazi Rosenberg which had long influenced him, to a study of the Bible and Christian theology.

Each viewer may get different impressions from the basic theme. But let us note certain facts which may aid our impressions and deepen our concern for the work of the church.

The design is along classical lines. Observe the many rectangles, squares and diagonal lines. A portion of a bronze twelve-sided frame is seen, which the Greek Pythagoreans declared to be a symbol of the universe. Above this structure in partly realistic, partly transparent fashion are shown two arms which seem to reach out embracing the universe. Above this nearly transparent figure there is no head. Does this suggest the risen Lord of the church?

Now note three circles: the hills rising out of the small sea, the encircling arms of the headless One, Christ with beckoning hands, seated while His disciples kneel as communicants around the table.

The Christ, both present and ascended, is there. The world with its boats, symbolic of its activity (the secular world), is there. So is the embryonic church bowing as it is being readied for Christ's death and its own life of service. The arms of the faceless Christ extend inclusively. As you stand before the picture, you feel yourself drawn in. The beckoning hand with arched forefinger and spread thumb is so very personal. How well it tells the gospel story. Christ is for all, but Christ is for me!

Then I see that the circle of disciples is not completed. I am asked to kneel, to join. Here is the little church with its Head waiting for those who are to be rescued into the new community.

Will we bring them to the communion table? Will we make the active life outside meaningful because of the redemptive fellowship inside? And here we face a continuing paradox: The world waits for us; the world could not care less about us! Tragically it is turning elsewhere for solutions. We must go out from communion to communication. We must by our witness in life and words make relevant the living Christ.

Then we can all say, "It is a great day to be alive in the world and in a changing, dynamic, relevant, holy and catholic church." Then we will all obey His command to "go," and will receive His greatest blessing, *"Lo, I am with you always."*

I Look at Me

It happens to each of us — moments when I see me! Many different things occur in those moments — things which make a difference and that make no difference. Suppose we think about this together.

I need a good mirror! I understand a stream was man's first mirror. We know the story of Narcissus who saw himself in a pool, pined away, and, in love with himself, was changed into the flower bearing his name. So being narcissistic came to describe a person who experienced undue gratification looking at himself. Then there was the dog with a bone. He trotted across some boards bridging a stream and looked down and saw a dog with a bone. In greed he pursued the "other" dog (with opened jaws), only to lose his own bone. Parables?

Then there is the mirror which greets me every time I step into the narthex of the church where I worship. It always makes me feel as if it was a huge mistake to get up. It is, I think, a distorting mirror. I hope I don't look the way it says I look. I find it a depressing way to begin worship. I think I have a better mirror at home. That is, I think I see me as I am.

That is what I need — a mirror that lets me see me in all my reality. I don't need a "house of mirrors" made to provide different and distorting reflections. That may be fun at times. I do need some laughs.

I need a mirror that is a proper mix of honesty, objectivity, and clarity. A good constructive, critical friend is part of the mix. I can also let the Bible be my mirror. I may have to ask it to do that for me. But if I ask, it will! Another element in a good mirror may very well be those moments of quiet reflection when I deliberately open myself to the mirror elements found both in the Bible and the personal ministry of the Holy Spirit. Yes, Lord, let me see me — warts and all!

I need to like me! I find Freud depressing. But Jesus! He is different. I'm sorry Freud missed Him. When Jesus put it all together for us He compacted the moral directives. Jesus saw three things intertwining — to like God, neighbor, and me. We dare not pull them apart. I can't like God and hate myself or my neighbor. I can't like neighbor and hate God or myself. I can't like myself and be indifferent to God or neighbor! So I need to like me. But if I am to like me I must have help. (Stop! Read John 3:16.)

Jesus was sent to change us right where it counts. It gets very personal. I can't like me unless I have Jesus to help me like the God who is like Jesus — and to like the neighbor who is so much like me — and to like myself who is both unique and yet so very much like other humans. The *great fact* is that Jesus died and rose again to make Himself available to me through His Spirit to give me this precise and needed help. Thank you, Jesus. I accept Your help. I want to like me.

I need to know what I am worth! Well, I am worth more than it appears. It used to be said that, if all I am is a carcass, I am worth about ninety-seven cents. But with inflation, that may now be up to three dollars! If all I am is "matter," it's not worth computing. I get no feeling of worth from the unlimited size and crushing power of the universe, nor from death, or the shortness of life, or the reach of my decision-making power, or how well I am known.

I believe I know a bit of my worth as I watch God risk making me at all. *I am God's wanted child.* This is the one very personal thing I can understand about the majestic, creative enterprise of God. *I am God's wooed son.* He pursues in lovingkindness. I rebel and alienate myself from Him and neighbor. The pursuit of God tells me something of my worth. *I am God's redeemed child.* God, acting in Christ, paid the kind of price I can but faintly take in so that He can communicate the fact of His love, release me from a self gone wrong, and restore me in loving reconciliation, fellowship, and partnership. Thank you, God — Father, Son, and Holy Spirit — for letting me know my worth. Help me to stand straight and tall because of Your estimate of me and effort for me!

I project me! I know it now, Lord. Help me to love — even to like — myself so that I *can* and *do* love every other human You bring my way. Help me to help by having a good self-image. I think, Lord, that will help me enhance the image and worth of other persons, whom You love as much as You love me. Thank you, God, for treating me like a person. That makes me feel good. Help me to treat others as persons whom You love.

Index Cards — They Helped Change a Life

I saw her recently. She has retired. She looked so vibrant that I didn't immediately recognize her.

But I remember a time when I was her pastor. She, her husband, and her daughter had experienced one crisis after another. Things had piled up. She was at the breaking point.

I came on a pastoral call. Immediately and with a look of distress she said, "I have never been entirely sanctified." She got to her knees and asked me to pray. I spoke gently. "Get up — I am going to my study to write prescriptions for you and will soon return."

I returned with Scriptures typed on index cards. I asked, "Where will you best see one of these cards in every room?" We walked together. One was placed over the sink, another over the mantel in the living room. The most prominent spot in every room was selected. And there we put an index card. She could not enter any room without confronting the Word of God.

"And now another thing. When you get up in the morning I want you to go immediately to your bedroom window. Look out and up. And regardless of weather or feelings, say out loud, *'This is the day the Lord has made, I will rejoice and be glad in it'* (Psalms 118:24, paraphrase). Repeat the words until something warming happens inside you."

Later this sensitive and intelligent woman reported, "I thought you were the strangest Free Methodist preacher I ever met. Who ever heard of one who would refuse the opportunity to pray with a seeker after entire sanctification?" But then with great seriousness she added, "If you had not done what you did I am sure that I would have been institutionalized."

She told me about the first morning after the prescriptions. She remembered the counsel. But it embarrassed her. She argued, "That's silly, and I'm not going to do it."

But then she said, "He is my pastor. I suppose it won't hurt anything." She went to the window and said the words again and again. Finally, something happened deep within her.

She began to face crises victoriously. She found help in the ever present and supportive Scriptures on the index cards. She became a vibrant person and for many years held a very responsible position.

God, I believe, has help for each of us in His Word. Try it. Start the day just as I recommended to my distraught parishioner. You may also say out loud, "Thank you, Lord, for loving me." Repeat. Believe that God accepts you as you are. Let Him be your friend. You are His both by creation and redemption. He has an investment in you.

Try Psalm 31:7. *"I will rejoice and be glad in your unfailing love: For You have seen my affliction and You have cared for me in my stress"* (LHK). Type Romans 8:38-39 (TLB) on an index card. Carry it for ready reference.

Do fears invade? Try Isaiah 43:1-3. *"The Lord says ... fear not: for I have redeemed you. I have called you by your own name; you are mine. When you pass through waters (troubles), I will be with you, even rivers (deep troubles) will not drown you. ... For I am the Lord your God ... your Savior"* (LHK).

Affirm with Isaiah (12:2): *"God is indeed my deliverer, I am confident and unafraid"* (NEB).

Write John 10:28-29 (TLB) on another index card. Let the words remind you that it is not your hold on God that makes the difference. It is His hold on you! Let Him hold you. *Rest* rather than *cling. "The eternal God is my refuge, and underneath you are the everlasting arms"* (Deuteronomy 33:27, LHK). *"Happy is the man who fears the Lord. ... Bad news shall have no terrors for him, because his heart is steadfast, trusting in the Lord"* (Psalm 112:1, 7, NEB).

Recast the words of the psalmist (103:2-5) as your affirmation. *"With all there is of me I bless the Lord. I remember with thanksgiving all You do for me"* (LHK).

Any troubled, sleepless nights? Remember — peace comes when there is trust! Again let the psalmist help. *"Now I will lie down in peace, and sleep; for thou alone, O Lord, makest me live unafraid"* (4:8, NEB). Or make Psalm 121:3-5 the source of a personal affirmation. *"The Lord himself is caring for me! He is my Guardian. ... He is never weary, never sleeps"* (LHK).

Personalize God's Word. God will become the First Reality, the First Intimate of your life.

Jesus' Invitation to Happiness

Now when he saw the crowds, he went upon a mountainside and sat down. His disciples came to him, and he began to teach them saying:

Blessed are the poor in spirit, for theirs is the kingdom of heaven (v. 3).

Blessed are those who mourn, for they will be comforted (v. 4).

Blessed are the meek, for they will inherit the earth (v. 5).

Blessed are those who hunger and thirst for righteousness, for they will be filled (v. 6).

Blessed are the merciful, for they will be shown mercy (v. 7).

Blessed are the pure in heart, for they will see God (v. 8).

Blessed are the peacemakers, for they will be called sons of God (v. 9).

Blessed are those who are persecuted because of righteousness, for theirs is the kingdom of heaven (v. 10).

Blessed are you when people insult you, persecute you and falsely say all kinds of evil against you because of me. Rejoice and be glad, because great is your reward in heaven, for in the same way they persecuted the prophets who were before you (vv. 11-12).

You are the salt of the earth. But if the salt loses its saltiness, how can it be made salty again? It is no longer good for anything, except to be thrown out and trampled by men.

You are the light of the world. A city on a hill cannot be hidden. Neither do people light a lamp and put it under a bowl. Instead they put it on its stand, and it gives light to everyone in the house. In the same way, let your light shine before men, that they may see your good deeds and praise your Father in heaven (Matthew 5:1-16, NIV).

The focus is what has come to be known as the "Beatitudes." In Matthew's record it is the beginning of the Sermon on the Mount.

Jesus sat down to teach. That to us is a surprising custom. A dear friend of mine living now in the Seattle area went to do an interim ministry in Wales. He developed cancer of the bone. He had shrunk five or six inches in a short time. But recently I was informed that he preached at Everett, Washington, seated. He did well. Why not? It was Jesus' way. It suggests closeness and relaxation.

Jesus' first word of proclamation was "Repent," and when looked at closely we discover it was a word of great inspiration and comfort. Jesus said, "Look, you CAN change! You are not locked into what you now are!"

Likewise, these words are not intended to be another harsh code. Jesus intends to free us to be what we were intended to be. So He tells us:

1. What pleases God
2. What is worthy of the Kingdom of God and, ultimately,
3. What is self-fulfilling

The problem is that our human perspective has been skewed. It is fallen man's perspective. We do not see life realistically nor hopefully. Jesus wants to change that — He wants us to repent, to change, to get a new thinking cap.

The KJV, RSV, and NIV translate "Blessed are ..."; the NEB "Blest are ..."; Phillips "Happy are ..."; and Barclay mixes it up and often speaks of the bliss certain attitudes and characteristics produce.

The Beatitudes are more than simple statements; they are exclamations. Barclay says, "O the blessedness, the bliss of ... ." Not pious hopes, uncertain prophecies, but congratulations on what is present reality with some.

The words are not pointed to the future. They are focused in the here and the now. Jesus does not describe something we may enter into in the sweet by and by but something one may experience in this life.

Taken together, the Beatitudes say to us: "O the bliss of being a Christ-person! O the sheer joy/happiness, the radiant gladness of the Christ-like life."

Blessed! The Greek is *makarios.* The Isle of Cyprus, in the Greek, employs this word and it means "The Happy Isle, lovely, rich, fertile, with all the climate, trees, fruits, minerals — all the materials for perfect happiness." A kind of Garden of Eden.

Jesus has in mind a way for us to have serene, untouchable, self-contained joy which is independent of the chances and the changes of life. The root for the English word "happiness" is "hap" which means "chance." So normal human happiness is dependent on chance and change. Life can give its good things; it can also take them away.

But Christian blessedness, happiness, bliss is that joy which Jesus said "*no man taketh from you*" (John 16:22, KJV).

It is not difficult to make out that Jesus sets all the commonly accepted norms of the world aside. J. B. Phillips presents a pagan list of beatitudes as follows:

- Blessed are the "pushers": for they get on in the world.
- Blessed are the hard-boiled: for they never let life hurt them.
- Blessed are they who complain: for they get their own way in the end.
- Blessed are the blasé: for they never worry over their sins.
- Blessed are the slave-drivers: for they get results.
- Blessed are the knowledgeable men of the world: for they know their way around.
- Blessed are the trouble makers: for they make people take notice of them.

God aims at turning our perspective inside out, down-side up! He suggests what must seem as a really topsy-turvy world for us earthlings. It is as though He said, "Look, friend, have you found bliss, blessedness, fulfillment in your accepted norms? Those standards, procedures you have established all on your own? Those man-made articles of faith by which, whether you are aware of it or not, you try to live out your life? Has your autonomy or self-directed life given peace, contentment, fulfillment, joy, satisfaction?

If it has not, then this is an invitation to listen to a new way, a new perspective which is not mere idealism, but rather pragmatic realism. Let's look at how Jesus shifts life's center of gravity. Let's just move down through His words and see what He proposes. The center of life-gravity is shifted.

1. **From self-reliance to unhesitating trust in God.** This has two results: It makes possible a life of obedience to God. Next, it makes a person a citizen of the Kingdom of Heaven (v. 3).

2. **The shift is from indifference regarding both corporate and personal sin and sorrow, to deep and responsible caring for persons** (v. 4). Now observe that the first Beatitude (v. 3) congratu-

lates those who are able to **detach** themselves from things, who are able to put things in the proper order of priority.

The second Beatitude (v. 4) congratulates those who are able to feel **attached** to others and able to live lives of concern and caring. It marks a counteractant to self-centeredness. So first there is **detachment** from **things**; next there is **attachment** to **persons**.

3. Now we are ready for the third Beatitude (v. 5). Here the shift is from **uncontrolled instincts and passions to self-control through putting God at control central.** "Meekness" also suggests deliverance from haughty self-deceit to realistic and humble self-appraisal.

4. The fourth Beatitude (v. 6). Next Jesus points to a shift from **filling life with the world's husks to the satisfactions of total righteousness — rightness, goodness.**

5. The fifth Beatitude (v. 7). He moves on quickly to the shift from **indifference regarding others to seeing with Another's eyes, thinking with Another's thoughts, and feeling with Another's feelings**, for that is precisely what Jesus did.

6. The sixth Beatitude (v. 8). **The shift includes moving from mixed motives to unadulterated, unalloyed, unmixed motives: pure motives.** When we allow that shift to occur, we begin now to get the beatific vision; we begin to see God now. Life begins to clarify, for we begin to see things as they really are and should be. The pure of heart see God, and go on seeing God, with ever-increasing clarity.

7. The seventh Beatitude (v. 9). Now Jesus moves from wanting peace as a sort of cessation of hostility to **making peace, from passively watching life's schisms and conflicts, to active participation in helping to establish right relationships between persons, wherever we can have a positive impact.** And it is in this, Jesus says, that we do the God-like work. For it is His main business also.

8. The eighth Beatitude (v. 10). Jesus is not through. He would move us **from self-protectiveness to willingness to suffer for the right.** One has said that Jesus "did not come to make life easy, but to **make men great**."

9. The ninth Beatitude (vv. 11-12). Those days soon after Jesus left this planet tested the mettle of all the Christ-persons He left behind. Those were not easy days. The political development of

Rome saw the emperor given God status. Worship of the emperor became the law of the land. **Christians were faced with a choice: Christ is Lord or Caesar is Lord.**

A poet spoke of our earliest Christian forebears as "the panting, huddled flock whose crime was Christ." God always matches us to our hour. Happy is the person who meets the test triumphantly.

What a very strange invitation to bliss, to true happiness our Lord offers. Was He right? Or are the ordinary norms and values of society right? Is it any wonder that once these early Christians were announced as "those who have turned the world upside down"?

Has most of mankind walked so long in an inverted posture that the words of Jesus seem like the ultimate distortion? Yes, Jesus in these words has described "the holy ones" for all who have eyes to see. Happy, joyous, bliss-loaded are these holy ones!

But what Jesus says next is, I think, of utmost significance in the light of what He has said in His invitation to happiness. Such holy ones are not only the happy ones. They are in fact the kind of persons absolutely essential to ongoing life on this planet. They are the planet's anti-pollutants.

Note what Jesus says about these blessed ones: (1) They are the planet's salt. (Salt makes thirsty.) (2) They are the planet's light.

Notice that I have said "they." And perhaps that is a source of temporary comfort. It removes it one step from "me" and from "we."

But dare we, and will we move it closer? Can we say, or can it be said regarding "us":

We are the salt of the earth.
We are the light of the world.

That puts it in the here and the now!

The happy holy are this planet's most needed citizens!

Key Biblical Perspectives on Tongues

Explanatory Preamble

This publication is a section from a book in preparation to be published and tentatively titled *The Holy: Holy Spirit, Holy Church, Holy Love.* (**Editor's Note:** The book was never completed and published.)

The principal word in the chapter title is "Biblical." There is no attempt to deal with psychological, historical, or other considerations regarding the tongues phenomenon manifest in either the regular "Pentecostal" denominations or in the new nondenominational forms. Neo-Pentecostalism is accompanied by a strong anti-institutional posture.

It is impossible to provide a detailed description of the Corinthian tongues problem. It is possible to note a connection between it and the modern movement — neo or regular. That connection is the usage of non-language sounds as a distortion of the gift manifest on the day of Pentecost. There is also a connection between this phenomenon and that which from time to time has occurred in other great religions as well as in utterly pagan worship.

Personally, I have knowledge (1) of those who could speak in tongues, at will, without a relationship with Christ as Savior and Lord, and at the same time intermingle obscene or blasphemous language; (2) of those who were delivered from the manifestations of demon possession and hence of the practice of tongues; (3) of those who were zealously missionary in promoting this error and loveless when rebuffed; and (4) of a few who practice tongues who do not promote the error and are gentle and peaceable.

The limited and relatively narrow scope of this chapter does not provide the needed larger framework of the Person and ministry of the Holy Spirit. The larger context will be supplied in the projected book.

What follows requires an open Bible before you as you begin to read.

Achieving a biblical understanding of a subject may be a simple or complex matter. When faced with an apparently complex issue it is essential to observe the rules of interpretation. We must compare scripture and try to gain as full an understanding as is possible. Proof-texting has often proved an inadequate tool. We must seek to understand the intent of the writer whose words were penned centuries ago to people of a very different culture and language from ours. We must ask, "How did the first readers understand these words?" Only after these and other technical procedures are observed can we safely move to apply the ancient message to our times, culture, and needs.

The combination of perspectives attempted will, it is hoped, provide an adequate basis for interpretation which is biblical in the fullest sense.

The problem is placed in the center. Let us walk around it viewing it from the vantage points provided by the Scripture. Only in this fashion can one hope to arrive at a biblical understanding of the problem.

Viewing Platform One: Perspective of Pentecost

From the perspective of Pentecost we see the importance of the tongue in the Christian era: the tongue that sat on each person; the languages used to witness to the mighty acts of God. The tongue was used in inspired but intelligible witnessing. To the foremost natural gift of God to man — speech — is now added the releasing and heightening work of the Holy Spirit.

The phenomena accompanying the Pentecost event did not become normative to receiving or being filled with the Holy Spirit. The infilling of the Spirit is a Christian norm. Purification of the heart by faith accompanies the infilling, and this is logical, since it is the work of the "HOLY Spirit." Believers filled with the Spirit were characteristically courageous, outgoing, and enthusiastic. Their understanding of the Scriptures was clarified and focused on Christ and how Christ related to man's salvation. The filling of the

Spirit affected the tongue. The use of the tongue produced conviction and repentance. There was amazement at the way the Spirit-filled spoke. The taunt of drunkenness does not connote the utterance of unintelligible speech; instead, it was free-flowing and uninhibited. These were released men! The ability to speak was heightened by the Spirit. The speakers at Pentecost were in control of themselves, yet free, as they had never been before. Their excitement and enthusiasm communicated. They were filled with the Spirit and spoke "as the Spirit gave them utterance."

There is unusual symbolic significance in the "tongues as of fire" which separated with *one* tongue coming to rest "on each *one* of them." One tongue to one person. The usual art representations are not accurate. They were not forked tongues! The significance is multiple: fire spoke God's presence; one tongue to each believer emphasized that all, not a special few, were henceforth to be filled with the Holy Spirit; the tongue shape announced the important role of the tongue in the new era of the Spirit; the confusion of tongues at Babel was reversible. James called the tongue "a fire ... set on fire by hell." And it is able, he says, to "set on fire." No wonder the tongue is prominent at Pentecost and in the ongoing work of the Holy Spirit. He would, indeed, make the tongue a fire set on fire of heaven, proclaiming the mighty acts of God. The tongue used by the Spirit "set on fire" the hearts of men. Observe the list of gifts in Romans and Ephesians and the preeminence given to gifts related to the use of the tongue! In fact, *intelligible* communications is dominant among the gifts of the Spirit. The "tongues" of Pentecost was languages or dialects.

Ecstasy and the rapture of new joy characterized both the "tongues" and the sermon of Peter. *But both were intelligible.* The invasion of believers' lives by the Holy Spirit, plus a new understanding and appreciation of the mighty acts of God, was enough to produce ecstasy and rapture. But there is no evidence that each witness was unconscious or out of control. Their spirits were subject to them (1 Corinthians 14:32). Even the preaching of deacons, Stephen and Philip, was marked by the Spirit's heightening of their natural powers and abilities of speech. The Spirit helps us to be more fully what God designed us as humans to be and more, rather than less, conscious. But all our powers are brought under the control of the Spirit. So Wesley sings, "Hear him, ye deaf; his praise, ye dumb, your loosened tongues employ."

Since the work of the Holy Spirit is so prominently linked to the Christian's use of the tongue, let us note an important matter about the natural gift of speech to mankind. The gift of language is the foremost distinction between man and animal. Learned between the ages of two and four, it is the most difficult achievement of a lifetime for any human being. It is essential to self-knowing, to civilization, and to the communication of symbols, meanings, abstractions, ideas, traditions, and so on. It is now known that the most primitive society has an exceedingly complex language which taxes the expertise of the best trained linguist to understand its systematic grammar, syntax, and so on. Linguists and anthropologists are at a loss to explain this phenomenon. The Christian may well rejoice in this special input on the part of the Creator. Apparently this gift cannot be explained in an evolutionary fashion by the evolutionary enthusiasts.

How does this relate to Pentecost and tongues? The God who made us in His image and endowed us with the extraordinary gift of speech, now at Pentecost completes His gift to us by adding a dimension of ability by the Holy Spirit so we may be effective witnesses of the mighty acts of God in Christ Jesus our Lord. That stirs my emotions with holy joy! Pentecost is the continuing acts of a creating God.

The tongues of Pentecost would pose no problem in the church. Clear, Spirit-anointed witnessing does not divide or damage the body of Christ. It unifies, edifies, and converts. (I know a man who received the gift of language to work with the Haitians. Later transferred to Africa, he had to learn another language. The Spirit did not give it to him.) It is "as He wills."

Viewing Platform Two:
Perspective of Acts – After Pentecost

We can discover no evidence for tongues being experienced that is different from that at Pentecost; none ever sought tongues; many are filled with the Holy Spirit with no evidence of accompanying tongues.

Acts is descriptive narrative while 1 Corinthians is teaching regarding abuse. Acts is the *only* record of persons receiving tongues. It is always related to the receiving or infilling of the Holy Spirit. But there are ten records of persons being filled with the Spirit without any record of their speaking in tongues. Only three events refer to tongues: Acts 2, 10, and 19. Acts 2 refers to languages. It cannot be dogmatically asserted that the other two incidents were NOT languages. The Acts 10 record is often referred to as the Gentile Pentecost. Peter reported at Jerusalem that *"the Holy Spirit fell on them, as on us at the beginning"* (11:15). And *"... they heard them speaking in tongues and extolling God"* (10:46, RSV). This does not support an "ecstatic and unintelligible utterance" conclusion.

The next descriptive narrative is Acts 19, which may be described as the Ephesian Pentecost. This concerns another distinctly different group. They were isolated followers of John the Baptist. They may have been early followers of Jesus who had not heard about the era of the Holy Spirit. The formula is a bit different. When Paul laid hands on them, *"the Holy Spirit came on them; they spoke with tongues and prophesied"* (19:6, RSV).

Language speaking is a fitting symbol for ushering in the era of the Holy Spirit with three distinct and significant groups. In each case the recipients are passive. They are not seeking the so-called gift of tongues. Flexibility is noted, for in chapter 2 the event follows ten days of prayer; in Caesarea it interrupts preaching; in Ephesus it follows baptism and the laying on of the hands of Paul.

You may examine the four passages which refer to receiving the Spirit but without indicating accompanying tongues: Acts 4:31; 8:17-19; 9:17b-18a; 13:52 (see RSV). Add to that six references to persons who were reported to be full of the Holy Spirit but without evidence that they ever spoke in tongues or practiced speaking in tongues.

Viewing Platform Three:
Perspective of Peter's and Paul's List of Gifts

Peter identifies only the two categories of gifts: speaking and serving. Peter and Paul are the only New Testament writers who provide lists. Paul, in letters to more stable churches and at a later date, does not list tongues. The Ephesian letter lists only gifts related to the special-

ized use of the tongue. Romans lists three speaking and four practical serving gifts. Three lists in a single chapter of 1 Corinthians are a measure of the abuse of the tongue by "tongues." (See Chart 1, page 196.)

Peter directs, *"As each has received a gift, employ it for one another, as good stewards of God's varied grace: whoever speaks as one who utters oracles of God; whoever renders service, as one who renders it by the strength which God supplies; in order that in everything God may be glorified through Jesus Christ. To him belong glory and dominion for ever and ever. Amen"* (1 Peter 4:10-11, RSV).

The gifts of the Spirit are in two categories: speech and service. Each Christian has a gift and is a steward. He has two purposes: use the gift "for one another" and that "God may be glorified." Peter's directives are important: *speak* the messages of God; *serve* in the strength of God.

The Petrine *categories* are useful applied to the *lists* of Paul. Each of the nineteen gifts listed by Paul is placed in the categories. A further division is made between the functions and the one who functions — call them "Stewards of Grace."

The language varies, but the intent is the same: God of His grace provides the twofold gifts to the church for its good and growth in order that it may witness effectively in the world.

Now look at Chart 1 on page 196.

Ephesians (A.D. 60-61) is Paul's last word on the gifts. The letter is really a treatise. The dominant theme is the church. That is important to note. It is systematic and encyclical — directed to a group of churches. What does Paul emphasize? Priority is given to the speaking gifts for the development of the church. (Note: not a hierarchical order of offices, but of functions.) Just before the list Paul shows concern for that Christian character which makes unity possible. Right after the list he states the purpose of the gifts: bringing the church to the *"unity of the faith, and of the knowledge of the Son of God, to mature manhood, to the measure of the stature of the fullness of Christ."* The negative purpose, he says, is to save the church from being tossed *"with every wind of doctrine, by the cunning of men, by their craftiness in deceitful wiles."*

Romans (A.D. 58) comes three years after the Corinthian letter. It also is important to this study, for it is a systematic and definitive writing about Christian faith and practice. Spirit-gifted use of the tongue is stressed; tongues is simply not there! Together with Ephesians it constitutes material of great significance. Paul provides three speaking gifts and four serving gifts. There is a touch, a dimension of the supernatural about these gifts if they are used properly. Any gift can be abused. For example, how often has the gift of giving been abused by the steward ceasing to have the attitude of a steward and taking on the role of a dictator in the church!

We see in the gifts a mingling of the human and the divine. A substrata of human capacity touched by the Spirit of God so that we are enabled to do more than we can do! The gifts are gifts only when they are the work through us of the indwelling Holy Spirit! Paul further regulates the gifts by relating them to the lordship of Christ (1 Corinthians 12) and the love of Christ (1 Corinthians 13).

Now note a peculiarity of the three lists occurring within a single chapter in 1 Corinthians 12. The list includes a few gifts which never recur anywhere in the New Testament as gifts. It may be that all of them were rather high in generating problems. Tongues, of a certainty, was a troublemaker. This rather different group we may call "the spectaculars," i.e., faith (that-moves-mountains sort), healing, miracles. Certainly they are the source of unusual temptation to pride, arrogance, and self-exaltation. They rank low on Paul's scale, which seemed to be at great variance from the scale used by the Corinthians. There is a reason for "tongues" being at the bottom of the ladder in the lists. It is at the top in chapter 13 in order that Paul can contrast it to love and do it immediately. It is up front in chapter 14 also. But again it is to put it down! It is placed in huge and repeated contrast with another use of the tongue — namely, prophecy.

Viewing Platform Four:
Perspective of Paul's Unit on the Gifts
(1 Corinthians 12-14)

From the perspective of the total unit, tongues receives severe treatment at the hands of the Apostle Paul. The unit shows the concept, context, and control of gifts. It shows their purpose and how they should behave. It shows that the work of the Holy Spirit is to make real the lordship of Jesus and to bring every gift under the equally controlling love which only God can give. The length, tone, and

procedure are a measure of the abuse of the tongue at Corinth.

"Tongues" was one of the problems at Corinth. It was one of Paul's pastoral concerns. The entire first letter Paul wrote to Corinth deals with many problems he faced as a pastor-counselor. The letters of the New Testament give us insight regarding the problems of the early church as it functioned in many locations with language and cultural differences. Many of the problems identified in the early church have been recurring. So the letters are of immense significance. Corinth appears to be the only early church with a "tongues" problem. And that is understandable when it is seen as a part of a multi-problem church. We may identify its problems in large categories: emotionalism, sensualism, secularism, disunity, disorder, and orthodoxy. The problems of orthodoxy are threefold: worship, morality, and doctrine. Pride, pushiness, and contentiousness caused division. They suffered from the results of their previous paganism in their behavior in matters of sex, lawsuits, abuses of the Lord's Table, and the spiritual gifts. Hardly the church to emulate!

First Corinthians 12-14 comprise a unit devoted to the *pneumatikon*, that is, the "spirituals" or the operation of the Holy Spirit in gifts. In this unit Paul turns from problems of the Lord's Supper to questions which had been raised with him regarding the gifts in general and "tongues" in particular. It appears he turns to the task sternly since he is irked at their childishness, immaturity, and love for excitement and the spectacular. He seems immediately to suggest, as a jibe, that they are ignorant about the gifts. The hint is that they really should know better. The gifts are wonderful; abused, they are hindrances to the church! The plan of the unit is masterful. Immediately he established the necessity of the lordship of Jesus, and that it is a reality only by the Spirit. Then he moves to demonstrate God's love of variety and His provision for it in the functions of the church. Variety and unity are essential. But this fuss over gifts is out of hand, as seen by the series of questions at the end of chapter 12.

The better way is described in chapter 13. *Character takes precedence over gifts in God's church.* And pity the church where love does not reign through the lordship of Jesus.

Again in chapter 14 the tongue is contrasted with tongues — the constructive with the destructive. In chapter 14 we see how love behaves in Christ's community. It is very specific.

Viewing Platform Five:

Perspective of 1 Corinthians 12

The purpose of the Holy Spirit is to exalt Jesus as lord of everything in the believer, including the gifts of the Spirit. The tests of relationship, reason, and usefulness are to be used. Gifts must contribute to the unity of the body; they are distributed as the Spirit wills; the answer to "Are all ... do all?" is NO!

ANATHEMA JESUS versus LORD JESUS — it is just like that in the Greek.

In the previous pagan life and worship, it was common to be carried into a mindless frenzied state in which one might cry "ANATHEMA JESUS." But the implication is that it is the business of the Holy Spirit to help us say, "LORD JESUS." The saying is not glib; it means that Jesus is Lord in reality and pervasively. The invasion or infilling of the Spirit is essential to His lordship in our thoughts, feelings, and will, and hence in both our words and deeds. He is Lord of the gifts — Lord of the tongue/speech in particular if it is the work of the Holy Spirit. The aim of pagan worship was release from reason, self-consciousness — a spiritual trip. By contrast, the Spirit heightens reason, self-consciousness, will, and feelings by release from ourselves to the lordship of Jesus. Anything the Spirit ministers to us, in us, or through us will forward the lordship of Jesus in our lives and in the lives of others. The problem apparently at Corinth was the tendency to drag the desire for a trip into the new worship. Against this desire and practice Paul places the ministry of the Spirit making Jesus Lord.

The concept of the gifts is provided. They are from the triune God who seeks variety in functions. The purpose emphasized in this chapter is "the common good" (v. 7). Variety in unity is described: baptized into one body by the Spirit, that very body illustrates the principle at work in the variety of the gifts. Lordship is emphasized in the distribution of gifts "as He wills" (v. 11). This and the body illustration is a blow to pride and self-assertion which was producing envy and division. An eye becomes a whole body — so we are reminded that the exaltation of the spectacular is grotesquely perverse. Paul had a sense of humor, irony, and the ridiculous. Rational, serviceable, intelligible communicating gifts get the favorable emphasis.

There are tests of *relationship, reason,* and *usefulness.* The questions are like this: Does the gift accept and forward the lordship of Jesus? Is wisdom and knowledge at the top? Is it for the common good?

By employing a writer's gimmick — a series of questions with an understood answer to each — Paul destroys belief in any gift being a sign of the baptism of the Spirit or of superior spirituality, or that one is to have all the gifts, or that tongues is for everyone. The Spirit "as He wills" will distribute gifts. The answer to "Are all ... do all ...?" is "NO!"

Viewing Platform Six:

Perspective of 1 Corinthians 13

Paul distinguished between higher and lower gifts. Prophecy rates higher and is open to all. But love is the director-general of any gift. It is in fact the greatest gift, for it sets a believer free to serve effectively. Tongues fade. The tongue, inspired and controlled by love, assumes great importance.

In the chapter transition Paul suggests that one should desire the greater or higher gifts (12:31). BUT there is a *better desire,* a *better way* than any or all of the gifts. Each does have at least one gift. But better be giftless than loveless. If your interest is excellence, then focus on a prime *fruit* or product of the Spirit — love (Romans 5:5 and Galatians 5:22-23). It is the gift of God by the indwelling Holy Spirit, and it is the fruit of the Spirit. It is expressed in unconditional self-giving. It is other-oriented. It is the only grace of the inner circle of graces which lasts into eternity — "never ends." Spectacular gifts and powers are placed in contrast with love, and tongues is the most fragile and least able to stand in the presence of the grace of love. Even rational powers will end, and knowledge will disappear in truth. Character lasts. Paul hints that Corinthian attitudes and priorities are childish.

Chapter 13 is the most magnificent expression ever penned of how Christian love feels, thinks, and acts! It is the Christian's touchstone and criteria. Without love *"I am nothing ... I achieve noth-*

ing" (2-3). The zealous tongues promoter is redirected. Then and now the church's real deficiencies are more notable in the area of love (character) than in gifts (functions).

Paul's summary is, *"Put love first; desire the higher gifts but especially that you may prophesy."*

Viewing Platform Seven:

Perspective of 1 Corinthians 14

The crucial chapter. It is a specific application of love in the case of a gift which is abused. It draws attention away from obsession with tongues to the inspired but regulated use of the tongue. It contrasts tongues and prophecy. It is a clarion call for the use of rationally ordered, Spirit-inspired, and intelligibly transmitted languages in Christian worship, whether private or public. The call is illustrated in three ways: a hypothetical personal visit to Corinth, musical instruments, the many languages of mankind. Forbidding women to speak in church is included in the tongues problem. The unit is an appeal for that which builds and for decency and order.

It has been made clear: love is the Christian's aim; the higher gifts are desirable; one gift all may seek and practice in church — to prophesy. Pride destroys the value of *any* gift and cannot dwell with love. In chapter 12 Paul uses the body as illustrative of this fact and of the usefulness of variety within unity. In chapter 14 he uses three illustrations to call for the rational and intelligible use of language, rather than unintelligible and mindless articulations. He illustrates how his coming to Corinth could be either a useful or a useless exercise (v. 6). Then he notes that in both music and language there is a system for intelligible communication. Each sender and receiver has a medium both understand. The illustrations are meant to contrast with the abuse of the tongue as practiced at Corinth.

Examine carefully Chart 2. Absorb the impact. There is an overwhelming buildup in argument against tongues and for the use of the tongue in inspired witnessing (prophesying). Observe the seeming contradiction in Paul's words. If the seeming contradiction is to be resolved, the thrust must be carefully noted.

Look now at two paragraphs which are closely tied together: 6-12 and 13-19. The punch lines are at the end of each paragraph —

"excel in building up the church." "I would rather speak five words with my mind, in order to instruct others, than ten thousand words in a tongue" (RSV).

"You are eager for manifestations of the Spirit" (v. 12). Apparently their zeal was without knowledge (Romans 10:2). There is rebuke in the words rather than applause. Paul has said love is our true objective, or "aim." By contrast to the desire for manifestations he exhorts, *"Strive to excel in building up the church."* Repeatedly he tells us what builds is that which should involve every Christian: love and prophecy. Look again at the lists in Romans and Ephesians. They stand quite apart from this abuse-oriented letter. The exhortation to excel is aimed directly against non-intelligible utterances! Excelling in the "building" gifts does not have a strong appeal to these lovers of the spectacular and the mysterious.

The new paragraph begins with "therefore," so one needs to reexamine the previous paragraph, 6-12. In the light of the uselessness of non-intelligible communication as illustrated in the previous paragraph, they better "pray for power to interpret" their meaningless sounds. Why? So that finally, though circuitously, intelligible words are uttered *even in prayer*! Wordless utterance despite accompanying ecstasy is not helpful to others, for the others cannot move along with the prayer to an appropriate "Amen." Paul insists the others should be edified (v. 17). Now we have the context for what on the face of it is an utter contradiction: verse 18 against verse 19. Is Paul in conflict with Paul? Is he the author of confusion? Not intentionally! He may seem so to us, but did the Corinthians understand the thrust and the seeming contradiction? Or was it clear and without even seeming contradiction to them? I am convinced they understood. They knew Paul, his many abilities and his background of education and experience. In a congregation of many languages he would be able to communicate, if necessary, in at least five languages — likely more. With all Paul has said to this point and faced with the Corinthian brag on "tongues," might he not have done as in other letters — bragged a bit on his own? It was a distasteful but necessary strategy for Paul. Could Paul have possibly bragged on mindless utterance in either public or private worship? Not in the light of the context he provides! He was altogether committed to communication which edified by being understood. His attitude, expressed in this paragraph, toward mindless utterances in prayer seems to preclude that he was boasting of tongues in his prayer life.

But let us say more about the problem of verses 18 and 19. Likely we have a language problem, or more precisely a word problem — one word with more than one meaning. The word is *glossa*. Some commentators always give the meaning, "languages"; others also give the meaning, "ecstatic, uncontrolled utterance." Most commentators use both meanings as one or the other appears to be required or as it appears to be the intent of the user. This is not an uncommon problem even in English — and what if many centuries had passed and someone was trying to determine our meaning? (I find it difficult enough to communicate in clear English so it is understood now, or three months later!)

It is very possible — in the light of the direction of Paul's argument — and indeed it cannot be ruled out that Paul is saying, "I speak in languages more than you all." The alternative is to believe that Paul spoke contradictions which cannot be resolved. Some find a way out in proposing that he meant his prayer life. From the above analysis, that appears very unlikely. He was a mature Christian and certainly would not be dependent on emotional non-language sounds to converse with the Lord Christ. Whichever choice is made of the alternative attempts to reconcile the verses, the following is clear: Paul opposes tongues as an exercise which does not build the church (v. 12); Paul prefers intelligible to non-intelligible utterances (5 intelligible equals 10,000 non-intelligible — the preference ratio is 2,000 to 1). Does, then, Paul *permit* tongues? If so, the low rating is clear. Perhaps we can survive permission on the basis of Paul's ratio of preference! However, what follows in the next paragraph makes permission less credible and the translation proposed more credible.

So we examine a crucial paragraph in a crucial chapter: verses 20-25. Right off he strongly suggests they have been acting as people who are children and immature in their thinking. Be babes indeed so far as evil is concerned, he exhorts. However, they had been quite experienced in evil and found it hard to shake even after coming into the church!

In verses 21-22 Paul, I believe, moves in with the *coup de grace* (the mortal stroke of mercy). With all the Old Testament available, why does he go to Isaiah 28:11? Could the strategy be to provide the final blow without appearing to be harsh to these converts and at the same time provide biblical authority and illustration? Look ahead, and you will find him concluding the chapter with a strong, dogmatic, even emotional assertion of authority for the words he has spoken — undoubtedly a measure of the difficulty of the problem and the intransigence of the tongues advocates.

Look at Isaiah 28:11 and its context. Drunken priests and false prophets have enticed Israel (the people of God — Church of the Old Testament) away from God. Israel refused to hear Isaiah even though he spoke clearly and distinctly the message of God *in their own language.* The message carried the promise of "rest" and "repose." Even though they were church members in the Old Testament, they were unbelieving members of Israel. In reality and ultimately they rejected God, not Isaiah. That rejection caused God to act in judgment. He will send them a plague of tongues. But He does it by sending the Assyrian troops which were composed of various nationalities and tongues and could not be understood by Israel. The languages of a conqueror became the language of judgment — *"that they may go, and fall backward, and be broken, and snared, and taken"* (Isaiah 28:13, RSV). Sad picture of the results of unbelief and failure to accept God's prophet speaking in words understood by the hearers. Tongues is by analogy a judgment on the unbelief of some errant church members at Corinth!

One must understand the Old Testament reference used by Paul to understand the thrust of the entire paragraph, verses 20-25. Observe that Phillips in translating alters the accepted text. Something, he concludes, must be wrong. Either Paul's pen slipped, or more likely a copyist erred. Not so. He should have studied Isaiah. Paul says, *"Tongues are a sign not for believers but for unbelievers, while prophecy is not for unbelievers but for believers"* (RSV). What tongues? The tongues of invaders come — so far as Israel is concerned — in judgment. Those unintelligible tongues were the sign of unbelief, which is rebellion against God. Tongues were a judgment on unbelievers in Israel. That is like saying, "Tongues is a sign of judgment on unbelievers in the church." And that is Paul's intent. The judgment was not intended against those who believed in the message (prophecy) of Isaiah. Prophecy, not tongues, was for believers. Believers welcomed the word of Isaiah in their own tongue. It was not for unbelievers. In unbelief and rebellion they rejected the words and thereby rejected the God who inspired the prophetic message! There is no escaping it. Paul's words are the strongest anti-tongues statement I have ever heard! The comparison is absolutely devastating. And when understood, it makes verses 23-25 perfectly understandable, with no conflict between them and verses 21-22.

Let us move on then with Paul to verse 23. Paul is now concerned with a very different kind of unbeliever — not a God-rejecting church member (Israel), but an outsider. He is a pagan, ignorant of the Christian message and way, and therefore an unbeliever. He knows nothing of the great acts of God in Christ which are proclaimed by inspired witnesses, for he has never heard the witness. So far such unbelief is excusable. Paul does not criticize him for his unbelief; rather, he condemns the church for making it difficult for such an unbeliever to believe. Paul's sympathies are with him if in a meeting where false tongues is employed the outsider concludes the company "mad" or, as Phillips translates, "insane."

Again the contrast between tongues and the tongue inspired in Christian witness (24-25); the verses hardly need commentary. The results of prophecy are such that they not only build the church, but they have a wholesome, redeeming effect on the outsider. Look at the results Paul identifies: the outsider is convicted; he is judged regarding his sins; his innermost needs are laid bare; he is moved to repentance; he worships God; and he comes to the conclusion about the group (and note the contrast): *"God is really among you!"*

Now if we are to believe that Paul is "soft on tongues," why does he resort to the extraordinarily strong passage from Isaiah and then immediately couple with it severe and judging contrast between tongues and the prophetic tongue?

Now remember — for it is important — that verses 26-33 have all that has gone before in the unit on the *pneumatikon* (chapters 12-14) as context. Here is a beautiful picture of a fully participatory kind of early church worship. But unfortunately we must keep to the subject: tongues. Two principles emerge: (1) Let all be done for edification; (2) God is not a God of confusion but of peace. Tongues has been declared as non-edifying. So what is Paul the pastor-counselor doing in the paragraph? In the last paragraph, with its strong condemnation of tongues and exaltation of prophecy, was he done, finished, through with the false tongues? It appears very likely. Having delivered the *coup de grace* to tongues, he can move on to liturgical concerns. Does he not now say what you do in a multi-language assembly? He must either use *glossa* to mean languages or non-intelligible sounds. In the light of what has gone before, I must opt for "languages." If in a multi-language congregation one wishes to speak in a language understood by a minority of the participants, let him do so if an interpreter is to be present.

Suppose it is still contended that Paul meant non-intelligible utterances by his use of *glossa*. If this is what he means or if one can still believe that after the strong words he has used, then Paul must be using a strategy appropriate to headstrong, emotional persons which carried out will doom their prized gift. How? By rigid liturgy, by control, by advance planning! It would go something like this: The one claiming the tongues gift would need to make certain that an interpreter was to be present, and then "only two or three" may participate within this strict order. It sounds very unlike any of the tongues in Acts where *all* spoke! — and no one initiated the gift! What is the net result? The excitement is removed, the emotion drained, and the so-called gift dies a natural death. Excitement demands more and more stimulant! I wonder if Paul was accused of being an authoritarian ecclesiastic who sets dangerous limits to the freedom, the blowing of the Spirit? It appears that Paul would argue that the Spirit moves powerfully, innovatingly, and convictingly. It is the role of the Spirit to build, to give peace, and to unite the body of Christ — not to produce confusion. He cites the objective of the primitive service — *"that all may learn and all be encouraged"* (31), as indeed all can *"prophesy one by one"* (31).

There is yet one more statement aimed at the so-called gift of tongues. *"The spirits of prophets are subject to prophets"* (32, Beck). The NEB translates, *"It is for prophets to control prophetic inspiration."* The literal: "And the spirits of prophets to prophets is (are) subject; for not is of tumult God but of peace." A twofold understanding is offered by the translations, and I think helpfully. Observe that even the prophet who has been applauded so vigorously by Paul must not abandon to ecstasy or get carried away so his utterances are contrary to the Word. Such a performance could contribute to pride in the prophet. He is always to be in command of himself — not carried into mindless trance or frenzy. The other and likewise important side of the coin is that prophets should be a mutual disciplining group. Private judgment and performance is disciplined by the rational (discerning) review of peers in Christ. There is individual and corporate responsibility for maintaining *"peace"* and stopping *"confusion"* (v. 33). There is also responsibility to submit to the other prophets as they *"weigh what is said"* (v. 29). To the Thessalonians Paul said, *"Do not quench the Spirit, do not despise prophesying, but test everything; hold fast what is good ..."* (1 Thessalonians 5:20-21, RSV). This is in line with the gift of discerning of spirits (12:10, KJV).

Now we come to the end of chapter 14. Verses 34-36 is the strongest kind of statement about the use of the tongue by women in public worship. My question is: How do tongues advocates interpret the passage? Why do they honor it more by an opposite practice? That is not raised to criticize their conclusion — that women can talk, even have prominence in the church. It is to ask what rules of interpretation they use to overrule the apostle, when with much less reason they enthusiastically promote tongues? It is a strange performance indeed! And to all who simplistically declare, "But the Bible says!" I reply that one needs to know much more than that certain words are said in the Bible. Context, culture, and all the well-established rules of interpretation must be called into action.

There remains one last hurdle. It is the last verses of the unit. *"So, my brethren, earnestly desire to prophesy, and do not forbid speaking in tongues; but all things should be done decently and in order"* (38-40, RSV). Here again is the problem of translating *glossa*. It cannot be translated "non-intelligible utterances" in the light of all that has preceded it; rather, "let various languages be used in the multi-language assembly, providing it is controlled according to the ritual of 26-33."

So now the subject has been viewed from seven points of observation. The bold-faced passage at the beginning of each perspective provides a summary. Put the perspectives together for a full portrait of the problem. Certainly nothing is found that is favorable to non-intelligible utterances in either public or private worship.

Some Implications of the Preceding Study

1. The tongue/speech is the greatest functional gift to man and is of paramount functional importance to the church when it is inspired by the Holy Spirit, operates under the lordship of Jesus, and expresses the love which is God's kind of love.

2. The purpose of tongue/speech is intelligible communication.

3. The purpose of Christian speech is the intelligible communication of the wonderful acts of God in Christ and all that that signifies for the person and for mankind.

4. The tongue/speech of the Christian needs the control of the lordship and the love of Christ.

5. Unintelligible uses of the tongue do not contribute to the common good or build the church.

6. God's gift of speech in creation, plus all the acquired skills of communication, plus another dimension of ability provided by the Holy Spirit, is essential to the effective communication of the gospel. We need to remember — every witness — that it is Spirit-anointed speech which carries the authenticating power of both Word and Spirit.

7. Pentecost was a beginning of the end of Babel. It is the work of the Holy Spirit to reverse Babel. It is cause for rejoicing that God has called so many to use their gifts in translating the message of salvation into the languages and dialects of the human race. We should avoid moving from Babel to Pentecost and back to Babel!

8. Luther emphasized "the priesthood of believers." Let us also emphasize "the prophethood of believers." A kingdom of priests and prophets can extend the lordship of our Savior Jesus Christ.

Summary of Author's Convictions

On the basis of careful exegetical search and interpretation of the New Testament passages which speak of "tongues," I submit my convictions that:

1. The gift of the Holy Spirit Himself in His fullness is our greatest need.

2. The impartation of God's kind of love by the Holy Spirit is more important than the gifts of the Spirit.

3. The Holy Spirit distributes, as He wills, gifts of speech and service devoted to the common good and the building of the church.

4. Gifts are to be exercised under the lordship and love of Christ.

5. Whenever there is a genuine gift of tongues, it is the supernatural impartation of rational, intelligible language as at Pentecost.

6. There arose a "tongues" problem in only one church identified in the New Testament, and it became a divisive issue noted three times in a single chapter and was never again mentioned in letters to the churches.

7. Tongues speaking was a problem at Corinth, rebuked by the Apostle Paul as being under the judgment of God and condemned in both private and public usage.

8. The New Testament fails to provide even one instance of a Christian seeking tongues.

9. The modern tongues movement tends to emphasize so-called tongues rather than prophecy or the full range of the gifts and, therefore, comes under condemnation of the Scriptures. Often tongues speaking is exercised at the will of the person rather than at the will of the Holy Spirit. It thus appears prideful and self-exalting. The modern movement does not emphasize language as the fulfillment of the gift. And the Apostle Paul deplores utterances which do not communicate clearly and rationally.

10. Nevertheless, we should extend the right hand of Christian fellowship to Pentecostal denominations in interdenominational associations, even as we do to other Christians with whom we are not in full doctrinal agreement.

11. Furthermore, we should seek to help those who may be caught up in this error. The modern manifestation may accompany immaturity. It may be a psychological phenomenon. In some instances it may be an expression of demon possession. In any case, the church should seek to teach, to promote maturity, or to deliver. But in no case should a person be permitted to promote the error within the church.

CHART 1

Gifts of the Holy Spirit in the New Testament – 19 different ones!✧

Peter provides the categories of gifts: "whoever speaks ... whoever renders service" (RSV). Peter declares each Christian has a gift, uses it for one another, is a good steward of God's varied grace, serves in reliance on strength God supplies that God may be glorified through Jesus Christ (1 Peter 4:10-11).

(11) SPEAKING

The communications and ministry system of the church: The verbal and body language of the church!

(8) SERVING

The Stewards | *Their Functions* | *The Stewards* | *Their Functions*

Ephesians 4:11 (A.D. 60-61)

Apostles
Prophets
Evangelists
Pastors
Teachers †

Romans 12:6-8 (A.D. 58)

Prophecy
Teaching
Exhorting †

Romans 12:6-8

Ministry (administration)
Giving
Ruling
Acts of Mercy §

Faith (mountain moving)
Healing
Miracles

1 Corinthians 12:8-10 (A.D. 55)

Speaking Wisdom
Speak Knowledge
Prophecy
Discernment
Tongues
Interpretation
(Discernment relates to prophecy and likely to the others) †

1 Corinthians 12:28

Miracle Workers
Healers
Helpers
Administrators (organizers)

"And God has appointed in the church first," etc.
Apostles
Prophets
Teachers
Speakers in kinds of tongues †

1 Corinthians 12:29-30

"Are All ... Do All?" Expected answer is

*"NO!"**

Apostles
Prophets
Teachers

Miracles
Healing
Tongues, Interpret

* NO! "But earnestly desire the higher gifts" (1 Cor. 12:31) ... especially that you may *prophesy"* (1 Cor. 14:1). BUT BETTER STILL "make *love* (chap. 13) your aim."

† Speaking gifts predominate, with certain ones having priority.

✧ Paul is not set on the number of gifts. He might name more if writing today.

§ Some *seem* very commonplace, i.e., acts of mercy, ruling (administration), helping, but when touched by the Holy Spirit they are full of ministry potential!

CHART 2

1 Corinthians 14

	FOR *Prophecy*	FOR *Tongues*		AGAINST *Tongues*	AGAINST *Prophecy*
1				"aim at love . . . desire to prophesy"	
2		"speaks to God . . . utters mysteries" →	but	→ "no one understands"	
3	"speaks to men for their upbuilding and encouragement and consolation"				NOTHING
4	"edifies the church" ←	"edifies himself" (not a compliment) →	"but"		
5	"even more to prophesy" ← "He who prophesies is greater → *Reason*: "church may be edified"	"I want you all to speak in tongues" →	"but" / than / "unless someone interprets" *Interpret then equals prophesy. Hence, tongues dependent upon a prophetic function.	→ he who speaks in tongues"*	
9				"how will anyone know what is said? For you will be speaking into the air"	
11			V. 12—So . . . strive to excel in building up the church" Inference: Tongues do not build the church.	mutual foreigners	
13				must "pray for power to interpret" (take the short road to communication: prophesy)	
14		"my spirit prays → (not a compliment—cf. v. 4)	but	→ my mind is unfruitful"	
			V. 15—Putting it together, pray and sing with *spirit and mind* (not with *tongues and mind*)		
				Others can't say "Amen" for they can't understand	

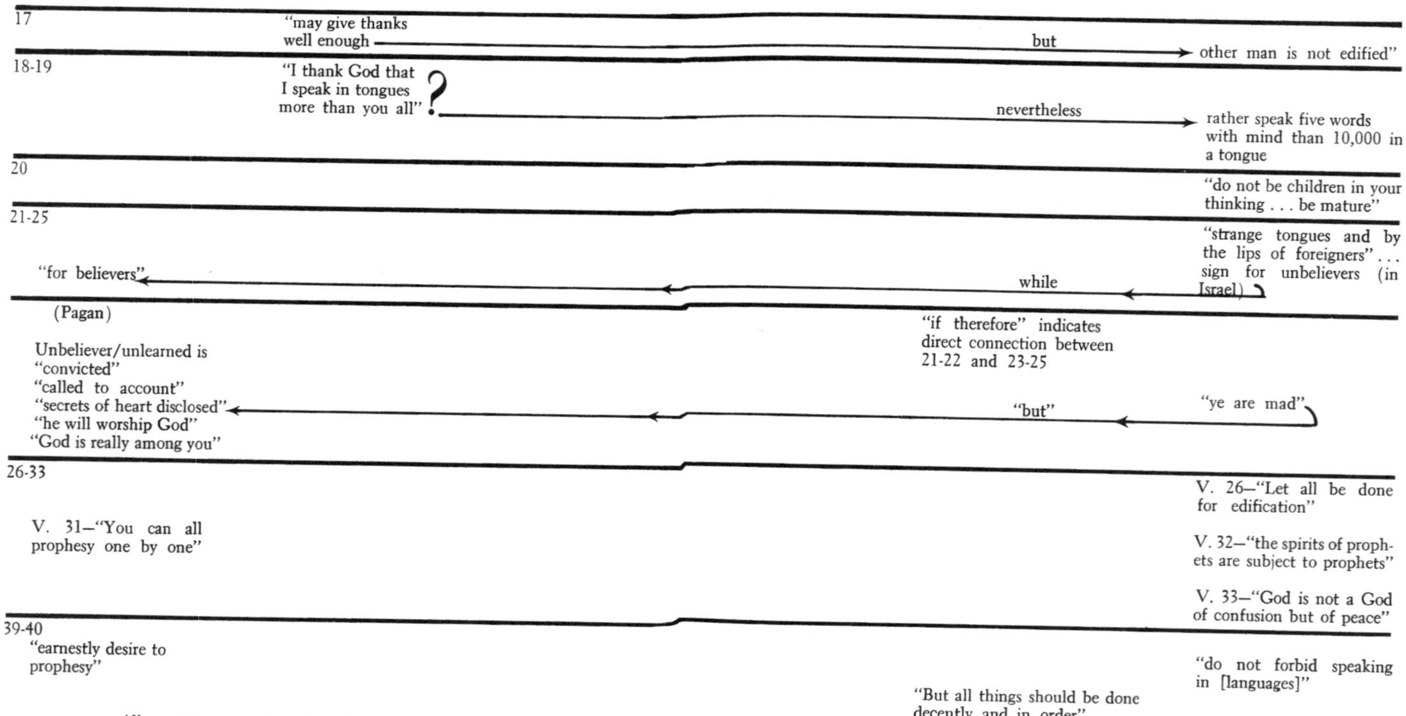

All quotations are taken from RSV.

Living Inside God's Purpose

We know that in everything God works with those who love him, whom he has called in accordance with his purpose, to bring about what is good (Romans 8:28, Goodspeed).

We marvel at the range of adaptation found in nature. But there is also a wonderful adaptation within the **will** and the **purpose** of God.

William Cullen Bryant caught the correspondence between nature's mystic adaptation and that possible for our own lives in the spiritual realm — under God.

Bryant wrote, "Ode to a Waterfowl" at a time of great need and anxiety. He was away from home and seeking a place where he might find work in his profession. As he walked over the Massachusetts hills at sunset, his meditative wondering caused him to write:

There is a Power whose care
Teaches thy way along that pathless coast,
The desert and illimitable air,
Lone wandering, but not lost.

All day thy wings have fanned,
At that far height, the cold thin atmosphere,
Yet stoop not, weary, to the welcome land,
Though the dark night is near.

And soon that toil shall end;
Soon shalt thou find a summer home, and rest,
And scream among thy fellows; reeds shall bend,
Soon, o'er thy sheltered nest.

Thou'rt gone, the abyss of heaven
Hath swallowed up thy form; yet, on my heart
Deeply hath sunk the lesson thou hast given,
And shall not soon depart.

He who, from zone to zone,
Guides through the boundless sky thy certain flight,
In the long way that I must tread alone,
Will lead my steps aright.

The God with whom we deal is a Person with all our limitations removed ... a person of power who uses that power for good purposes. He is, indeed, the Creator of a heaven and earth that is good beyond our knowing, even yet!

We are discovering that God's task is unfinished. And we are His appointed assistants to finish His purpose. The words of Jesus are the appropriate words for us, *"Not my will but thine be done."* On Dwight L. Moody's tomb are these words: *"He that doeth the will of God abideth forever."*

Success is achieved when we make the most out of the stuff God gave us. And He gave abundantly. Like the Prodigal Son in Jesus' story, too often we have wasted the good stuff! It is sad that more humans have not yet discovered that it is most important to find out His purpose and His will for our lives.

You may recall that it was Abraham Lincoln's concern, not whether God was on the side of the North in the Civil War, but that the government seek to be on God's side. He gave practical emphasis to that concern. He was in a church service. The minister reported that the War Department had ordered churches commandeered for hospital use without his knowledge. He arose in his pew and spoke. "I rescind that order. We must keep the churches open to keep the stars shining in our skies."

Woodrow Wilson made a comparable moral, spiritual statement. He said, "I'd rather lose now in a cause that will ultimately win, than win now in a cause that will ultimately be defeated."

Let us just remind ourselves of a number of characteristics of living inside God's purpose:

1. It is sustained living.

Living inside God's purpose anchors us. A lesson is in the pendulum of a clock. It is useful when attached to the works, and only then. Only as it is attached is it free. Life must be attached to something bigger than it or us: **The purpose and works of God!**

2. It is lighted living.

The purpose of God sheds constant light on the path we take in life. God wants to light our lives. He does not want us groping in darkness. Again, the light bulb is useless unless in full contact with an electrical source. Light that is found in God's purpose provides wisdom for life.

One declared that human affairs are only a struggle in the dark. And indeed it can be just that, but it need not be.

3. It is guided living.

Keeping in focus the will of God provides constant guidance. We have to reset watches in new time zones — not so a compass. The purpose and will of God is our essential compass. Fitting is Cardinal Newman's hymn, "Lead Kindly Light":

Lead, kindly Light, amid th' encircling gloom, Lead thou me on!
The night is dark, and I am far from home; Lead thou me on!
Keep thou my feet; I do not ask to see
The distant scene; one step enough for me.

I was not ever thus, nor prayed that thou shouldst lead me on;
I loved to choose and see my path; but now, Lead thou me on!
I loved the garish day, and spite of fears,
Pride ruled my will; remember not past years.

So long thy power hath blest me, sure it still will lead me on
O'er moor and fen, o'er crag and torrent, till the night is gone;
And with the morn those angel faces smile,
Which I have loved long since and lost awhile!

4. It is inspired living.

Often we think of God's will as restricting and constricting our lives. Not so; it liberates! It inspires!

Likely there is no greater musical composer than Johann Sebastian Bach. He found inspiration in Martin Luther and his magnificent accent on faith. Bach's music was indeed an interpretation of justification by faith. There is a calm, a peace not in other music. Some say that it is beyond them. Likely it is, for on all his music appears the words, "Only to the Glory of God" or "By help of Jesus."

Finally ...

5. It is victorious living.

The story of the only survivor of a shipwreck is apropos. Thrown on an uninhabited island, he managed to build a hut in which to place everything he had saved from the wreck. He prayed for deliverance and every day scanned the horizon to hail any passing ship. One day, returning from a food hunt, he was horrified to see his hut going up in flames. Everything he had was destroyed. From his perspective, the worst had happened. But the next day a ship arrived. The captain said, "We saw your smoke signal."

Our lives lived in the center of the will and purpose of God are safer than anywhere else. We may not always get what we want or think should be. But we will discover that God is at work with those who love Him and that He works toward achieving what is good.

At the center of God's purpose and will is His son, Jesus. He is God's centerpiece, and ours. He informs our minds and hearts regarding God's will and purpose. So we need to know Him, and more and more. It is here that we get to know the mind, the plan, the heart of God, and the word of God in its best form.

Do we want to know Him more and more to make our lives conform to God's will and purpose? This touches us regarding what we desire.

To know and to live in God's purpose and will is to understand Paul when he writes: *"And the peace of God which passeth understanding will garrison your hearts and minds through Christ Jesus"* (Philippians 4:7, Goodspeed).

The Lord of the Lampstands

Revelation 1:9-20

Before I read the passage I want to say a few words about the Book of Revelation.

1. A better title would be, "The Unveiling of Jesus Christ," or "The Revelation as Recorded by John."

2. It is apocalyptic/picturesque literature, employing a kind of imagery and symbolism which is oriental in character and not characteristic of our Western way of thinking. We must bear this in mind in any proper interpretation/understanding of the book.

3. The dual purpose of the book: (1) to unveil Christ; (b) to comfort persecuted saints.

4. Method: Drama which often employs enigmatic imagery — apparently some things in that imagery we may never fully understand. Enough is clear for our faith and our life as Christians. Drama in itself can perhaps be the most powerful form of communication. This drama has extraordinary significance for the Christian. Given during a period of extreme persecution, it is full of hope, comfort, assurance. It not only tells those who can understand the outcome of the drama of the human race what cosmic power will be triumphant, but it also tells our personal and corporate destiny as Christians.

5. Drama Overview:

A. FRONT OF STAGE: Church and world locked in mortal combat.

B. BACK OF STAGE: CHRIST and SATAN in horrible warfare. IF Christ wins, His Church wins! IF Satan wins the World wins!

So if we want to know the outcome of struggle in foreground, we need to watch the large figures in the background of the stage. For here we'll find a clue to how things are coming out. Do you read the back of the book? Well, that is one way to read this book. For at the back of the book we know the end. Do you like good endings? Then you'll like this — IF YOU ARE CHRIST'S.

6. It is a cosmic struggle! The principal in the drama is Jesus Christ who is demonstrated as Cosmic Lord.

7. The principal cosmic figure — Christ — is the principal figure for the Church — Christ Lord, Head of Church. The One who created the world is in the process of re-creating. And the startling truth according to this book and according to Pauline writings is that the redemption of the Church, of persons, is tied to a re-creation which cannot be described in any lesser terms than COSMIC.

Caird says that to take apart the symbolism in the Book of Revelation is to "unweave the rainbow."

John's allusions are not code in which each symbol requires separate and exact translation. Rather, each symbol is used for its EVOCATIVE and its EMOTIVE power.

Here we do not have photo art. Rather, it is a series of pictures to set echoes of memory and association ringing. It incites the imagination. It aims at producing a humbling sense of the sublime and the majestic which men experience at the sight of a roaring cataract, a Niagara Falls, or a midday sun!

Such experiences are viscerally, emotionally the nearest equivalent to what must have been experienced by the first readers. It is the awe evoked by a vision of the divine, the supernatural, the Transcendent One. It is the awe of one who gets a vision of the Risen Christ clothed in the attributes of deity — even if these attributes are expressed in imagery rather than in straight prose.

Think of John, the primary receiver of this vision! It must have been an almost overwhelming, annihilating wonder which he experienced in prophetic trance on the Island of Patmos! No wonder he writes, "I fell at His feet as though dead."

I'd like us now to briefly look at the Two (Twin) Visions and the TWO REALITIES.

Vision One is of the Lord of the Universe and the Head of the Church ... "Someone like a son of man."

Vision Two is of the Earthly Church which replicated as nearly as possible the Church as it exists in the mind of its Creator and Head.

Note that in verse 20 we are offered some translation of the imagery employed. Obviously there must be no misunderstanding of this particular imagery. The very fact that it is translated into the prosaic is testimony to its priority, its significance.

SEVEN STARS, SEVEN GOLDEN LAMPSTANDS:

The STARS are the angels of the seven churches — real, functioning churches in Asia Minor.

The SEVEN LAMPSTANDS are the seven churches.

Note one more thing in the verse. The little but important phrase, "in my HAND"!

What is to become of the Lampstands, the churches? Their fate quite clearly is tied to the relationship between the lampstands and the Lord of the Lampstands who moves constantly among the stands, watchfully, helpfully, hopefully, as the Sovereign of them all!

Look ahead to chapter two for just one verse, the fifth. The chapter begins with a message to the church located at Ephesus, and in this verse is an awe-inducing warning, "Remember the height from which you have fallen! Repent and do the things you did at first. If you do not repent, I will come to you and remove your lampstand from its place."

The very existence of the lampstand depends on the approval of the Lord of the Lampstands.

The Lampstands are at times in need of repentance. When, I wonder? When they are not pleasing to the Lord of the Lampstands? When they are not fulfilling their original purpose set out by the Lord of the Lampstands? When Lampstands go beyond their functional intention and become institutionalized to the point of living for themselves and not in service?

Now look at the TWO REALITIES:

1. Seven Lampstands (churches) represent the whole — entire — universal church. Perfect number — church universal.

2. Seven Stars (angels, messengers) are symbolic of universal sovereignty. Found on the Imperial Roman Coins, they suggest the universal dominion. This points to the seven angels, to the churches as a divine reality — to the Church as it in fact is in God's eyes and therefore is and eternally shall be.

The seven Lampstands point to the churches as historical reality, functioning on earth at a certain time and place as the light of the world. Jesus had said to His disciples, and He says yet to us, *"You are the light of the world. A city set on a hill cannot be hidden"* (Matthew 5:14, NIV). In fact, the word "stand" is used, upon which you put light, rather than under a "bushel." It likewise gives the purpose of the unhidden, shining lights, that the world may see good works and *"give glory to your Father in heaven."*

Then Paul, writing to the Philippians, reminds us that we function in an unfavorable environment —"*a crooked and perverse generation.*" But it is in this setting that "*you shine as lights in the world, holding fast the word of life, so that in the day of Christ I may be proud that I did not run in vain or labor in vain"* (2:15-16, RSV). Surely Paul is expressing the very feelings and concern of the Lord Who sacrificed Himself on Calvary!

3. The TWO REALITIES are inseparable — the divine/human and the spiritual/temporal bond together in mission and ministry in the unfavorable environment we are to reach for Christ.

The words to the churches tell them to be in their human actions what the church by divine action really is. Somewhat as we both rebuke and encourage one another when we say, "Be yourself."

So these are words of recognition, rebuke, correction, praise, promise, threat.

Let the Lord of the Lampstands be ignored and the lampstand is removed! What then is left? Institution only. A social/financial organism, human only!

Let the seven churches hear and heed. The seven churches were earthly realities. They were all found on a Roman road which ran northwest from Ephesus to Pergamum, turned inland and southwest to Thyatira, Sardis, Philadelphia, and Laodicea.

These were all towns and centers where the Cult of the Emperor was fostered. We can understand then how much they needed John's vision!

Look and listen to what John saw and heard (verses 12-20)!

1. Heard voice like trumpet. (ATTENTION!!)
2. Turned to SEE a voice. But what he saw was:
3. Seven golden lampstands — valuable, precious, of worth!
4. One "like" a son of man — reminiscent of Daniel's vision
5. Long robe
6. Golden girdle about the breast
7. Head and hair — white as snow, *like* wool
8. Eyes — *like* flame of fire
9. Feet — *like* burnished bronze

10. Voice — *like* sound of rushing waters
11. In right hand — seven stars
12. Out of mouth — comes sharp double-edged sword
13. Face — like sun shining in full strength (like in Egyptian desert at Luxor)

IT WAS JUST THE VISION the seven churches needed. And we, too, need to see the Lord of the Lampstands.

And even in the shadow of our great need to see Him, I believe in the church because it belongs to the Lord of the Lampstands. The church is not the creation of man but of God. God has chosen to invite us to partnership in its mission.

I must look at the earthly church; but I must also try to see the church of the stars — the divine reality — the reality as it exists in the mind, purpose of the Lord of the Lampstands. Most of all, I must fix my vision on the Lord of the Lampstands.

Again, I believe in the church because the world desperately needs the light which can come from the lampstands.

Now let me do one more thing before I read our passage. I turn to literature different from the Drama — the Church's most famous Creed — the Apostles' — which is an early distillation of the basic, commonly accepted beliefs of the Christian Church, all of which our present *Discipline* affirms.

The language is concise, compacted, precise — no frills, no imagery. BUT the thrust is in common with the Revelation! The creed is the outgrowth of two things interacting, the Scripture and the living laboratory of the Church in time!

The Creed begins, "I believe in God, the Father Almighty, Maker of heaven and earth, and in Jesus Christ His only Son our Lord." It recites detail of life and death; of resurrection and ascension, and session. It concludes with these lines:

"I believe in the Holy Spirit; the holy catholic church; the communion of saints; the forgiveness of sins; the resurrection of the body and the life everlasting. Amen."

I, John, your brother and companion in the suffering and kingdom and patient endurance that are ours in Jesus, was on the island of Patmos because of the word of God and the testimony of Jesus. On the Lord's Day I was in the Spirit, and I heard behind me a loud voice like a trumpet, which said: "Write on a scroll what you see and send it to the seven churches: to

Ephesus, Smyrna, Pergamum, Thyatira, Sardis, Philadelphia and Laodicea."

I turned around to see the voice that was speaking to me. And when I turned I saw seven golden lampstands, and among the lampstands was someone "like a son of man," dressed in a robe reaching down to his feet and with a golden sash around his chest. His head and hair were white like wool, as white as snow, and his eyes were like blazing fire. His feet were like brass glowing in a furnace, and his voice was like the sound of rushing waters. In his right hand he held seven stars, and out of his mouth came a sharp double-edged sword. His face was like the sun shining in all its brilliance.

When I saw him, I fell at his feet as though dead. Then he placed his right hand on me and said: "Do not be afraid. I am the First and the Last. I am the Living One; I was dead, and behold I am alive for ever and ever! And I hold the keys of death and Hades.

"Write, therefore, what you have seen, what is now and what will take place later. The mystery of the seven stars that you saw in my right hand and of the seven golden lampstands is this: The seven stars are the angels of the seven churches, and the seven lampstands are the seven churches" (Revelation 1:9-20, NIV).

Mistakes We Can't Afford to Make, Part 1

Someone in the crowd said to him, "Teacher, tell my brother to divide the inheritance with me."

Jesus replied, "Man, who appointed me a judge or an arbiter between you?" Then he said to them, "Watch out! Be on your guard against all kinds of greed; a man's life does not consist in the abundance of his possessions."

And he told them this parable: "The ground of a certain rich man produced a good crop. He thought to himself, 'What shall I do? I have no place to store my crops.'

"Then he said, 'This is what I'll do. I will tear down my barns and build bigger ones, and there I will store all my grain and my goods. And I'll say to myself, "You have plenty of good things laid up for many years. Take life easy, eat, drink and be merry."'

"But God said to him, 'You fool! This very night your life will be demanded from you. Then who will get what you have prepared for yourself?'

"This is how it will be with anyone who stores things up for himself but is not rich toward God" (Luke 12:13-21, NIV).

How amazing the way Jesus strikes hard at the very things that plague contemporary society, that eat at the vitals of the church, that threaten future generations.

In a rather connected series of statements and parables going on through verse 48, Jesus challenges the accepted standard of values — then and now — because it is the invention of twisted man. Yet Jesus is no killjoy. He does not advocate the pursuit of poverty, contentment with a dull, unexciting, meager existence.

Rather, He intends to make it clear that our usual ways do not secure the rich, full and fulfilling life. It is rather our own perverse inclinations which lead us to futureless, hopeless pursuits.

Jesus points out three fatal errors we humans continue to

make generation after generation. We have been guilty of these errors, our kids make the same mistakes, our neighbors do the same. Institutions which are the shadows of men make the same fatal mistakes. Churches get caught up in the thinking that characterizes these errors. We stand constantly in need of the probing words of Jesus if we are to experience true life.

A tricky, deceiving thing about these three errors is that they are so common that we conclude they can't possibly have serious consequences — even when we see the consequences daily on TV. In fact, these errors are so prevalent that we too frequently conclude they are cherished concepts and not errors at all!

The reason is that these errors walk among us dressed in the finest clothes, move in the best circles, are often industrious, frugal, successful, progressive, and full of ambition and foresight. Sometimes there is a bit of social awareness that invades and parades among these errors.

These errors are incarnate in members of institutional boards of commerce, industry, science, and even the church. These errors are so well dressed and so seemingly wise and wealthy that their advice is sought — they are so practical, so logical. So they are sought out for these reasons rather than for embodying faith in God or submission to God's will.

So these errors are devilishly subtle. And even when occasionally bemoaned they are stubbornly pursued. They may be condemned, yet we find them seducing us.

In the end, these errors prove deadly, disastrous. They are inversions of values. They are a misconception of the meaning of life. They represent a perversion of human desire.

Look at the man of the story: He accepted the body, man, things, and time as the supreme values. Philosophically, these are the mistakes of materialism, humanism, naturalism — regardless of whether the expression is base or refined.

Putting **body**, **man**, **things**, and **time** in first place requires the denial of **God**, **soul**, and **eternity**. So Jesus puts His finger on the fatal follies of those He addressed and upon us here and now.

What is so wrong? Jesus tells us the wrong lies in a bad choice of the terminal destination, or objective. These choices are wrong because they are **not big enough** for **who** and **what** we are.

Self and the urge to autonomy took over. "I," "self," my,"

"mine," were exalted to the throne room. Strangely, we never seem to learn the consequences: reduced life — little, cribbed, cabined. The poet is accurate:

Lift up the curtain: for an hour lift up
The veil that holds you prisoners in this world
Of figures and of men who trust in facts ...
Where men with blinded eyes and hobbled feet
Grope down a narrow gorge and call it life.

This describes well the man of our story. In verse 19 he addresses his "soul," but his real concern is temporal contentment and security.

He mistook his body for his soul.

He dies a spiritual beggar despite "barns," "fruits," "goods." He supposed he had an eternal quit-claim deed to it all!

Just how can we live long and still seriously believe that stuff, inheritances, gadgets, wealth, progress, science, industry — that these things produce contentment and security? Too late, we discover that these taken alone do not secure social justice, enduring good, or personal peace or joy.

These do have their place in life, but put first they become poor substitutes for the "soul." "Plenty of good things" can't satisfy our deepest wistful desires. The rich man's standards were inadequate. So the real answers escaped him.

Measuring for life by possessions is using the wrong tool. Such assumptions are weighed in the balances of ordinary living and are found fatally faulted. The American Translation has verse 15 saying, *"Man's life does not belong to him, no matter how rich he is."* It's so easy to ignore that wisdom!

We don't belong to ourselves. We belong to our ancestry and our posterity. Here and now we also belong to our neighbors. Just try isolation and independence and we settle for all that is less than human. We owe something to our forebears. We owe something to our successors. What will we bequeath them? We are here because of our forebears. We endure largely by what we can pass on of that which is good, and fine, and godly.

And we should now know that more than all else, our life belongs to Christ. Life's full meaning is not discovered apart from commitment and loyalty! Christ above all others deserves our loyalty — a loyalty born out of a loving relationship.

We learn from Jesus' story that market mentality is not good enough for a rewarding life. Oscar Wilde said that cynics see the price of everything and the value of nothing.

His error was body for soul and means for end.

So he lived in moral and spiritual confusion. You can't call him criminal. We hurl no insults his way. He gathered his riches in customary, legitimate ways. Who would point an indicting finger at this big man in the community? He had made it good. He gained respect. He was likely unduly honored for his amassing abilities. He was likely elevated to seats of position and honor and responsibility.

He looked so wise, his methods so reasonable. One is reminded of the exuberant wish of Tevye in "Fiddler on the Roof." If only he were a rich man. Men would think him wise and pious. He'd get the best seat in the synagogue. Looking heavenward, he wonders why the Lord couldn't make him rich. He even takes off into a fantasy of the kind of house he'd build which would have one staircase going nowhere — just for show.

The record seems clear that *means* became *ends* in this man's distortion of reality. Truth is the "end" which ennobles or degrades the means we use. The Bible does not condemn *things* or *flesh* as inherently evil. They acquire their character from the use to which they are devoted.

It is not recorded that this man wanted the material for philanthropic or social purposes. The consumer was to be "I." He talks to himself, "You have plenty of goods laid up (exactly the problem) for many years." He was secure in his materialism.

Could we predict that skilled, advanced, technologically superior civilizations can be built but not maintained without more than material objectives? Is this when men and nations lose their "souls"? Here is why I conclude that Communism has within itself the seeds of its own destruction.

But lest we become self-congratulatory, let us ask if we are not in the same danger when we make materialism our god and decreasingly emphasize moral and spiritual values?

This man was a magnificent materialist. We understand him. We relate to him. He tore down. He built greater. We all gather around to applaud.

A friend of mine recently was taken from a poverty-stricken church to vacation in a luxurious Seattle home overlooking Puget Sound and with around-the-clock guard protection. The friend sent me pictures of the exterior and interior and said, "Would you believe it? They are planning to tear this down and build greater, plushier. They want to really fit into this restricted neighborhood." The owner's wife finally confided some uneasiness about the whole thing since she did profess to a faith in Christ.

Yes, we understand this man of Jesus' story.

But what *he* built and what *we* tend to build are *containers*. We make cisterns for storage, but they turn into cesspools. Life, like love, is gained by giving. There are two seas in Palestine: Galilee and Dead. One lives because it gives. The other is dead because it hoards.

The real problems of persons and society are *always* spiritual. Strip away the overlying and deceiving layers and we find a spiritual source for our failures. Our problems and fears are but symptoms of our real illness. Our ingenuity about "things" seems to far outrun our wisdom about objectives.

We boast of our realism in politics, industry and business, only to discover that we avoid realism when called to face up to our fundamental problems of living. These are usually relational, and so, traced back one more step, they turn out to be moral and spiritual.

We are realists, we are logicians, we are rational in things material. We are weak, incompetent, bankrupt in things moral and spiritual. We are street-wise, market-wise, social-wise, but afflicted with low SQ's — spiritual quotients.

Science becomes a god and becomes a destroyer. Wealth takes over and selfish, damaging relationships are embraced. Destructive industries, like alcoholic beverage, tobacco, drugs, are justified because they provide employment or pour money into the economy. Every day we hear morally twisted reasons for doing what we perceive to be of economic advantage. And often the advantage is really a will-o'-the-wisp.*

Amazingly, things that are proven destroyers of persons, life, and character are fought for and cherished and promoted ... and

***Editor's Note:** This sermon predates legalized state-sponsored gambling, but it is remarkably prescient, considering the rationale is used in its promotion and in the reality of its effectiveness.

defended. It's pure and simple moral madness, a kind of insanity more dangerous, finally, than loose psychotics.

Education and religion receive our tips, our pittances, while sports and amusements receive our billions. We have a fundamental twist and an inherent taint. It is called "sin."

We are a lost society without the intervention of Christ. We shall fail to find the spiritual power to control the nuclear power our age has unleashed, apart from obedience to the lordship of Christ. It is amazing! The hell we moderns threw out the door as offensive to our delicate sensitivities has crept back through the windows of our man-made terrors.

It has been suggested that it is no longer "Sinners in the Hands of an Angry God," as Jonathan Edwards thundered in his famous sermon, but rather God in the hands of angry sinners!

Our strange and twisted logic now declares that we have made such a miserable mess of things that we glibly conclude that the only hell we can ever experience is the one we know right here and now.

We need place no confidence that we shall escape the moral judgments consistent with the moral structure of our universe.

Playwright Paddy Chayefsky indicted our culture: "I don't know what Hollywood stands for, but if it stands for current values I am dead against it. American values are all wrong — the pursuit of security and comfort, with everyone plugging away to be as ordinary as possible. It's like Rome. I can hear the clanking of the barbarians at the gates."

Mistakes We Can't Afford to Make, Part 2

Luke 12:13-21 and Daniel 4:29-37

The person in Jesus' story made three common but fatal errors. We dealt with one of those. He mistook body for soul, means for ends. And we need reminding, it seems to me, that man is more than flesh and blood and brain.

When I say, "I," if I think about it, I know that "I" speaks of a being with powers, capacities, potentials, beyond the ability of science to enumerate, explain or to reduce to some kind of formulae. This "I," this soul, is beyond analysis.

One writing about discoveries made during the course of surgical efforts in the study of epilepsy reveals the amazing capacity of the mind to store experiences, record them permanently, and reproduce them upon proper stimulation. The conclusion is important. It is doubted by men of science that the mind of man can ever fully know the mind of man.

This "I," this "me" has potential for time and for eternity that only an adjustment for life on a moral and spiritual basis can foster, and that adjustment is not achieved through a code of ethics, as such, but through a new and a personal relationship by being, what Jesus in this story called, *"rich toward God."*

In part, beyond the scope of our passage we find clues to true riches. We find that it is by seeking the kingdom of God, putting that first and foremost, rather than through self-interest (verse 31). It's made very clear that this is a law of life. Putting kingdom first, in fact, is the thing that works in our own best interest.

See verse 34: True riches come as we reject the flat, the horizontal interests and investments in favor of heavenly investments. Life lived with sensitivity to the perpendicular, Jesus is saying, pays — it pays in this life. In verses 35-40, we discover that life is enriched by our waiting and our watching and our working readiness for the coming of the Son of Man.

I wondered as I read this if Judas was present to hear this story that Jesus told, for how like the man of the parable was Judas. Were not their attitudes and their sins identical?

There's no contentment apart from commitment. L. B. Jacks once wrote, "There's a coward and a hero in the breast of every man." The coward seeks security, safety in things; the hero seeks victory through commitment.

Selfishness eventually robbed this man of Jesus' story of what he wanted most. It always does. It blinded him to any helpful insights. Not for a moment did he contemplate what good productivity could accomplish with what the Lord had blessed him with. Instead of turning his good fortune outward in helpfulness, in benevolence, in philanthropic adventure, he experienced the self-deceit of false hope.

Too late, he discovers he has fewer hours of life than he thought he had years. His story is not an isolated one. It is not an ancient story.

Now let's move forward to look at another mistake this man made:

He mistook man for God.

In very few words we get a look inside the soul of this man. He thought *within* himself, what shall *I* do, what will *I* do? *I* will pull down, *I* will build greater, *I* will bestow — but notice that he's not intending to bestow it on anyone else. I will bestow it on myself.

Now having chosen this ill-considered course of storage for self, he talks to himself again. He says, "Now, you, self, have plenty of the good things put by for many years. Take your ease, eat, drink and enjoy yourself." Now there's a great goal for life, isn't it? See the emphasis. He had what one could call "I" trouble; he was egocentric. The accent, in other words, was entirely and completely on the human, on self.

There was indifference regarding the blessing of God. He was neither caring nor innovative. He could think of nothing better than creating a greater storage place for a bumper crop. Clearly, when we disregard God it soon follows that we lose regard for the need of persons.

Olin Curtis has what I regard as a classic statement regarding the Fall of Man. He said, "Man did not care enough about God to do His will." He did not love God enough, he did not care enough about God. He cared about something else — he did not care enough to do His will. And the story of that is continued into this congregation yet this morning.

We need this story. We need it now. We need it this morning. We need this theology. It's the story of our human race. It's the story of Lucifer, the fallen angel, the mistake of not caring enough about God to do His will and to see in that the biggest benefits of life that can be acquired.

There's the mistake of thinking that we can be independent of God, even rebellious against Him:

His proud independence of God

Further results or consequences in the ancient world are made dramatic in the story of the Tower of Babel — proud independence of God. It is this very proud independence that brings tortures to our own souls. How easy it is for the very virtues which have made for material and technological progress to become debased into a pride of self-sufficiency.

Is this proud independence of God that which taints our culture? Is this what taints what we are living with every day? Is this what corrupts our legislature, and Wall Street, and industry, and education, and — religion? We've had enough of that in the news, haven't we?

We live in what often seems like a miracle world of technological advance, but it can also become an easy and great sin. We are bombarded with an amazing world, and all brought into our living rooms. What is there that now can amaze us? We're past being amazed. Changes come so fast that we easily lapse into an apathetic mood.

Indeed, how can we escape the feeling of being clever, and ingenious, and self-sufficient? In our society, the farther we move away from the soil, our sense of daily dependence upon God fades. It's hard for us to feel the urgency of the prayer given to us by our Lord, *"Give to us this day our daily bread."* We have so much to eat and consume; we cannot have any sense of urgency. But there are parts of the world today where there is a sense of urgency and a meaningfulness in that prayer.

Perhaps we need the sobering reminder of the boast of one

drunken man with his own sense of power and importance and accomplishments. You listened to it this morning in the reading of the Scripture, *"Is not this great Babylon, which I have built by my mighty power as a royal residence and for the glory of my majesty?"* (Daniel 4:30, RSV).

Even as the boast was uttered a voice was heard, *"Nebuchadnez'zar ... The kingdom has departed from you"* (Daniel 4:31, RSV). What followed those eerie words? Confusion, derangement. Moral madness grips us in the same way today as it did Nebuchadnezzar. We are equally vulnerable. And finally Nebuchadnezzar learned his lesson, and with the learning of the lesson he was returned to greater power and honor and glory.

Now let us hear the regenerated, the renewed, and the restored Nebuchadnezzar: *"Now I, Nebuchadnez'zar, praise and extol and honor the King of heaven; for all his works are right and his ways are just; and those who walk in pride he is able to abase"*(Daniel 4:37, RSV).

It was a testimony of humiliating experience. Our proud independence of God, however, stretches beyond material matters, and science, and business, and politics.

Increasingly, people feel that they can have the ethical refinements, can be humane without the Christian faith. And we in our pride want to be humane, and we want to be decent, and we want to be good. But we want to do it all without God and without religion.

We say, "Give us the good fruits, but let us not bother with the roots." That great Quaker, Elton Trueblood, reminds us that we consequently live in a cut-flower civilization, a rootless sort of thing — beautiful for a time but destined to wither and die because severed from the sustaining root of a great faith.

We shall find it difficult to maintain the dignity and the value of the individual, the person, apart from the deep faith that every one of us is made in God's image and is precious in His sight, and yet is utterly, utterly dependent upon Him.

Finally, we shall rediscover that we cannot be humane apart from a proper relation to deity. The need of our hour is what it has always been — a burning faith in God that makes an absolute and personal commitment to a personal God.

We really should not be surprised that our precious ethical convictions — that we have thought of as profound and central and essential — are curiously ineffective and seemingly impotent in the face of dedicated materialism and communism.

Our human tragedy is that we can prostrate ourselves — we have the ability, in fact the inclination to prostrate ourselves in utter dedication before that which is false and which is eternally destructive. And such dedication can be terribly effective against all that is good.

G. Campbell Morgan spoke of those at Pentecost as people who were possessed of "the mighty enthusiasm of an overwhelming conviction." Only that can turn back the tide of the errors of mankind. The church, moved by the Holy Spirit-inspired conviction, turned the world upside down once. It can do it again.

A few summarizing statements:

◆ If we persist in the pride of self-sufficiency, God will see to it that we are brought low.

◆ If we attempt to maintain high ethic ideals without relation to the lordship of Jesus Christ, we discover that we cannot for too long be manly or humane. In fact, the tendency is to sink below the level of the beast.

◆ A form of Christianity that is only intellectual or creedal or formal lacks that mighty inspired and enthusiastic faith in Christ that carries with it utmost commitment and consecrated action. And this will collapse before the onslaught of a less than human but inspired attack.

◆ At this very moment that I speak and you listen, we are culturally and spiritually going through bankruptcy. Our dividends are spent, our ethical flowers are drooping for lack of sustaining rootage. Days of judgment are upon us as sure as they were on Nebuchadnezzar. The feet of undertakers sound closer and closer. Only a gracious God-sent renewal and revival across the nation and the world can spare us from moral disaster.

Finally, I turn for a brief look at the third mistake that was made by the man in Jesus' story:

He mistook time for eternity.

It's small comfort that many are still doing this. How often we are sheep-like. It's no wonder that the sheep picture is used of the human race in the Scriptures. We gather a sense, seemingly, of security heading for a precipice because we are in a crowd headed in the same direction. "Follow somebody," seems to be the word of advice.

We seem to actually believe the old saying that, "A million Frenchmen can't be wrong." And with a shallow shrug we believe we are thus magically relieved of personal responsibility.

But we must insist again that these are fatal errors. Irrevocably, they damn the soul that makes them. Multitudes behave as though they were to live forever. Whatever the future holds for each of us, of heaven or hell, it must bear a marked relationship to the character of our present living.

Tragedy — tragedy begins with a disregard of God. Then it is that eternity loses its hold on our lives. The man Jesus tells about seems to have thought that the number of his days was under his own management; the ground he worked, the fruit, the vines, the fields, the barns, were his, and they were his alone without restriction, without limitation. He thought his own soul, his own pleasure, and his own time were indeed his and his only.

Before the end of life's little day there should have been regard for the ultimate question. But we have an aversion, you see, to ultimate questions. The question is, *"Whose shall these things be that You, You have provided?"*

God help each of us to face that question squarely. It will elicit, I am sure, a sense of dependence on God, a recognition of our responsible stewardship in the world.

The rich fool's concern was with the wants of "I." He should have been concerned with the wants and wishes of God, which in the long run are in our interest.

Give Him your all, and give it to Him now! Then there will be no startling terror at life's end when the call comes to another world.

"His will be done," we say, with sighs and trembling, expecting trials, bitter loss and tears. And then how does He answer us? With blessings in sweet rebuking of our faithless tears!

My Philosophy

Reduced to a sentence, the philosophy I have desired to make increasingly mine was first given expression by a well-educated Jew of Tarsus and Jerusalem. When as a consequence of his meeting Jesus Christ face to face, he finally became the Apostle Paul. He wrote that for him "to live was Christ, and to die was gain." I realize that those words expressed more than a philosophy. It was a matter of experience. Still, a true philosophy must be wrought out in experience. And increasingly I realize that such a sentence philosophy requires many paragraphs of living. However, it does indicate that life is a whole of which Christ is center, circumference, and segment.

I have discovered that such an experience and viewpoint make heavy demands on the quality of life I must live. But it also furnishes me with immense satisfaction of mind and peace of heart.

I am convinced that these words of Saint Paul are not meaningless mumbo-jumbo. They have a very practical bearing on life. For one thing, it furnishes me with a satisfying view of the universe. To be convinced that the Christ, who has become your first love, bears an intimate, creative, and sustaining relation to the universe brings a feeling of "at ease," and delivers me from a feeling of loneliness in the world.

For I have the conviction that the Christ who is so complete a revelation of moral love could not have created and would not sustain other than a friendly universe. Even its inexorable laws, I come to realize, are for my well-being, and thus I desire to make intelligent adjustments to "my Father's world." This view has produced in me a growing, ever-deepening appreciation of God's lavish hand manifest in nature.

Parenthetically, I might say that the beauties and wonder of New York have done something to me. I cannot help but feel inwardly expanded and enriched. There are many things about the universe I do not understand. However, I believe that knowing the creating Agent, I can trust it to be orderly, purposeful, and friendly if I understand it and obey.

To believe that "to live is Christ" requires for me some very definite attitudes. There is my attitude toward the universe which has just been covered. There is my attitude toward God. Because of Christ I think of God as a wise, loving, personal "heavenly Father."

When I wish to visualize God I remember Jesus. Again, such a viewpoint is a source of contentment. Yet it makes demands on me. It demands that I manifest a great loyalty to God. It demands that I be willing to be like His supreme revelation — Jesus. It demands that I honestly seek to know and do His will. It demands that I seek His fellowship which alone can raise me toward the ideal.

Such a philosophy demands certain attitudes toward myself. It becomes important for me to know myself, and I discover that if Christ is my life He makes self-knowledge much more probable and likely more accurate, for He helps to free me of blind spots and rationalizing habits that would tend to hypocrisy. I must live with myself and be true to myself, and by being true to Christ I discover that my own company becomes more enjoyable.

He helps me to discover within me a very interesting and needed world. He helps me to be self-reliant and resourceful without being proud or independent of God or my fellowmen. I believe He helps me to be more nearly "a real person" as Dr. Fosdick would say, and that I do believe is very important business. I come to dislike pretension, hypocrisy, fraud in people and to desire honest, straightforward dealings.

I find that to live comfortably with myself, when Christ is really my life, demands from me honest toil and the best of my effort in worthwhile pursuits. I discover the tendency is to eliminate not only the bad and half-bad, but things which are lesser though not evil. I find constantly opening vistas of the good and the wholesome so that my great regret becomes the shortness of the life span for exploration and understanding.

I am persuaded that if I devote myself to the good alone I shall not have the time or capacity to know its possible enrichment of my life. Life, hence, is not a narrowing road, but a gloriously expanding experience. The necessity of comfortably living with myself, I find, does demand a searching honesty and an unflinching willingness to know the truth and obey it from whatever source or angle it may come.

"To live is Christ!" For me that involves my relation to others and my attitude toward society. It gives me a heightened respect for personality. It means I must do more than love "souls" in the abstract; I must like, respect and help people.

It means that I have a genuine respect for those who have had different background, experience, education, and advantage, hence a different outlook and attitude toward life. I may not, often must not, endorse their philosophy or conduct, but I must try to understand them without pitying. It means I must be rid of the pride and prejudice of race, religion, or color, for Christ, I believe, stands above distinctions of this order and dwells "in the midst" of each to give Himself where possible.

When Christ becomes my life, I am honest, courteous, kind, forgiving, and perhaps most of all understanding. Love is not love unless it is understanding! As leader or employer it demands a full recognition of the rights of followers and employees. As servant and workman, it demands work done as in the presence of Him who is my life.

With Christ as my point of reference I believe it possible to get a more objective view and perspective of contemporary life and civilization. I believe that above time and change, wars, and the struggle of classes, stands the Christ who has a purpose and is working out that purpose for man, and that there is a special providence working in the lives of those who love Him and seek His will and purpose.

This saves me from the spirit of the mob, from the fear of those whose hearts fail them in troubled days, from the fear and dread of tomorrow, from despair at the prospect of standing before a Perfect Judge at an ultimate judgment. It saves me from a sense of futility and disillusionment. Such living and outlook makes me an optimistic realist, not a religionist hunting a storm cellar by denying the reality of the ugly and sinful, nor one who momentarily expects an arbitrarily enforced solution of problems I am expected to help solve with the aid of Him who has become my life.

I believe I must be interested in the social and political betterment of the race, that I must attempt a global rather than a provincial view. The resources of the holy must be brought to bear on the contemporary scene.

Another important attitude concerns the church. I am naturally so self-centered that I realize that which properly directs my energies and attention away from myself is healthful. Since I must give myself to something, I choose to give it to the cause which is dearest to Him who has won my loyalty.

With all the church's imperfections, the imperfections of humanity and not divinity, I give myself to forwarding His cause in the world through the best possible human means, recognizing that that human becomes in a sense divine by His presence and power operating through it. It provides me with the highest form of fellowship.

A philosophy of life includes a view of death. Paul said death "is gain." Christ transforms my attitude toward death. Because of Him I cannot feel that death is a dead-end street. My aspirational longings must and shall find fulfillment. He assures me they shall!

All that awaits beyond the narrow stream of death is beyond my ken, but I am secured by His Word and by an inner persuasion that I shall be with Him, like Him, and shall joyfully serve Him. Worship and work shall be bound together in a glorious and satisfying activity that shall be free of weariness, worry, monotony, sin or distress. Such a view makes much in the modern funeral seem strangely incongruous and pagan.

Just two items in conclusion. First, I believe it consistent with such a philosophy and religious experience that I bring all the educational training, experience, and talents possible and devote them to the cause of Him who is my life!

Second, I believe that His presence is at work within me when I am not conscious of it, that He is there working His will so long as I am willing, and that He increasingly becomes the great integrating factor of my life.

Editor's Note: This was the response from a University of Rochester professor: "This is one of the clearest, most concise and at the same time comprehensive statements of a Christian philosophy I have seen."

New Life in Christ: No Condemnation! No Separation

Therefore, there is now no condemnation for those who are in Christ Jesus, because through Christ Jesus the law of of the Spirit of life set me free from the law of sin and death (Romans 8:1-2, NIV).

The old life is a vicious circle of sin and death: no breakthrough, no break-out. In Egypt today one can still see oxen going through the endless, monotonous threshing circle ... around and around. The old life runs a Samson-like circle — eyes out, enslaved, pulling a load without hope.

The old life is not only a circle, it is an unresolved dilemma (7:21ff). Paul reports the dilemma as he had known it. He knew the good, but what he wanted to do he did not do. What he rationally rejected he nevertheless practiced. Two warring forces were at the center of his life. He felt defeated, enslaved. The old life is a circle of sin and death. The old life is an unresolved dilemma.

And at the end of Chapter 7 he provides a horrible illustration of his condition. He likened it to the inhuman practice in extreme situations of attaching a dead person, body to body, face to face with an accused criminal until the criminal died. Sin, Paul says, is like that! And he cries out, *"Who shall deliver me from the body bringing me to death?"* But no sooner is the situation described, and the memory of the old life relived, than we hear him fairly shouting out the good news: **There is a way out!**

He is not preaching. He is witnessing. He is telling what happened to him. The hermetically sealed circle of sin and death can be penetrated from the outside! There is deliverance. There is escape from that monotonous, death-dealing circle. It is possible to be truly human like one is designed to be. There is escape from the *"body of death"!*

His shouted testimony resounds through the years to us here

and now: *"I thank God there is a way out through Jesus Christ our Lord!"* (Romans 7:25, Phillips).

The way out is found in a Person — One who did more than complete an objective historical act on a real cross sunk in real Middle Eastern soil surrounded by both sympathetic and antagonistic onlookers. Indeed, He did do that for Paul and you and me. But the true glory is that somehow by that death He — the Christ of God — can be released into my life!

By that act He can break through the hermetical seal, reach the cords binding me to the body of death and cut them. The Lord Christ Alive can relate to me now in person! And I can relate to Him in a way that is genuine, intimate, natural.

It is this mutuality of relationship to each other — Christ to me and me to Christ — that Paul calls being *"in"* Christ Jesus. That was a very meaningful way for Paul to describe what had happened that was so glorious.

Christians through the centuries have been able to identify with Paul. They have in fact experienced the **lifting relationship with Christ.** There is powerful thrust in this new relationship, like power to escape earth's atmosphere. March down through Chapter 8, and you will be able to see all the freedoms, the lift, Paul said he experienced by his new relationship *"in Christ."* Let's go together ...

Freedom from condemnation.

Freedom from base pursuits, from the lower nature, the lower level (basement living), the instinctive actions, the carnal — animalization of life.

Freedom from death — the worst death of all deaths — separation from God.

Freedom to obey the promptings of the Holy Spirit.

Freedom to experience life and inward peace — he speaks as though this was a great difference from the past.

Freedom to get going *"on the way to real living"* (v. 13, Phillips).

Freedom from paralyzing fear — the fear produced by guilt (v. 14).

Freedom to be the sons of God the Father (v. 14).

Freedom from slavery (v. 15).

Freedom of heirs — those who belong and have something still coming that is good and valuable — heirs with Christ (v. 17).

Freedom to suffer with Christ (v. 17), freedom to choose this as a kind of glorious privilege.

Freedom to be glorified along with Christ (v. 17).

Freedom to entertain genuine hope (23-25) even redemption of our bodies.

Freedom from debilitating, defeating pessimism (18-25).

Freedom from defeat and defeating adversaries (31-37).

Now let's go down through the chapter again quickly, noting that the new life Paul found through a revolutionary, lifting, freeing relationship has at its heart a marvelous TRINITY.

The Son Relationship

There is a way out through Jesus Christ our Lord. He is the way out (7:25)! He (the Son) lifts me out of the old circle by moving into my life. Paul says our problem is *"the weakness of human nature."* But we need not be in despair. *"God has met this by sending his own Son Jesus Christ to live in that human nature which causes the trouble."*

He, the Son, is not a remote God. He does more than empathize. He moves in with reinforcement, enrichment. He plugs the gaps, strengthens the weakened tissues of our human nature. He helps us, He comes alongside to make us increasingly what we were designed to be. He moves in to remake us. Now note:

The Spirit Relationship

Look first at verse 9, *"the Spirit of God finds a home within you."* The first part of the sentence gives us both the negative and positive consequences of the Spirit of God dwelling in our house. You are not carnal. You are spiritual. You are adequate. You are alive — really! By living in a responding relationship with the Spirit we really *"live,"* or as Phillips correctly translates, *"You are on the way to real living."* New life! New direction! And more to come! But let us go on, for Paul knew God also as Father.

The Father Relationship

In fact, it was the Spirit who whispered the reassurance of the Father relationship of God (v. 14 ff). Did the Spirit say, *"You know the Son, you know Me, but you must also know the Father"?* At the heart of the universe is a wondrously kind Father. He made the grain of the universe. He knows how you work and how it works. He therefore knows what is best for each of us. With Paul, I rejoice that I'm a child — that does not degrade or downgrade me.

I'm a son — with the assurance of loving care and direction and discipline.

I'm a son — I have identity, status, confidence.

I'm a son — I am loved.

I'm a son — I have been given a stake in life and a promise of more to come. I am an heir.

I'm a son — and do you know who my Father is?

If you did know, you would know why I do not fear! Why I stand tall! Why I do not fear another human being regardless of title, station, function, or position! Why I am important! Why I have a sense of meaning and direction! My Father gives me that! I am not lost! I am found! My Father knows me, knows exactly where I am and what I am! He watches me! He tells me He wants me! He wants me forever! No wonder I can respect others! I am respected by my Father!

The new life in Christ is based on a threefold relationship with God: **Father, Son** and **Spirit**. Paul sees as tremendous:

The Benefits of the Relationship with God

The benefits are immediate: No condemnation, no separation; deliverance from the circle of sin and death; a whole bunch of freedoms — freedoms from (the negatives); freedom to (the positives); freedom to be and become!

The benefits are also future: (See vv. 20, 24, 25.) No storm cellar religion which retreats from reality, whether the retreat is found in Christian Science (which is neither Christian nor science), or is found in some more likely heresies which ignore the realities of this world when they are not to our liking. Paul experienced, accepted, and coped with *"the sufferings of this present age/time"* because they were so much outweighed by the hope of *"the glory that is to be revealed in us."* But immediately he asserts that glory to be revealed in us is part of a coming cosmic renewal and glory.

ALL creation is to be redeemed — made new and free from *"bondage to decay," "the tyranny of change and decay"* (Phillips) *"and have its share in that magnificent liberty which can only belong to the children of God!"*

What a hope! Where does it come from? It grows out of

Paul's relationship with God as Trinity! It is a blessed hope! No blueprint is given. Trust in God precludes the necessity of a blueprint! The glorious end is clear! The "how," the means, the timing, is none of my business, but it is all God's wonderful business!

Then to hope Paul appears to add a wonderful kind of new knowledge — new to pagans; new to Israelites — *"in everything God works for good with those who love him* [God]" (RSV), *"everything that happens fits into a pattern for good"* (Phillips).

Now this is all true because by our new relationship and new life we have become a part of a new destiny. We are destined *"to be conformed to the image of His Son"* (v. 29). And step by step we move from God's plan of good for us — His call to us, His putting us into right relation with himself — to all that is meant or imagined by Paul's word, *"glorified"!*

Finale (vv. 31-39)

Paul moves to the grand climax. In fact, he seems to move from peak to peak in this great passage. But this is it — the finale. Because of our relationship to God — Father, Son, Spirit — we move from *"no condemnation"* to *"no separation"!* These are the Christian's twin experiences! They can't be pulled apart without ruin to the whole affair. No separation is the cause of no condemnation. And no condemnation secures no separation. And with no condemnation and no separation there is release to growing fellowship and togetherness with God!

And the great truth is that *"no condemnation, no separation"* is not only the rhythm, the mode of the present but also the guarantee of the tomorrows — so linked to hope! So how does Paul conclude? This way: In a life characterized by *"no condemnation ... no separation"* there can be:

No defeating adversary (31-32)
No defeating circumstance (35-37)
No separating event, person, power — either now or in any tomorrow — from the *"love of God"* (38-39).

Note the last words of Chapter 8: *"Christ Jesus our Lord."* That becomes an affirmation of both love and loyalty! When Christ Jesus is Lord, there is *"now no condemnation — no separation!"* It is now clear how Paul could write the Philippians (4:13, Phillips), *"I am ready for anything through the strength of the one who lives within me."*

Our Creed

The Articles of Religion of the Free Methodist Church are in the tradition of the creeds of the church or churches through the centuries. I shall therefore shorthand reference to the articles as "our creed." The creeds have appeared in both long and short forms. They show evidence of the struggles of the day in which they were written. Despite these differences there is a remarkably uniform central core that shows in each.

For us our distinctives are accented, but what is dominant is that believed by most Christians through the centuries. For example, the Reformers — Luther, Calvin, Zwingli and others — show in their creeds the concerns they had in the break from Rome. They also display certain doctrinal emphases which we cannot follow, although we are certainly children of the Reformation in the sixteenth century.

But we are likewise the theological descendants of both Anglicanism and the Evangelical Revival which came to England two centuries after Luther and Calvin. That fact shapes us in many subtle ways. Anglicans did not represent as severe a theological break with Rome as did the Continental Reformers. We are inheritors of the 39 Articles of the Church of England. This gives us a sort of catholicity. But we are also the inheritors of the Evangelical Revival of the eighteenth century and especially of John Wesley. Until the Revival, England was in the grip of far-reaching religious rot. Noted historians judge that it was the Evangelical Revival that saved England from a bloody revolution which was experienced just across the channel in France.

Wesley gave heart as well as head to the creed. Stress upon the availability of inward assurance and cleansing along with concern for the life-style of the Christian added a much needed dimension to the creeds. The creed must become internalized, real — a part of the daily living experience in relationship with both God and men. Our creed embodies this balanced emphasis — the intellectual, the spiritual, the moral, the practical. It does not mark a departure from the main-line of creedal development, rather, the supplying of missing dimensions.

Most have likely observed a change of form in the 1974 restatement of our creed. The old form was propositional. These were straight out statements. The new form is confessional. Each article begins with the words, "We believe." The general conference received the articles set out both ways and, as I believe, wisely chose the confessional form. The creed then is not something which "they" put in our mouth. The creed is rather what "we" say, we believe. There is a subtle, but I believe real shift from "they" to "we." Again I think the impact should be to help us internalize the creed. It should be a tool of personal and corporate refreshing, of reorientation, direction, and of examination. So now in our creed we declare, "We believe!"

And we believe is —
what we think
what we feel
what we will
our life affirmation
our commitment
our mission.

So our Articles of Religion are more than creedal formula, more than another statement of lofty philosophy. They are the expression of our church's understanding of the meaning of Scriptures — an attempt to put into words a total faith and life view. It is our view that the Bible sits in constant judgment upon creed and not the other way around. Creed is a distillation of theology, biblically based, and terse and precise. Since creed is compressed, it does not say everything and does not elaborate. Therefore the writing of creed requires extreme discipline and care. Creed is an attempt to get to the major concerns, not to touch every concern.

Creed is not intended to be abstract, but concrete and intensely applicable to daily life. Our faith may take rise in heaven, but it flows in lives that touch pavement and dust. So what we truly believe is *only* that which is translated into living. Our creed, our faith is for incarnation, for enfleshment; it is real when it reaches our nerve endings. The faith must be taught; it should also be caught. It is a matter of both head and heart.

So Charles Wesley's excitement and hope are well expressed — "O that all might catch the flame," and Auden's little phrase is compelling to the company of believers who are to "show an affirming flame." To this we are called: to catch and show the flame. That is more than intellect, certainly. But in Christianity the heart is reached through the head. And the head is influenced by the heart. Together head and heart must yield appropriate action.

Creeds are the record of how the church has theologically interpreted the Bible in the past and the present. But in turn, creeds become authoritative guides to hermeneutics (the science or rules, principles of interpretation) in the present. Creeds flow out of the life of the church as body and back into the life of the church. Creeds are the intellectual consensus of the church regarding what is essential to faith based on the church's current best understanding of the meaning of the Scriptures.

The rise of heresy gave rise to much of our New Testament literature but finally to the formulation of creeds. The reappearance of a variety of historical heresies in new combines and dress continues to give urgency to the need for theology and hence the creeds.

May I rather parenthetically note another important fact. The Christian church has never been non-creedal. Any attempt to be non-creedal spells the end for that group. The church has always been both creedal and organized, and there is no avoidance of these two characteristics. Our theology is the source of our life, and theology (creed — condensed theology) flows out of the commingling of God's word written and the daily life of its believers.

Creeds are the church's attempt in a particular historical time and place to state concisely what it believes. Theology is an expansion and extension of the creedal expression. Creeds are likely sharpened and improved by the threat of heresy. Often lengthened!

Creeds are the record of the churches' intellectual struggles, affirmations, and denials. So reading the context which brought each into existence makes fascinating reading.

But a Christian creed is more than an intellectual exercise. Creed emerges from the Bible, from personal and corporate experience of God and life, and from how each relates to other realities of life.

Creeds do more than emerge. They thrust back on the daily life from which they, at least in part, spring.

Ronald Knox taught the Roman Catholic creed to a class of displaced girls housed in a convent during the dark days of World War II in England. Finally, he put the teaching in a book which he called *The Creed in Slow Motion,* by which he meant he had attempted to be simple in explanation.

But what I strongly wish to urge on us is that the Creed is not window dressing, not infrequently used reference items. But rather that the Creed is the very stuff of daily action. Creed immobilized is useless adornment. Creed that never becomes enfleshed is hypocrisy. The creed incarnate and in motion — not slow motion — in the daily course of life is what should concern us.

Let me say it this way: Our creed
constitutes the song of the church,
the standard of the church,
the battle cry of the church,
and the witness of the church to the world.

The Creed does not have written on it a label which says to its users, "For Internal Use Only."

Now may I offer some other brief statements regarding creed. They are kind of staccato points to be made.

1. The Word of God stands in perpetual judgment on every human word even when spoken *in* and *by* the church. So no matter how useful and necessary creed may be, we never make it an idol.

2. Creed must be expressed in the language of specific times and places to be effective.

3. Creeds are the result of history and they make history. Piety, worship, and cultural involvements help to form and are formed by Creed.

4. The theological reflections placed in creeds form the memory bank of the church. No great creed was ever formulated without regard for the thought and expressions of previous generations in the church.

5. Ultimately, creeds are confirmed or rejected by history, especially by "the common-sense wisdom of the Christian community." Creeds therefore represent consensus for those living in or under them.

6. The great doctrines of the church were tested and lived in worship and experience and consented to before they were put on paper or voted by a "council" or officially "authorized." They are

not solo performances; rather, they are the products of the community of faith.

7. The corporate confession of the creed is appropriate to the communion of saints. At the same time it reinforces the faith and practice of the individual within the communion.

8. In creedal confession we make outward and overt what is inward and covert. It is a declaration of loyalty, an act of courage.

9. While the creedal confession is a matter of mind, of intellect, it is more. It is a commitment of the whole person and the entire life. It is an offering of one's self to the Creator-Redeemer.

SAY IT AGAIN

Rearticulation is the obligation of each generation. The following is from *We Believe: Insights into the Beliefs of Free Methodists.*

Say it again!

Our church wisely delegated reformulation of the "Articles of Religion" to a Study Commission during the last quinquennium. The commission received substantial input from our scholarly community. The result of this huge effort is presented here.

I have in my library several collections of Christian creeds as they have developed through the centuries. The church has always been in the process of resaying its beliefs. It is a sign, not of weakness, but of strength. A review of the creeds ancient and modern is a testimony to the dynamic, the intelligence, and the insight of successive generations of Christians.

To "say it again" is not an easy task. No two persons trying to express the essentials of the "Articles of Religion" would use the same words. Certain words will always be more pleasing or less pleasing, according to our language tastes. So it is not easy to secure a document that a large delegated body finds suitable. And editing by a large body exposes to possible loss of document integrity and felicity of expression.

The appearance of these Articles is once again evidence that they always grow out of the very life of the church and feed back into its life. For such Articles are the corporate affirmation of faith. They are the corporate response to heresy. The "councils" and a General Conference confirm they are what is normal in the life of the church. This is a historic reality. So the Articles must be restated from time to time in ways that reflect the language and the insights of time and place.

The "Articles of Religion" are the indispensable tools for the church as it

teaches,

preaches,

worships,

and witnesses.

Creeds have always taken on new significance when there have been foes within or without the church. Threats have always served to sharpen the thinking and the experience of the church. Reexamination of the foundations usually is a reassuring experience. We thought they were good. We find them better than we could have imagined. They bear examination! The creeds are essentially affirming. And it would be wrong to overemphasize the crisis nature of the creeds.

Yet one can and should use the creeds as does one Indonesian church. Article by article it affirms its faith, but at the end of each article says, "And with this article we deny and reject ... ." That church thinks the procedure necessary to its life and teaching program. And indeed the positive affirmation includes the existence of an opposite, or a negative. We are *for* some things; therefore we are *against* other things. But the reaffirmation of our faith is evidence that we refuse to be "beleaguered by ... negation and despair." It is our corporate declaration of hope and confidence.

Our Theology

Our theology should be:
Relational
Revelational (biblical)
Systematic
Life-changing

Relational is a suitable term to describe (1) the objective of revelation; (2) the acts and words of God; (3) the content, direction, and meaning of Christian living.

Revelational is an appropriate term to describe what we have in the Bible as text and what we find in the Person of Christ as Incarnation. Our theology is what we have to say about the self-disclosure of God.

Systematic is useful, since we must finally organize our understandings for improved communication, ready reference, and the coordination and refinement of insights based on our revelation. Preference: Biblical

Life-changing is a term which reminds us of the objective of revelation and relationships. It is also an antidote to mere theory and ideology which removes itself from life as it is and as it should be lived day by day.

The Responsibility of the Preacher

In the context of our subject I believe every minister of the gospel has a serious responsibility to:

1. Know his Bible through both inductive and deductive study. This is unquestioningly a lifelong pursuit.

2. Know himself with as rigorous and objective honesty as he can manage. This too should reflect growth.

3. Diligently bring to bear all natural and acquired skill in communication to the preparation of mind and heart so that he can share effectively his best insights regarding the revelation of God and the way it relates to daily life.

4. Motivate both himself and his people to a life of maturity in relationship with Christ.

5. Recognize the total process as involving his whole person in utter commitment to the lordship of Jesus Christ — intellect, emotions, will.

Our Times: His Hands

A Meditation

Just a moment, now, you who say, "We are going to such-and-such a city today or tomorrow. We shall stay there a year doing business and make a profit"! How do you know what will happen tomorrow? What, after all, is your life? It is like a puff of smoke visible for a little while and then dissolving into thin air. Your remarks should be prefaced with, "If it is the Lord's will, we shall still be alive and will do so-and-so." As it is, you take a certain pride in planning with such confidence. That sort of pride is all wrong. Well then, if a man knows what is right and fails to do it, his failure is a real sin (James 4:13-17, Phillips).

Do not boast about tomorrow, for you do not know what a day may bring forth (Proverbs 27:1, RSV).

I can recall people both saying and writing about their plans, "D.V.," which are the first two letters of Latin words that mean "the Lord willing." Perhaps that was a good custom. It caused one to stop and think about the role of both providence and accident in our daily lives.

James and Proverbs both remind us of the importance of a thing we call time and of the unpredictableness of our own future. If you have been told rather straight-forwardly, as I have been, that your chances of being alive very long were slim, you get a new appreciation of that commodity we call time and the uncertainty of our tomorrows.

James is calling us to attention. Each of us needs to hear his words. I remember my mother seemed to function as though she was to be here eternally. Well, she was not and neither are we. Not one of us knows what the morrow may bring of good or ill, of sorrow or of joy. So the whole thing is to live so that uncertainty is not a threat. Let's live in such a way that we show forth a new appreciation of the life God gives us.

An unknown has written:

If I had but one year to live;
One year to love; one year to bless;
One year to better things
One year to sing; one year to smile;
To brighten earth a little while;
One year to win my Master's praise;
One year to fill with work my days;
One year to strive for a reward.

So, if I have a year to live
Or just one day in which to give
A pleasant smile, a helping hand
A mind that tries to understand
A fellow-creature when in need
'Tis one with me — I take no heed,
But try to live each day He sends,
To serve my gracious Master's ends.

How we treat time is of utmost importance. St. Augustine said a terse truth when he wrote, "Time never takes time off." Another said, "Time is the most valuable thing a person can spend."

Well, what if you had but a day, a week, a year to live? Martin Luther said, "If I thought the world was coming to an end tomorrow, I would plant my apple seed today."

V. Y. Laramore had a good word:

I've shut the door on yesterday —
Its sorrows and mistakes;
I've locked within its gloomy walls
Past failures and heartaches.
And now I throw the key away
To seek another room,
And furnish it with hope and smiles
And every springtime bloom . . .
I've shut the door on yesterday
And thrown the key away —
Tomorrow holds no fears for me,
Since I have found today.

I like the following, of another unknown:

> If you have work to do, do it now.
> Today the skies are clear and blue,
> Tomorrow clouds may come in view,
> Yesterday is not for you. Do it now.
>
> If you have a song to sing, sing it now.
> Let the notes of gladness ring,
> Clear as song of bird in spring,
> Let every day some music bring. Sing it now.
>
> If you have kind words to say, say them now.
> Tomorrow may not come your way.
> Do a kindness while you may,
> Loved ones will not always stay. Say it now.

Arnold Bennett wrote: "The supply of time is a daily miracle. ... You wake up in the morning, and lo! your purse is magically filled with twenty-four hours of the unmanufactured tissue of the universe of life. It is yours! the most precious of your possessions."

The late Bishop J. H. Vincent repeated to himself each morning these words: "I will this day try to live a simple, sincere, and serene life; repelling promptly every thought of discontent, impurity, and self-seeking; cultivating cheerfulness, magnanimity, charity, and the habit of holy silence; exercising economy in expenditure, carefulness in conversation, diligence in appointed service, fidelity to every trust, and a child-like faith in God."

So what if you had but one day, one week, one year to live? We really do not know, do we? Love more, complain less. Enjoy more of the free things of life. Quit worrying about all or most of what now bothers us. Be more patient with children and others. Quit complaining about what others have and you don't have. Invest more in persons and less in things. Spend less time in prayer for self and more for others.

Heavenly Father, our times are in Your hands. You do not guarantee me tomorrow, so I thank You for today. Help me to live as though I had no more than 24 hours, and work as though I had another 50 years. Amen.

People of Purpose

"We know that in everything God works with those who love Him, whom He has called in accordance with His purpose, to bring about what is good" (Romans 8:28, Goodspeed).

Our Christian faith rests on the assumption that this is an ordered universe with a God of purpose at the helm. We believe that God's glory is our glory, and that His good is our good. If God knows where He is going and what He is doing, then great is our assurance, and that gives us stability in a shaking world.

Amidst the conflicting purposes of men, in the face of world confusion, we believe God is working out His own wise design. And that design realized will be His highest glory and at the same time be for our highest good.

Paul assures us that God is at work in everything. In the dust clouds created by our human striving, it is often hard to see or to believe that indeed God is at work in everything. The truth that goes with this God at work, Paul says, is that God is in partnership with *"those who love him."*

His purpose is ours; His goal is ours. Just as God at creation stepped back and *"... saw that it was good,"* so now the purpose God pursues is to *"... bring about what is good,"* and that in the here and now.

So we pray and we act as Jesus taught us to pray and act. We do this together constantly, *"Thy will be done, thy kingdom come on earth as it is in heaven."* What we long and pray for arms our efforts and drives our spirit. God constantly seeks to take us into His active purpose. He wants a people of purpose, a purpose like His very own.

God works with His people, the church, to establish basic, fundamental convictions in our minds. Let me cite four which we share in carrying out the purpose of God on earth.

1. The Reality of God

John Ruskin a century ago said, "There is need, bitter need, to bring back into men's minds that to live is nothing, unless to live be to know Him by Whom we live."

Thomas R. Kelley states, "The deepest need of men is not food and clothing and shelter, important as they are. It is God. We have mistaken the nature of poverty, and thought it was economic. No, it is poverty of soul ... ."

Too often quickened interest in God comes from the wrong reasons — threat to material security, fear of impending danger, personal sorrow, coincidences of affliction or deliverance, rather than from any sense of deep spiritual need and lostness.

We do not need sermons of "proofs" of God. We need the proclamation of God's aliveness by our works and by our words. A. J. Balfour said that men want a God "Whom men can love, a God to Whom men can pray, Who takes sides, Who has purposes and preferences, Whose attributes, however conceived, leave unimpaired the possibility of a personal relation between Himself and those Whom He has created."

What then is our task in partnership with God? It is to constantly affirm the reality of such a God, with the aid of the Holy Spirit. And this will most often be intuitively accepted. God has built us with this intuitive ability. This is something within humans that is on the side of our evangelizing.

2. The Fact of Sin

This is our second deeply held conviction. The wars and turmoil of our century have not altered any part of our Christian faith or duty. We are overwhelmed with the loss of masses of humans. But the fact remains: **You can account for the wickedness of the whole world when you can explain one man's ability to do wrong.**

The problem of dealing with **one** man's evil-doing in relation to the character and the power of God, is just as great as dealing with crimes of army, nation and empire.

In the face of this fact, what is our task? It is to unflinchingly declare the sinfulness of sin. And having done this, we trust the Holy Spirit to do His convicting work.

3. The Ability of God

The reality of God, the fact of sin, and now the ability of God. We need awareness that God has already, long since faced the fact, the dilemma of human sin — the false use of our human freedom.

Bishop McConnel said, "When a man makes a bad choice God carries out the bad choice to its appropriate course in the play and interplay even of havoc working forces." Sinful decisions have consequences which even forgiveness cannot change. God can, with our cooperation, work out new situations which modify the full damage of consequences. That is indeed the grace of God at work in our sin-damaged lives.

And we need to proclaim the ability of God to forgive, to change us, to rehabilitate, to transform, to heal and restore wholeness to persons. Our great work for the world is not the wickedness of men but the sufficiency of God to deal with our sin and brokenness.

At Calvary, God gave His best demonstration of His ability to deal with sin and to dispense "love divine all loves excelling." Our task: to declare the atoning, cleansing blood of Jesus and a grace that is greater than all our sin.

We go to the world around us with these convictions:

The reality of God

The fact of sin

The ability of God, and finally ...

4. The Certainty of Victory

The first word spoken came from God. What He spoke, created. And it was good. We can rest assured that the last word of our human drama will also be His word — and it will be good. The redemptive accomplishment of a good God will be even greater than the creative accomplishment. The final word does not and will not come from science, the humanities, psychology, or all the other human "ologies."

When Ben Franklin was 81 — a not very pious womanizer — he wrote, "The longer I live, the more convincing proofs I see of this truth: That God governs in the affairs of man."

Our task is to assure fellow humans that "the ultimate forces determining human history and life are the purposes of a righteous God."

We have a choice: accept the idea of the steady, **un**hurried,

unhalted march of a God of purpose to whom we yield our total lives and then find our little purposes brought to highest fulfillment by accepting and doing the Father's will.

The other choice: accept the chances, uncertainty, purposelessness of an evolving world, a world of whim in which the course of Jacob becomes our course: trial and error, fail now, try a **new** but yet human approach, until at the end of our human wits we realize — intuitively — that all our struggles are vain and we surrender our affairs to the One All Sufficient, Ever Able Christ Who changes us from Jacob to Israel.

Finally, hooked onto the purpose of God, I am at rest, assured, and secured. With God, there is personal victory. Hear Masefield's "Everlasting Mercy":

I did not think, I did not strive,
The deep peace burned me alive;
The bolted door had broken in,
I knew that I had done with sin,
I knew that Christ had given me birth
To brother all the souls on earth ...

O glory of the lighted mind,
How dead I'd been, how dumb, how blind.
The station brook, to my new eyes,
Was babbling out of Paradise,
The waters rushing from the rain
Were singing Christ has risen again,
I thought all earthly creatures knelt
From rapture of the joy I felt.

Thus Masefield celebrates the joy made possible by our Creator-Redeemer. And so indeed we feel at home in the universe because we are at one with the guiding **mind** and **heart** of the universe. We are God's victorious children here and now. No longer are we orphans, estranged, alone.

Justice Oliver Wendell Holmes said it well for us, "You have a feeling of intimacy with the inside of the cosmos." So we Christians are the people of God's purpose in the world. That is the source of our special brand of optimism in a deadly, sinful world. Pessimism, from whatever source, "discourages us from moral conflict and weakens the urge to unselfish activity."

So we come back to those significant words of Paul, the apostle to the Gentiles: *"We know that in everything God works with those who love Him, whom He has called in accordance with His purpose, to bring about what is good."*

So we go to the world with the word that ...

God is real.
Sin is our number one problem.
God is able to deal with the harsh realities of life.
God assures of final victory!

Prayers

Good evening, Father, God.
Thanks for inviting us to be with You
and to sit at Your table spread with everything good.
We are glad You accept us, love us, care for us.
We acknowledge with gratitude that we are neither
autonomous nor automatons.
You have not left us to ourselves, nor have You coerced us.
So now we freely, gladly confess we are not our own.
And just as freely and gladly we offer You ourselves
for whatever use seems good to You.

We offer our praise, our adoration, our love, our worship.
How glad we are that You are distanced from us, and
greater than we are — for we constantly need One
who can help us.
And how glad we are You are nearer to us than hands,
or feet, or breathing.
Thank You, Father, for being to us the matrix in which
we both begin and grow toward all that is
intended in our being "human."

And now we also recognize with gratitude that other womb
You provide in the living Church of Jesus Christ.
We are happy to be enveloped in its love and fellowship
and service.

We now earnestly pray for the well-being of Your church
around the world.
We place each functioning part of that church imaginatively
in our hands and hold it up for Your blessing,
for the anointing of Your Spirit,
for the healing of wounds,
for the effectiveness of service.
So we circle the globe with our minds' eye — a globe, a church

which is within the circle of Your love, Your care.

With our hands we lift to You now:
the nationals and missionaries in torn, suffering Africa;
the Christians in the other America, Central America and the West Indies;
the Asians — teeming populations of China, Japan, Hong Kong, Korea, Taiwan;
the struggling Christians in the Middle East;
the suppressed Christians in Communist countries;
the Christians who struggle for new vitality in Britain, in Europe;
the church trying to meet the challenge of great metropolitan areas in America and around the globe;
the leaders and followers and partners in Your enterprise, O Father, we lift them all to You.

You, Father, are needed in our midst. We who stand here in Your presence need You and want You.
Teach us, Father, how to make Christ Lord of our individual lives and head of our corporate lives — the church.

Don't take us out of the way; just keep us from running something that doesn't belong to us. Help us to learn Your signals and cues and respond to them quickly.

Finally, we give thanks, Father, for this gathering which in a way symbolizes the church universal. Help us to reach around this room and beyond in our love and concern.

In Jesus' Name, Amen

O God of steadfast love, we come in this hour of worship mindful of Your great grace. God of love, suffering and saving love, we offer our hearts to You in gratitude.

Our hearts leap with thanksgiving for the sense You are granting us of Your presence among us, for the moving of Your Spirit in Your church. You are making us all the more aware of how dependent we are upon Your action in our individual lives and among us as a believing people.

We are indeed grateful that You look upon us, Father, as Your children. We rejoice that we are Your sons and daughters. You help us to stand tall as we think of this wonderful relationship.

But we must also confess we are not always pleasing to You. We do not always act like we are sons and daughters of the Most High God. Father, help us to be good members of the body of Christ. Make us increasingly sensitive to the pressure of the Holy Spirit. May we never grieve Your Spirit. Forbid that we would blemish Your name by either act or attitude.

Help us to receive the grace You are trying to pour into our lives. Help us to experience more and more the gift of Your love so imparted to us, so embedded in us that it blossoms in beauty in our daily lives.

We confess our human weakness. We are neither strong enough to cope with what we meet in life, nor to be Your witnesses in the world unless we know Your strength rising within us.

> O God of grace and God of glory,
> On Thy people pour Thy power
> Crown Thine ancient church's story,
> Bring her bud to glorious flower.
> Grant us wisdom, Grant us courage,
> For the facing of this hour,
> For the facing of this hour.

Father, come with rebuke to those who need it; come with forgiveness to the penitent; come with healing to our bodies, minds, and spirits. Those with urgent needs we bring to You. Those facing chronic failures, bring about real change — deliver from a seemingly hopeless cycle of defeat. We come knowing You as our Father. You are always faithful. You never fail. Amen.

Invocation:

O God, how great You are; how small we are. How infinite is Your wisdom; how limited is ours. How everlasting You are; how brief our span of earthly life. How high and good are Your ways; how selfish and impure are our tendencies. Touch us again in this hour as we turn our faces toward Your face. Touch us with Your transforming power. Amen.

Our God and Father, we turn our hearts, our faces, our minds to You. We want now to see You. We want now to hear You. We want to sense Your love probing, disturbing, awakening us. Let Your holy love burn away our dross, purge our unloving thoughts, attitudes. Let Your holy love make real people of us.

Deliver us from hypocrisy. Deliver us from self-deceit. Deliver us from thinking we are better than those who are in some way different from us. Help us to remember that we are what we are, if we are anything at all, by the grace of God. And if we have been responsive to Your grace, it is because You have helped us to continue a repenting posture and attitude.

Father, we want so to be like Your Son. We want so to reflect amidst the daily stresses and strains of life the love of Calvary. And so often we are uneasily aware that we didn't quite make it. Forgive us. Teach us to love with Your love. Disturb our contentment with small progress. Keep before us goals of loving yet unreached people.

We confess, Father, we are still conditioned by our social environment; we still reflect, though unbidden, the prejudices of our own kind; we still have vestiges of prejudice and unreasonable biases that in moments of holy and loving thought shame us.

We confess, also, that we are ignorant and unskilled in the ways of love. We often want to show love and do not know its graces. We may, Father, have learned something of manners and socially acceptable performance, but we still have a ways to go to be genuine, to be a real person, to know the words, the looks, the tones that convey Your love. We need so much for Your grace to reach us, teach us, and transform us. Amen

---

Father God, God of grace, God of love.

We come now to ask You to teach us to love. Teach us to love like You love. We have so very much to learn of the costliness of Your love, the perseverance of Your love; the steadfastness of Your love.

Grant us the wisdom of love.
Grant us the power of love.
Grant us the personal transformation of Your love.
Grant to Your people Your love which alone makes us the true heavenly community living in the midst of a society indifferent to You and Your ways.

We confess that too often we are unlike You in our feeble attempt at loving.

We confess that we are in constant need of Your Spirit to shed abroad Your love in our hearts, deep within us. O Father, fill us with love by the indwelling of Your Holy Spirit within us.

We confess that too often we are not sensitive to the needs around us. Forgive us we pray and make us more sensitive.

Too often, Father, we are driven by law and not by love. Assist us in our moral and spiritual development to climb out of law and legalism and live in the fresh air of love.

May we feel both the freedom and the demands of Your love directing our lives, shaping our decisions, and sweetening our service to You and to others.

Father, send an awakening to Your very own people. Send it because we need it. Send it because the world is waiting for us to show who and what You are.

Make us a force for good and not a farce in this world.

Transform us so we may contribute to healthy changes in the larger society about us. Transform us so that by our prayers, our acts, our votes we change the quality of our representatives at all levels of government. Transform Your church so it impacts on world leadership.

Help us, O God, to believe in the power of Your presence in Your church to change the world for the better.

We turn our faces, our whole beings toward You now asking the blessing, the impartation to us of Your love. Let Your love cleanse us and make us whole. We remind ourselves that You are always faithful, always responsive, always giving. We thank You for never failing us. Amen.

Father, we have great reason to pray this morning. We stand amazed at who we are by Your creation. You formed us. You breathed Yourself into us. You wanted me and You wanted us — the people of God, a special kind of community. You gave us a task, a partnership in the management of our environment, of ourselves, of our gifts and of Your very own grace.

We are more than amazed. We stand here in utter awe at this amazing assignment. We give thanks for the honor, for the trust, the expectation found in Your assignment.

We know that as a race of created humans we have quite miserably failed in Your purpose for both planet and people. But again we are full of gratitude that You've not given up on us. You followed us. You came to us in Incarnation. You gave Your best in Your Son on Calvary. You've shown us Your wounds, the wounds of hurt love. You've shown us what You think of sin. You've shown us Your heart of holy love.

This morning as Your children we want to say that we crown You Lord of all, of everything. Not a mite would we withhold. Help us to get first things first. We give thanks for our dependence. We praise You that we are given all things and yet own nothing. We rejoice in the abundance and riches of Your grace and in the same riches and abundance of Your earth.

Not only are the cattle on a thousand hills Yours, the hills and valleys are Yours, the mountains, and the seas. We renounce proud independence. We only claim to be Your servant-stewards. And, Father, we have often not been very good at the job you've given. We have often not loved You enough to do a good job. And when we did we've been tempted to pride. Forgive us.

We would renew our covenant with You this morning. Help us to shape up under the impulse of Your holy love. Help us to bring purpose and plan into all our efforts. Help us to plan with bended hearts, opened ears, and quickened minds. Send Your Spirit to make us capable of discharging our debt of love.

Help us to get Spirit-guided discipline into our lives so we fail neither You nor ourselves. Help us to systematic, proportionate giving of our money and all else we have. Grant us a vision of what could be done if we were in fact Your good steward servants.

Make us count in a world that needs the righteous, the Spirit-moved managers. May our lives and our various offerings to you bring forth a fragrance that shall perfume our lives and all those we meet.

Father, we are really not up to this, so send us Your Spirit with the help You see we need. Through Christ, our Lord, Amen.

Here we come, Father God, accepting Your invitation into Your holy of holies. We come to make an offering of praise, of thanksgiving, of adoration. We bow our hearts in awe that You, King of the universe, willingly, lovingly designed Your most wonderful entrance into our lives, into our human dilemma and into our destiny by coming to us as a baby, and coming by stable and manger.

We stand here this morning enveloped in a mystery beyond our vocabulary to express or our minds to grasp. We rejoice that this mystery of Incarnation is not that of a cold and silent universe, impersonal and uncaring. We rejoice in a mystery that is full of warmth, caring, compassion, and love.

O God, we need another miracle. We need it in our personal lives and in the body corporate. We plead for a miracle of love and understanding to be worked in each of us. Enter our lives, dwell in us, live Your life in ours.

We bow with a sense of distress and shame that we so often fail to give expression to Your love in our various relationships. We are too often too quick to criticize, to take offense, to grieve Your Holy Spirit. We humble ourselves before You.

Transform us by grace divine. Christianize our consciences, our attitudes, our behavior. Conform us to the image of Your dear Son. Forbid, O God, that we would ever lose sight of Your Face by indulging in looking at the failures of others, measuring ourselves, our consecration, or even our effectiveness by how others perform.

Forgive us! Forgive us! Forgive us!

Father, we do again bow at your manger-throne in contrition, in love, in devotion, and in the determination that You shall be seen in our lives as we live them in home, work, and marketplace.

O Christ be Lord. We want You to be. All of this we confess and request knowing You are always faithful, dependable, trustable. Amen.

O God, our Father and the Father of our Lord, Jesus Christ, we give thanks for welcome into Your presence. We do now remind ourselves that You only are God: holy, majestic, sovereign. We want to worship You in spirit and truth. We place our little crowns before You so we can crown You Lord of all!

In mercy and in grace You have visited us in Your Son Jesus Christ who through His life, ministry, death, and resurrection has brought life and salvation to light.

We do in these moments give thanks for that incomprehensible love manifest in Christ, that while we were enemies and full of hostility You loved and died for us. And in these moments we seek Your renewing grace, forgiveness, and healing for each of our lives.

We rejoice in the offer that You constantly make to grant us wholeness, peace, and to fill us with joy in believing.

Help us by Your Holy Spirit to sense Your presence now in a wonderful, joyful, refreshing way. Grant us wisdom for life, devotion to service, love for neighbor. We do give thanks for every temporal and spiritual blessing we constantly experience.

Father, for those who bear unbearable burdens, suffer from loss of loved ones, are devastated by wayward family members, who know the despair of loneliness, and who struggle against adversity, grant the comfort of Your Holy Spirit.

For those concerns which press hardest against us, we now take time to pray silently.

Thank You, Father, for hearing and understanding us in our cries and concerns.

Afresh we commit ourselves to You for loving service. Unfailing Comforter, assist us to continue to worship and live for You.

May Your word and inspired song strengthen each of us according to our needs. We pray in the strong name of Jesus Christ our Savior and Lord. Amen.

Eternal God, our heavenly Father, we seek Your presence; show us Yourself. Make us to know that we stand in Your holy and loving presence.

We offer our praise the best we can. We recognize the limitations of our thoughts and words; we struggle against the intrusions of the world on our thoughts even in Your presence; we acknowledge both our humanness and our sin which beclouds our vision of Your majesty, sovereignty, holiness, and compassionate love. Forgive us, we pray. And help us to worship You in both spirit and truth.

We do give thanks for every working of Your spirit in our personal and corporate lives. Without this operation of Your grace we would be completely undone and helpless. So we acknowledge with thanksgiving that we are dependent on You for the human life we live, for the breath we breathe, for the bread we eat, for seedtime and harvest, for victory over selfishness and all manner of sin in our lives.

We give thanks that You, O Christ, are alive! You are alive this moment in our lives. Help us to lean on You for every need of our days and nights.

Deliver us from temptation. Strengthen us when and where we are weak. Motivate us when we are indifferent. Assist us by Your Spirit to love You with our whole person, to love ourselves properly and to care for others as we care for ourselves.

O God, we pray that You will rebuke every demonic force that works in us and in our society; we pray for the peace of mankind, for the leaders of nations, for the operators of bureaucracies. Restrain, O God, the flood tide of evil that surrounds us, destroying our youth, bringing death to marriages, and rupture to so many valued relationships.

We pray for those just now whom we know have special need — physical, spiritual, emotional. We reach out with mind and faith to support them and pray for the release of Your healing power in their lives.

Assure us again of Your steadfast love, Your unfailing and persisting grace. Amen.

O God, our heavenly Father, we come this morning grateful for the disclosure of Who You are. Sovereign, personal, creative, concerned, loving, and holy! We bow our minds, our hearts, and our will before You.

We acknowledge Your sovereignty over our lives, our nations, over all that exists. But best of all we recognize the Lordship of Jesus Christ in our lives and His headship in the church He bought with His blood.

We give grateful thanks for every expression of Your grace toward us. We depend on Your grace to save, to keep, to mature us. We discover that we are not sufficient to manage ourselves or to run Your church — none of us. We need Your lordship, Your headship if we are to be truly Your community in the world.

Pour out Your grace upon our lives we pray. Forbid that we'd be content with being half-Christian, half a Christ-person, half committed to You and Your purposes in the world. Help us to have a deep desire for receiving from Your hand of grace all the transforming power we need to make us victorious in every area of life.

O God, forbid that we should be so defeated in any area of living that we should hinder the coming of Your kingdom, that we should be a block to the faith of another person. Make us your servants, loving and faithful, models of what the church of Jesus Christ should be living in a dark, cancerous, damaged, ill-lighted world. Make us candles in the gloom of our day. May, O God, You live in us and manifest Yourself through us.

Our Father God, we come with praise. We come gladly into Your presence. We sense a bit of how much You have cared for us from eternity. You have loved us with a steadfast love. We bless Your name for You have blessed us with uncounted benefit to body, mind, and spirit.

We rejoice that You have redeemed us at unlimited cost. You have reached toward us and for us to the very limit of our sinfulness, our waywardness. You are the Shepherd ever-searching — not for the ninety-nine in the fold and safe — but for us who have wandered away and are lost. You seek us in our lostness, our sin, our estrangement, our alienation, our purposelessness, and in our hopelessness.

O God, we recognize we are not inherently good. We need You to transform us and make us good. And those You are making good, we acknowledge need to be made better. We recognize that it is only by Your marvelous grace that we are as good as we are. Only by Your grace can we become truly human and what You aspire for us to become.

In this very congregation we admit we need You deeply, urgently, and in some cases desperately. But You are right there to meet that need, in a moment, in the twinkling of an eye. O God, do for us what we are unable to do for ourselves.

We recognize that we are blessed with more of You and more of Your good things than most people who wander on this earth. We readily admit it is not ours by merit. We, most of us, were born in an advantaged country. In most cases in an advantaged environment. We've had a headstart over most of the peoples of the earth.

God, help us to never be heady about our advantages which are mostly not of our own doing. Grant us a vision of those deprived persons who need You and what You do for them. Flood our hearts with caring concern. Show us how we can be Your ministering servants, in things both large and small. Help us to see what we cannot do by ourselves we yet may accomplish in union with other members of Your body.

We rejoice that You offer us useful employment in Your kingdom, that there is something every one of us can do. Help us to see we count and can count for You.

Look into our hearts. Look deeply Lord Jesus. See our damaged souls, our impaired vision, our unbending wills, our inner illness, and heal us by the touch of Your Spirit upon our spirits. Make us not only good, but good for something, and good for You and Your kingdom.

Make us, this congregation, all You really want us to be. Send us to someone with a bit of good news. Give us the gift of giving of ourselves for Your sake. And Father, we will be grateful for all You can and will do for us, for we now offer You ourselves for Yourself. Thank You for Your faithfulness to every one of us. Amen.

With Onesimus and Philemon, Father, we bow in Your presence conscious of Your patience and Your steadfast love. We degenerate into uselessness, O God, unless by Your transforming grace You make us useful and useable.

We bow in awe and in gratitude when we get glimpses into the way You work in lives to bring about Your salvation, Your reconciliation.

Thank You, Father, for what You are doing among us this very moment. Come with healing, pour in the balm of Gilead where there is hurt, bruises, cuts, and pain. Comfort those who need comfort with Your great comforting power. Then as You comfort us make us able to comfort those who need us.

Where there is estrangement, bitterness, come with Your reconciling love.

Where there is frustration and a sense of lost direction, come with Your counsel and guidance.

Where there is pressure, moral and spiritual, come with the inward support of Your presence and grace.

Where there is resentment, remove the cause by the cleansing work of Your Spirit.

Where there is a critical spirit, come with the healing of greater understanding.

Where there is the malaise of general dissatisfaction with life, help us to get ourselves caught up in the significance of being Yours and serving for You.

When we get tempted to self-pity and an overconcern for our own welfare, wants, and needs, remind us of Calvary.

When we become headstrong and think we know what is best, rebuke the arrogance of our self-will and cleanse us deep within.

When we lack in compassion and concern for others, come with warmth to our hearts. Give us a vision of how Your Son served and how He felt.

When we are tempted to grow weary in well-doing and feel unappreciated, help us to draw strength and refreshment by drawing closer to You.

Hear our prayers. Incline Your ears to us. And give us obedient hearts. Thank You for never failing us. We rest ourselves in You ... through Christ, our Savior, Amen.

Privileges and Perils, Part 1

Hebrews 10:11-39

Day after day every priest stands and performs his religious duties; again and again he offers the same sacrifices, which can never take away sins. But when this priest had offered for all time one sacrifice for sins, he sat down at the right hand of God. Since that time he waits for his enemies to be made his footstool, because by one sacrifice he has made perfect forever those who are being made holy.

The Holy Spirit also testifies to us about this. First he says:

> *"This is the covenant I will make with them after that time, says the Lord. I will put my laws in their hearts, and I will write them on their minds."*

Then he adds:

> *"Their sins and lawless acts I will remember no more." And where these have been forgiven, there is no longer any sacrifice for sin.*

Therefore, brothers, since we have confidence to enter the Most Holy Place by the blood of Jesus, by a new and living way opened for us through the curtain, that is, his body, and since we have a great priest over the house of God, let us draw near to God with a sincere heart in full assurance of faith, having our hearts sprinkled to cleanse us from a guilty conscience and having our bodies washed with pure water.

Let us hold unswervingly to the hope we profess, for he who promised is faithful. And let us consider how we may spur one another on toward love and good deeds. Let us not give up meeting together, as some are in the habit of doing, but let us encourage one another — and all the more as you see the Day approaching.

If we deliberately keep on sinning after we have received the knowledge of the truth, no sacrifice for sins is left, but only a fearful expectation of judgment and of raging fire that will consume the enemies of God. Anyone who rejected the law of Moses died without mercy on the testimony of two or three witnesses. How much more severely do you think a man deserves to be punished who has trampled the Son of God under foot, who has treated as an unholy thing the blood of the covenant that sanctified him, and who has insulted the Spirit of grace?

For we know him who said, "It is mine to avenge; I will repay," and again, "The Lord will judge his people." It is a dreadful thing to fall into the hands of the living God.

Remember those earlier days after you had received the light, when you stood your ground in a great contest in the face of suffering. Sometimes you were publicly exposed to insult and persecution; at other times you stood side by side with those who were so treated. You sympathized with those in prison and joyfully accepted the confiscation of your property, because you knew that you yourselves had better and lasting possessions.

So do not throw away your confidence; it will be richly rewarded. You need to persevere so that when you have done the will of God, you will receive what he has promised. For in just a very little while,

> *"He who is coming will come and will not delay. But my righteous one will live by faith. And if he shrinks back, I will not be pleased with him."*

But we are not of those who shrink back and are being destroyed, but of those who believe and are saved (Hebrews 10:11-39, NIV).

This is a chapter worthy of serious and thoughtful consideration for every Christian believer. It is needed! In the paragraph of verses 11-18 is the essence of the discussion regarding the old sacrificial system and the way it impacts on our Christian lives in the days of the New Covenant.

The emphasis is on the "one sacrifice" rather than the repeated Old Testament offerings and sacrifices. The sacrifice is "for all time." And this sacrifice is the basis for our perfection and sanctification. *"For by a single offering he has perfected for all time those who are sanctified"* (RSV). Or as Phillips has it, *"For by virtue of that one offering he has perfected for all time every one whom he makes holy."* There is no question of making further atonement. That is done for all time.

So Christ's atonement is the basis of our privileges and responsibilities. But there is one other accent. See v. 12b and 13. **Christ's session** at the right hand of God is the second strand, as it were, in the basis for our Christian privileges, expectations, hopes. He reigns now, but not all enemies are defeated. Potentially — yes! Predictably — yes! Enemies will finally be "footstools."

Mark carefully the foundation these two events or facts provide the Christian. What assurance! Mark carefully that the atonement and the session of Christ make possible a marvelous transformation in our Christian lives — one which the law failed to make.

1. The Covenant Privilege

God enters into a new agreement or covenant with us! Behold what it accomplishes (all based on the atonement and reign of Christ). The atonement begins to take effect. The reign of Christ begins to take effect. But how? The answer is clear:

"I will put my laws in their hearts, and write them on their minds" (v. 16).

God acts by the Holy Spirit to internalize His will in our lives, at the very center, core of personhood. There is no other way the Christian life can come off successfully. Here is complete God-dependence giving internal controls. We're not dependent on some spiritual boost to keep us going. God has done and keeps doing something deep inside of us. There is no other way to spiritual security.

It is more than of passing interest that forgiveness is mentioned after v. 16. Let me suggest that continuous flow of forgiveness is made a possibility — a reality — because right has been internalized. In other words, God is free to trust us because we are not the same inside! So let us re-cap.

Remember, the writer is talking about the new covenant God will make. God's part is to **write** or **impart** His laws, to **forgive** our sins. And that, we are told, is the reason the Old Testament sacrificial system is ended, is no longer needed. What was outward has been made inward.

2. The Worship Privilege

"Let us draw near ... ." Worship should be the natural inclination of those in whom God has placed His laws, and those who have assurance of sins forgiven.

Worship is our coming into the living presence of God. Except for His forgiveness and for what He has wrought in us, this should be a scary thought. BUT note what our passage tells us:

We draw near to God with **confidence**. The basis for this confidence is a vivid sense of freedom from all fear as we enter the sacred area of God's presence. (The word suggests in the Greek, "exulting boldness.")

Blood and flesh suggest the atoning death of Calvary and the true historical human experiences Jesus knew as true man. Christ has pulled aside the separating veil between us and God and has in fact escorted us personally into the sanctuary. He is our *"great priest."*

So we come to worship with **confidence** and with **full assurance of faith**. The appropriate posture as we come is described as with a **sincere heart**, sincerity in the innermost being, without doubt or misgiving. The heart that is sprinkled clean and the body that is washed with pure water further suggests that worship is only successful when we are conscious of Christ's atoning sacrifice and the forgiveness of sins.

3. The Confession Privilege

"Let us hold unswervingly ... ." Here the stress or accent falls on the continuing relationship of those related to God in the New Covenant. Our confession is one filled with hope, because it centers in the faithfulness of God, *"for he who promised is faithful"!*

Our confession ultimately does not rest on what we do for ourselves, but on what God does in and for us! It is a tragedy to see those who seemingly throw aside this great confession for trivial reasons. Where is your hope, your confidence? **It must be in God alone!**

4. The Privilege of Mutuality

We are to *"encourage one another."* Perhaps here is a good place to note that each **privilege** is therefore a **responsibility**. We have the privilege of **mutual ministry**.

First Corinthians 14 is a marvelous picture of people coming to worship in a little home church with a clear sense of needing to contribute something, rather than with the attitude, "Let's see if the preacher or the service can do something for me — for me — for me." And the problem is just there, it is "ME" centered. Indeed "ME" needs help. We all, including preacher, need all we can get, but too many are waiting for someone else to work a miracle in their life.

Rather, how wonderful if we become each other's ministers, servants, helpers! Verse 24 begins, *"And let us consider."* Our mutual ministry requires thoughtfulness, thinking about how we can help another member of the body of Christ!

Mention is made of specific things we should try to achieve in this mutual ministry: *"let us encourage one another,"* not to division, gossip, but to good works. There is much to be done together. Some have bad habits — there are some good grooves we need to wear in our life-style. We depend on the faithfulness of God. He has a right to depend on our faithful habits. We are to *"encourage one another — and all the more as you see the Day drawing near."* "Go-it-alone" Christianity is unthinkable to the writer of Hebrews!

Finally, note the familiar New Testament trinity — what a wonderful trio they are! Faith, Hope, Love (vv. 22-24).

The great privileges are based on God acting toward us in Atonement, in Covenant, so we have **Covenant Privileges, Worship Privileges, Confession Privileges,** and those of **Mutuality.** Do you need to renew your awareness of the basis for your faith, hope, and love, the very life and blood of our Lord? Is your worship a drag or a spiritual privilege in which you rejoice? How are the confession and the mutuality dimensions of your Christian life? Do you stand in need of renewal?

Privileges and Perils, Part 2

Hebrews 10:11-39

We have noted the great privileges set out as belonging to Christians: Covenant, Worship, Confession, and Mutuality. Now turn to the somber part of the chapter — to the **Perils**. Even so, the chapter has the ending wished by the writer. See v. 39. But first, in v. 26 we note the great —

Peril of Deliberate, Knowing Sin

The writer has just noted the coming "Day" — a day of judgment which leads him from exhortation to severe warning. It is the sort of transition we mostly neglect in these tolerant, easy days. It is possible, says the writer, for one who has received *"knowledge of the truth,"* to sin deliberately, which really means willingly, without compulsion.

It is possible to come to a place where, through constant sinning, the attitude becomes one of continued conscious resistance to all one has experienced of the goodness of God and all he had been taught.

He becomes psychologically hardened until he sees no redeeming value in Christ's death and treats the *"blood of the covenant"* as a common thing. Since he has rejected the only possibility of atonement, he can only expect and receive judgment.

Hebrews 3:13-14 (NIV) reads: *"But encourage one another daily, as long as it is called Today, so that none of you may be hardened by sin's deceitfulness. We have come to share in Christ if we hold firmly till the end the confidence we had at first."*

Two results of such apostasy are declared (v. 27):

"**Fearful prospect of judgment**," final and irrevocable.

"**Fury of fire**," which consumes.

These results are worse to contemplate than those experienced by law violators under Moses. Why? Because we now live under a new, better, higher covenant with greater privileges, as we noted before.

We may today ask, "Whatever happened to hell?" Well, here in the Hebrews writings our feet are put near the fires! Why the greater judgment? Under the New Covenant are greater advantages, possibilities, opportunities, provisions.

What do you think about appropriate punishment? What has our degree of light to do with it? Should it be less or more? To answer we must describe the situation under the New Covenant when sin is wilful, deliberate, voluntary, and continuous.

But first, let's look at v. 30-31:

- Punishment is God's responsibility entirely. No more stonings as under Moses. *"It is mine to avenge. I will repay."*
- Judgment belongs to the Lord and to Him alone. And, of course, we know that it will be on a fixed and future day.
- But the punch line is v. 31: *"It is a dreadful thing to fall into the hands of the living God."* The "hands of God" are here of particular interest, as we will see. But let us ask, "Who are in danger of falling into the hands of God?" A dreadful experience is clearly indicated.

1. Those Who Reject Life's Primary Relationship

"... who has trampled the Son of God ... (v. 29). Why is this such a heinous thing to do? Because it —

Rejects the **culmination** of God's self-disclosure (revelation to the sons of men).

Rejects the **best**, what God has designed for us.

Rejects God's **utmost**.

Rejects **Love Incarnate**.

Rejects **God's way** to restore relations with Himself. Jesus is the **way** to God.

The Bible clearly teaches that God is primary in all interpersonal relationships. To reject this is to foul-up all life's relationships and leave us with a hell to go to hell in!

"Spurned" (RSV). A strong word: wilful, deliberated, knowledgeable decision. Self-conscious decision. Uninfluenced decision. It does not describe one "overtaken" in a sinful act. Next:

2. Those Who Deny the Very Basis for a Redeeming Relationship with God!

Those *"who profaned the blood of the covenant ..."* (v. 29, RSV). They poured scorn upon *What*? The only means to cleanse us, change us. It is the blood of Christ which is the covenant blood. Life was in the blood. So they profaned the very life of God Incarnate. The words are a graphic way of saying they did not want anything to do with Christ. They made it clear that they placed no value on Christ's sacrificial death, even though aimed entirely at their own benefit, their highest interests. They join the mockers at Calvary.

Those with a theology which denies blood, who eliminate any reference from hymns and teaching material, who think talk of blood to be vestiges of a barbarian, savage period — these only ask for **greater savagery** in modern life. Denial of Christ's blood is no way to lessen man's inhumanity to man. In fact, it is by the blood that we have hope of becoming truly human.

Who else is in danger of falling into the hands of God?

3. Those Who Insulted the Spirit of Grace

For those who *"... insulted the Spirit of grace"* (The Holy Spirit), it is a rejection of both Son and Spirit and ultimately a rejection of the creating, redeeming Trinity. The givingness (grace) of God receives insult!

The consequence is that we find ourselves in a Fatherless world and therefore a cold, uncaring, mindless universe, and living on a globe that is suddenly nothing more than a jungle ruled by the laws of the jungle ... survival of the fittest ... a snarling, violent environment. This is exactly what society becomes when God's Son is spurned, His blood profaned, His Spirit of grace insulted!

How many are opting for a **jungle** rather than a **God-ordered** society, a God-designed paradise?

"Spirit of grace": think of the beauty of the phrase! How well it describes God, the Holy Spirit, in His outgoingness, His givingness, His graciousness, His loving ministry — this is "holy love" indeed.

There's an old poem by Gertrude Manly Jones which pictures the work of the Spirit in the different periods of a person's life:

(paraphrased)

The Spirit once came to an innocent child
And pled in the tenderest tones — "Give me your heart"
But the child answers, "I want time to play
Go Spirit, go your way — some other day!"

The Spirit returns to the tall slim youth, asks
for his heart.
But the youth replies, "It's time for fun,
so much else to do.
Not now, Spirit — return some other day."

Then the Spirit does return to the mid-aged man
busy with toils and burdens and pleads for his heart.
But again the answer is made, "I'm too busy now to pray.
Some other day! Come back kind Spirit."

Once again the Spirit returns to the man enfeebled by age
and again the Spirit pleads for the heart.
But now he is too weak to pray.

Finally the song concludes:
No other day!
No other day!
The Holy Spirit has gone to stay!

Sad the day when the capability or inclination is gone, when the course of life is set irrevocably and in the wrong direction. No wonder then that it is *"a dreadful thing to* ***fall*** *into the hands of the living God."*

And what a shame that the very wonderful words, *"living God,"* should become a **terror** rather than a **tender** assuring phrase. We see the visage of God change before our very eyes, His face clouds, the sadness of love rejected registers in the lines of His face, and the hurt of the eyes — the face of the living God.

Finally we must look at —

4. Those Hands of God

Hands intended to be symbolic of His love — making, molding, shaping us, even as in Eden, protecting, leading us. How wonderful the hands of God!

In Jesus we see the intention of God's hands as He touches children, the ill, and Mary — healing, helping, touching Hands!

But how those wonderful wholeness-giving hands are transformed by deliberate, wilful sin, AND how terrible they become for the wilful rejector. One is reminded of that strange phrase, the *"wrath of the Lamb."*

Hands! Hands of the Living God!! The God who is near and approachable — as we saw in the first of chapter ten — is also the God who judges; the God who can be a *"raging fire"*; the God whose fire consumes *"the enemies of God."*

We have the choice of being God's friend or adversary.

But there is a **grand alternative** regarding **Hands!!** We can **NOW** place ourselves in His hands, know His presence, blessing, peace, joy, fulfillment, direction, usefulness, eternal bliss!

Which will you have? Will you **place yourself** in His Hands? Or will you **fall** into His Hands? **The choice is ours!**

We are encouraged to make the first of the choices. Note the end verse, 39. *"But we are not of those who shrink back and are destroyed, but of those who believe and are saved."*

Powerful indeed. There are no words to top that!

A Prodigal Comes Home

He died of AIDS. He was twenty-nine. He had chosen the gay life-style. His church memorial service was a celebration that participants will never forget. It was a celebration of grace. It was a shout of triumph through tears.

We experienced the stark contrast between sin's tragedy and grace's downward reach and upward pull.

The tragedy was played out in the context of a loving Christian family. Jim (not his real name) from birth had the benefits of a warm, loving family and parents. He loved sports. He was God-gifted in music.

The family moved often as he was growing up. In his high school sophomore year he attended a very large school. He was active in drama. Out of two thousand students he became part of a select group of twenty madrigal singers. Always the perfectionist, he was the punter for the football team.

Jim went to a Christian college for part of a year. He dropped out and moved to a very large Midwestern city and pursued a variety of sales activities. At some point something began to go wrong. He made a series of choices that took him deeper and deeper into a self-destructive path: alcohol, drugs, and the gay life-style.

Sin, now very much alive in Jim, took its deceptive, ugly course. A handsome young man with a charming personality was changing into one with a wasted, haggard appearance. Attempts to escape habit's clutches proved futile.

Loving parents finally became aware of something very wrong with their beloved son. They lived through several years of profound pain, despair, and bewilderment.

Questions plagued them. Had they failed? What could they do? Could they not find a way to rescue him? Jim was an independent adult now with a mind of his own.

His father is a loving, "fix-it" type person accustomed to solving industrial problems. In anguish of heart, one expensive effort after another was made to turn Jim's life around.

But sin always seemed to take a tighter grip and conquered. The downward step increased in tempo. Fear and despair gripped Jim's parents.

Four major hospitalizations followed for Jim. Then came the words of doom: "Jim, all your immune cells are gone. You have nothing left with which to fight this disease." It was over — all but the dying.

Parental love and concern turned with even greater urgency to the vital issue. What about Jim's eternal destiny? Sin's decisions had completed their deadly work.

But Christian hope turned to the possibility of one more and greater decision. Faith reached out. God alone could help. *"Oh God, take hold of Jim in mercy and grace!"* his parents prayed.

In the last weeks when movement was still possible, Jim appeared several times on three television channels. He made it clear that he had loving parents and that he loved them. He had a public concern: more help for treating the disease. He made no defense of the life-style.

Two months earlier he had gone to the dedication service of his home church. The fact that he wanted to go was a positive sign to his parents. And Jim was reading and marking his Bible. These passages were marked in his Living Bible:

"Lord, how you have helped me before! You took me safely from my mother's womb and brought me through the years of infancy. I have depended upon you since birth; you have always been my God. Don't leave me now, for trouble is near and no one else can possibly help" (Psalm 22:9-11).

"Lead me; teach me; for you are the God who gives me salvation. I have no hope except in you. Overlook my youthful sins, O Lord! Look at me instead through eyes of mercy and forgiveness, through eyes of everlasting love and kindness" (Psalm 25:5-7).

Three weeks before Jim died his father telephoned. "Jim, it is getting very serious. Tell me, son, has God forgiven your sins?"

"Yes, Dad, He has."

Then came a marvelous pause. "Son, if God has forgiven you, then there is no reason I can't."

Two weeks before his death Jim was thinking about Jesus and commented, "Jesus suffered more than I ever will." Jim was reminded of the thief on the cross and the words of assurance Jesus spoke.

Three days before he died Jim's old friends tried to contact him. He refused to see them.

Charles and Lois (not their real names) were constantly with Jim in the hospital — to love their son, to touch him, to read to him, to talk with him. Others around Jim were also dying with AIDS but without such parental love. The family's witness had impact on doctors, nurses, and others.

Time was very short. Led of the Spirit, Lois stood beside Jim. With her fingers she gently made the sign of the cross on his brow and softly said, "In the name of the Father, and the Son, and the Holy Spirit." Indeed it is the way of the cross that leads home.

Minutes later, as the Lord's Prayer was being prayed, Jim lifted his weak hand and said he saw a path. Lois squeezed his hand and held it up and said, "Yes, Jim, Jesus has your hand. He will lead you up the path to Himself."

Peacefulness settled over Jim and the room. Numerous assurances had been given that the "Hound of Heaven" had caught up with Jim.

Finally, father and nurse stood at Jim's side and each closed an eye in death. Jim was a forgiven sinner, a forgiven son. And after terrible detours he had made the right decision and was now safe in the arms of Jesus.

Charles and Lois shared the story with their ministers. They wanted the memorial service to be a ministry. The services for several recently promoted saints truly had been celebrations. And it was agreed that Jim's memorial could not be so.

However, later it seemed as though God spoke to me. The word came, "You can, too, celebrate! You can celebrate what every redeemed person can, the *grace of God!* No one is saved without that grace."

The hymn "Marvelous Grace" came to mind. God's grace. "Marvelous grace of our loving Lord. Grace that exceeds our sin and our guilt." At Jim's service that great hymn was both read and sung.

Jim, the prodigal, had come home. Seen coming in the distance, the Father greeted him and gave him ring, robe and feast.

Charles and Lois had modeled how Christians should cope.

They did not hide. They shared the truth, the pain, the hurt, and even the anger. They found loving support in the body of Christ.

They had to learn how to release Jim to God. It wasn't easy. And they had to forgive themselves. Doing so was difficult, especially for Jim's father, who is by nature an enabler. Charles had previously developed high stress and heart problems as a result of his son's struggles. The Twenty-third Psalm became the key through one of the pastor's sermons. Charles experienced the healing of the Great Shepherd amidst deep water.

The openness of Jim's parents is a ministry to others who emerge from closets of shame to talk to them. Release begets release; openness encourages openness. One person shared with Charles and Lois regarding a lost son, "I can't even talk to him, but you have encouraged me to try."

Hope resides in Christ and in loving the sinner. Let each of us pilgrims on the journey of life remember with humility and gratefulness, "There, but for the grace of God, go I."

Prophecy and Our Christian Heritage

How can a Christian be in Israel, and especially in Jerusalem, and not think of the prophets and of prophecy? How can one be here and not think of both the past and the future? Jerusalem is a marvelous place to become contemplative. I'd like to live here a few months and think and write. I like the air. I am enchanted by the environment — more by that which is ancient than what is modern.

If you have not been led astray by muddled interpreters, you cannot think of the future within the framework of your Judeo-Christian heritage and be a pessimist. But we are — if true to our tradition — *realistic optimists.* Our optimism about planet earth is not based on humanistic striving but on a combination of God working in and using history, and God breaking into history to accomplish His purposes in and through His people.

But a Christian cannot, in my understanding of the biblical disclosures, give up on either tradition or the planet, for both are involved inseparably in redemption, which is in fact a recreation.

Perhaps parenthetically but with good purpose we should note that the Incarnation has so far been God's greatest vertical intervention in our history. But we should also quickly observe that Incarnation did not fit in with the expectations of most Israelites. It was too quiet, too unpretentious, too unpolitical. Perhaps we should prepare ourselves for God's surprises tomorrow.

I was interested in an interview of Norman Cousins, a modern Jew, by Hugh Downs. Cousins was being probed about his attitude toward the future. He uttered this gem: "No one knows enough to be a pessimist."

Cousins spoke of the difference between a pessimist and an optimist and used the complexities of our day as a focus. The pessimist sees the complexities and gives up. The optimist sees the same complexities and tackles the task before him. He somehow views his role as being a problem solver. I resonate to that. But Cousins was not speaking or thinking biblically — at least not consciously.

But I discover Christians read the Bible and emerge from their reading with different attitudes — some as pessimists, some as optimists. However, I say the Christian's basis for hope — which is likely the better word — is confidence in a God who has acted, is acting, and shall continue to act in nations, churches, groups, and in individual lives.

Well, here we are in Jerusalem. Isn't it marvelous! This is my third trip, and I'd come yearly if I could. I was here in 1965 before the barbed wire no-man's zone was removed and before the Wailing Wall was cleared to its present depth. I was back for the Jerusalem Conference on Prophecy in 1971. Much had changed in the interim of six years.

But I think I shall relate two experiences of the first trip. The second one will bear on my assigned topic.

I was not with a tour group in 1965. I had a full day tour of Jerusalem, Jericho, Bethlehem as the only client of an Episcopalian Palestinian — an Arab. He had been a businessman with considerable education and culture. He had been violently dispossessed of home, fortune and business. Some in his family had been killed.

He was a bitter man. He helped me get the perspective of a Palestinian — these people who care not at all for Jordan's King Hussein, but care less for Israelites. They are the people without a country, caught in the middle. Many are in the refugee camps and have been for years. It is hard for them to keep hope alive.

I met and conversed at length with two graduates of Greenville. My oldest son Edward knew them well. They too were Palestinians. Their story added up to the same total as that given by my guide. I have never forgotten those experiences in my personal attempt to evaluate the tangled Middle Eastern situation.

But the experience which was so vivid and which related to the topic at hand occurred east of Meggido in the plains where countless armies have funneled East and West on their slaughtering missions. For land vehicles and marching soldiers it was the inescapable path used by Assyrians, Babylonians, Egyptians, Greeks, Romans, etc.

I was in a bus with people from England, Italy, the U.S. and likely other counties. The tour guide ordered the bus stopped at a strategic point on the plain. He lectured about all the great armies that had marched here, about the conquerors and the conquered. And then he drew forth his Old Testament and read about Meggido and its environs.

Then the guide called an English gentleman forward to read passages from the Book of Revelation. He said something to this effect: Some read these passages and understand that the last great war, the Armageddon, will occur here. There was a kind of electricity in the moment. But he ended it with a smile and said, "We certainly hope they are wrong."

Well, you are here where these and other kindred thoughts must occur to students of the Bible. Prophets and prophecy plus apocalypse constitutes a significant part of our biblical literature as measured by both quantity and quality. We should not ignore the literature. We should understand it and profit from it. No pun intended!

For a few moments let's glimpse the role of the prophet, prophecy, and apocalyptic literature as it relates to ethics, righteousness, obedience, eschatology, and the Christian's hope. The hope expressed in the Old Testament is *historically oriented.* The Old Testament prophets saw God's reign (Kingdom) as the consummation of God's working *in* history. The prophets' concern rooted in a *present* and *pressing* historical situation involving the people of God. Of course, their message concerned other nations as well.

History under God may be like our looking at the wrong side of the weaving. Some day God will, we believe, let us see the design side and we will understand what we do not now. That of course is a faith assertion based on our understanding of the entire trend of the biblical disclosure of the progressive redemptive program of God.

Prophets were primarily concerned with God's will for His people in the present. Their burden was more forthtelling than foretelling, more present than future, more ethical than speculative.

The essence of prophecy is not prediction but the declaration of moral and spiritual reality as it impacts on persons, groups, and events in a particular slice of history. In any detailed fashion, prophets were normally predictive in a near rather than a far sense.

Prophet: from Greek *prophetes:* pro — "before" or "for" and *phemi* — "to speak." So prophet is one who (a) proclaims or (b) speaks for or on behalf of another. In this case, God. He is not a magician attempting to coerce God. Rather, under inspiration he is used of God to utter God's will.

It is God who initiates the work of the prophet by summoning, inviting, impelling. God puts words in his mouth (Deuteronomy 18:18; Jeremiah 1:9). He is a God-inspired man. But inspiration does not suppress individuality. God uses prophets who differ in culture, character, and status. Also, there were writing and non-writing prophets.

Some divide the prophetic writings into these categories:

a. those concerned with the internal destiny of Israel — they speak of judgment, mercy, restoration.
b. those described as Messianic, i.e., Micah 5:1, and Isaiah.
c. and eschatological prophecies — last days in which God's rule will be set up on earth.

The final, *culminating* visit of God was always in the background of the prophets' perspective. What creates problems for us in relation to the prophetic vision and expectation is that the prophets did not make strict chronological differentiation. In other words, time for them collapsed and they viewed the ultimate *eschatological* hope related to the *immediate* historical future. They apparently did not share our modern and Western interest in chronology, sequence, time.

In *Jesus and the Kingdom*, George Eldon Ladd says of the prophets, "They viewed the immediate future in terms of the ultimate future without strict chronological differentiation and thus proclaimed the ultimate will of God for His people here and now."

Ladd says the reason for this prophetic WORD perspective — confusing to us — is that they placed their hope "not in the future but in God." Their hope was single, but also complex. The God who would act tomorrow or today would finally consummate His actions. All His acts were of one piece. The fabric was an unbroken single weaving. The weaving was and is redemptive. The redemption is a mix of mercy and wrath, of warning and blessing, of judgment and recovery.

The normal role of the prophet was to function in an actual historical situation and address the situation. Their proclamation of what was ultimate was intended to be guidance for what was current. They pronounced God's will for His people as they faced a here and now set of circumstances. Their constant concern was with the special relationship between God and God's people.

It was a relationship which if not kept alive and sensitive would suffer gravely. Not to cultivate that relationship could produce a fracture. And a fractured relationship would have dire consequences: political, economic, social, spiritual. The ultimate, future good must be made present and only by this could or would God's reign be a reality for Israel.

They were not speculators nor philosophers. They were a general sort of theologian, for they spoke *the* word about God, man, sin, or salvation which was needed now and quickly. The predictive element of the prophetic ministry grew out of their theology. Believing what they did about God and sin, about the will of God and righteousness, it was inevitable from a prophet's perspective what results would accrue from sin and disobedience.

The whole prophetic mission was, in other words, terribly ethical and moral. But it was an ethical concern which was inevitable, given its theological base. And the theological base was found in the God whom we are to worship and to whom we should relate in genuine fellowship.

This God in essence was holy love. And that essence was likewise the essence of the relationship of God with man and by extension man with man. It seems to me not too much to say that holy love was the basis for and clue to understanding the ethical quality of the prophets' work and message, his concern for Israel, and the predictive element of his ministry.

The future was only *absolute* in the sense that God's will would ultimately be done by His people. All the futures between now and an ultimate, consummate day were *relative.* And these intermediate futures were relative to the responses God's people made to God, to His holy love, His will, and to His proclaimed Word.

Scripture is clear in its vivid expressions that God *did, could,* or *would repent* providing a people made suitable responses. Such expressions were not understood as picturing a vacillating, changeable God. Actually, it was a clear expression of the unchangeableness of God's character and His judgment of moral matters. His attitude toward right and wrong never wavered.

What could alter radically was the condition and situations of His people when they either *did* or *did not* do those things which fostered or fractured relationship with God. God was so dependable in His response to humans that — you'll recall — some of the covenant people complained when God accepted the responses of the people of Ninevah and spared them. Suddenly these religious ones appeared more holy than God Himself.

The frequency of prophet reference to historical events, nations, leaders made clear that the prophets were existentially oriented, sensitive, alive. Out of their depth of awareness — of sensitivity to both situation and God — they interpreted the *present* in the light of the *future* and light of the nature and demands of God.

The prophet's concern as he addressed Israel or Judah is twofold (really two sides of one reality): *relational-behavioral*. The two could not be separated. To love God was to behave as lovers of God. To forget God was to behave like those who've forgotten God's place, forgotten the relationship, or not cared enough for it. To love was to act. Acceptable behavior without loving was an incongruity hardly anticipated. A loving relationship begot behavior consistent with and worthy of love.

We must keep clearly before us that the prophet is concerned with the ethical rather than the chronological. The future, or the Day of the Lord, is used by the prophet as a way to underscore the ethical. It impacts as an ethical exhortation to Israel. The prophet in a fashion attempted to face us with ultimate reality, to bring the last day to the moment and let it speak!

Because we do not think as the prophets thought, we may tend to focus on their seeming chronological failure. But for them God did act. The Day of the Lord did come, yet the Day of the Lord as an eschatological event remained for an undated future. There frequently appears to be a near and a future "Day of the Lord." He will act now, but in the long look He'll act again and consummately. The historical and the eschatological congeal in the prophet's vision and proclamation.

In Isaiah 13, God's visitation on Babylon is the "Day of the Lord" (4-6, 17). That is historical, but there is also present in the chapter the eschatological judgment of *all* mankind with disaster to earth and disruption of the heavenly order (9-13). Judgment came to nature and man. Yet the prophet sees it as but one day.

We must not force our thought forms on the prophets. They had no problem with an immediate historical future and at the same time an ultimate eschatological goal. They centered on the acting God, not future chronology. God is the King who comes and will come. The prophetic proclamation was designed to bring God's people into renewed relationship to God and into active obedience to their true King.

The catastrophic is never the ultimate objective of the prophetic. Jehovah's coming is not because the world or age is going to end, but to begin a new order after disaster. Prophet expectations were related to the working out of historical forces in which God's hand could be seen, but it also included a vision of a dramatic breaking into history. God Himself will visit His people. His kingdom is both historical and supra-historical. It is this dimension of the prophetic vision we may associate with the expression, "Day of the Lord."

This, if it be the *final* "Day of the Lord," is the eschatological dimension of the prophetic vision. Whatever the shape of things on earth after this final visitation, it marks the consummation of God's redemptive purpose. Again, whatever the shape of that future the prophet sees it as consummately good — as good as God can do!

For Israel or for us to focus too much on the future with its dates and details misses the mark and may lessen concern for the present and the present doing of God's will as an expression of our love and worship. God is, we must remember, Lord of both the near future and the far future.

The peculiar prophetic outlook needs emphasis. It is a perspective difficult for us. It relates to our attitude toward a paradox, a seeming contradiction. It is difficult for us to adopt a truly biblical view if we cannot entertain a paradox. So we may find difficulty in achieving the prophets' ability to "hold the present and the future in a dynamic but unresolved tension" (Ladd).

Much interpretive conflict ensues from an inability to maintain in our thinking a tension between *imminence* and *delay.*

If we are to understand the prophets we must think as they thought: The prophets' message often included past, present, and future. The inner unity of the message was found in the prophetic objective, to establish the supremacy of Jehovah or the Kingdom of God. The messianic prophecies were part of the overall purpose to see God's rule made effective on earth.

The prophetic vision, whether in Old or New Testament, includes the earth. Even fire does not end planet earth, but makes it new. The vision, though ill-defined, calls for new heavens and earth.

The *new* is associated according to Peter with "the day of the Lord," the passing of heavens and earth in cataclysmic heat. But then Peter declares, *"Nevertheless we, according to his promise, look for new heavens and a new earth, wherein dwelleth righteousness"* (2 Peter 3:13, RSV). (Compare Isaiah 65:17; 66:22; Revelation 21:1.)

Isaiah 65:17 (RSV), *"For behold, I create new heavens and a new earth; and the former shall not be remembered nor come into mind."* What a picture of a future so redeemed as to erase all sad memories! What precisely is meant by this newness need not overly concern us, or divide us. The great vision of Old and New Testament prophets is of a future in which God establishes His rule, righteousness is its chief characteristic, and its delight is so great as to eliminate memory of an earth in which unrighteousness prevailed.

Let us now note that the biblical view of the future is not Greek — a bodiless, nonmaterial, purely "spiritual" redemption. Earth, nature, body are related to a moral universe and to the moral life of man.

Paul makes this clear *and* that earth is to share in final redemption. God's glory will be perfectly manifested when the human heart, society, and nature are purged of evil and the effects of evil. Isaiah and Paul sound a common note (Isaiah 65:17; 66:22 and Romans 8:21-23) and share a common vision.

Earth is more than the staging area for man. Man and world are wed in a common order of creation, and earth participates in man's history and destiny. The world is affected by both man's sin and righteousness. Again and again the Old Testament provides dramatic expressions of this close relationship — fish, fowl, cattle, and grasses suffer from human wickedness.

Man and nature are inseparably related in both creation and redemption. Both depend on God for their existence, continuance, and their future. Though man stands apart from other creatures by virtue of his creation in the image of God, he never transcends his creaturehood. His urge to autonomy, to independence is the measure of his loss of love for the Creator and an index of his sin.

So salvation viewed biblically is not release from his creatureliness but the redemption of his creaturehood. Redemption must involve the whole man, and this resurrection of the body, not immortality, is an integral part of our biblical hope. This again relates to the biblical concept of all creation sharing in the blessings of redemption.

The world is not evil *per se.* Our salvation is not to be found in escape from earth or body — no Greek dualism here. Nirvana is not our destiny. God's good designing holds out a hope for more than cipherdom. We are, rather, designed for a kingdom in which God is happily central. How different this is from the other great religions of mankind. For them the best has been, is past and gone. To become a cipher, a zero, nothing, is the goal of much of earth's religions. Furthermore, the golden age is past. For them there is not even a small "millennium" of glory, let alone a larger, longer hope.

If Communism is a religion, as many believe, it is the only other religion with an eschatological hope. It has this hope because it is a bastard child of the Hebrew-Christian perspective. Its error is in placing its hope outside of, independent of, and in defiance of God. God is reduced to matter. Man's eschatological heaven will be achieved by conflict and will be man's doing — not God's!

So let's not close with the gloom of Armageddon but with the Christian hope expressed in Revelation 21:6 (NIV): *"He said to me, 'It is done. I am the Alpha and the Omega, the Beginning and the End. To him who is thirsty I will give to drink without cost from the spring of the water of life.'"*

Redemptive Rebels

(Commencement Address, Wessington Springs, 1966.)

Bernard Iddings Bell used the term "Redemptive Rebels" years ago. I think it is still a pertinent and provocative phrase. Perhaps we could just as well talk about "Redemptive Revolutionaries."

Whatever the term, let us be clear that I mean the positive, progressive, forward-looking, hopeful attitude and action!

There are "reactionaries," "inactionaries," and "revolutionaries."

Reactionaries

For example: Communism is not a revolutionary force in the world. It is reactionary and consequently has in it the seeds of its own disintegration and death. Communism attempts to paint a future utopia which cannot become reality. Nothing anti-human, anti-personal, anti-ethical, nor anti-God can provide hope in this world, much less hope for the world to come.

Just as the paranoiac personality is self-defeating due to its unhealthy suspicions, so a system of society which is paranoiac cannot, ultimately, produce a sound human system of government and society. *Fear, distrust,* and *suspicion* are *reactionary* characteristics. It should be clear that a Christian cannot be a reactionary.

Inactionaries

But what of the inactionaries? They are a peculiar affliction of our day. They are the product of fear, sloth and the paralysis of a task that has grown too big and complicated for the person to feel he can do anything about it. The inactionaries shrink from involvement and responsibility because there are penalties attached. They cost. So we have the strange behavior of human beings doing absolutely nothing, not so much as phoning the police when horribly brutal, inhuman and murderous acts are committed before many eyes. No one acts. Not even *one* daring Good Samaritan. And there are facts that stack up on the side of the inactionaries. But where is the courage that acts in spite of consequences?

Then others do nothing, it would seem, out of sheer sloth. Sloth, you may recall, has traditionally been one of the seven "deadly" or "capital" sins along with pride, envy, covetousness, lust, anger, gluttony. These sins have been called "capital" because they are the kind from which other sins are spawned. They are root or source sins, so the theologians have told us.

Josef Pieper, a Roman Catholic theologian, says sloth means that man "renounces the claim implicit in his human dignity." This renunciation leads to all sorts of inhumanities, separations, estrangements. Sloth is the refusal to be a man as God intended when He created Adam. To be a man in a biblical sense "involves personal, social, and cultural initiative and responsibility."

God wanted stewards when He made man. So He created in His own image and endowed with a capacity for management toward God-like ends. Too frequently man has fallen short of his design and God's expectations.

Jesus, you will recall, was in line with the intention of creation when He repeatedly used the role of a steward, or a manager, as an illustration of what a man should be in conduct and attitudes. He portrayed not only the good but the bad steward and His listeners could easily identify the evil. Jesus would understand when we say that too often church members are characterized by escape from responsibility.

Our belief in the freedom and responsibility of man — whether Christian or not — has too often been set within the context of overt, willful, sensual sins. This is not a wide enough context. What we do not do is as important as what we do. We cannot safely ignore the sins of omission. Man is placed on this planet with managerial responsibility and with definite guidelines as to what he should do, what he should not do. He is responsible for his external environment and for his interior environment.

Scientific and technological advance in geometric progression should be clear enough evidence that God intends man to control his environment. Never since Adam has it been clearer. The borders of the unknown have been pushed back and with it the fear of the unknown. We are placed here to manage our own affairs and that of our environment.

But it is quite apparent that we have managed badly. Ignorance has contributed much to the mismanagement. Fear and suspicion have had their role. But the principal failure all the way from the individual and his conduct of a personal life to those who manage nations, is the unwillingness to recognize the beneficent Presidency of God in our affairs. Self-centeredness has been man's ruin whether expressed in sensuality, pride, or other well-known labels, or whether that self-centeredness expressed itself by an unwillingness to be in control, to manage, and to make better what God in His goodness has given.

The story, then, of the farmer may not be so irreverent after all. One looking at his neighbor's wonderful, bountiful, and beautiful crops said, "What wonders God hath wrought here." And the farmer's retort was, "Yes, but you should have seen this place when God had it all alone." Indeed, there is no good harvest without the blessing of God's nature, but neither is there a good harvest without man's management and investment of himself.

The scientific and technological advance is something we should be grateful for. Let us not knock it. It has brought us comfort, and it has created the opportunity for all of us to be creative, to open new frontiers. We have enough leisure to permit us, if we will, to enrich our own and others' lives. But we should be grateful for another reason. This remarkable advance is a reminder of the unlimited horizons of man's managerial function on earth.

BUT we should also be reminded that God's delegation of management in man did not permit the usurpation of God's place in the whole affair. A proud independence of God dooms any of our efforts to failure. We are not here to build Babels. We are here to build the City of God, the Community of the Redeemed. The contrast in the Book of Revelation between Babylon (Babel) and the New Jerusalem is much to the point.

It is, significantly, the leaders of science and technology that see, perhaps more clearly than those in the pulpit or the pew, the need for man to manage, but in a far wider area than has been imagined heretofore. They see that we need an ethical answer. In our salute to the flag we now say one nation under God "with liberty and justice for all." This phrase, "under God," is the thing which must be translated into action. Its mere recitation is hollow, if not blasphemous, if our acts do not match.

The same is true of those who sign, sing, or say the creeds of Christendom. We must move to manage more than machinery and dollars and people for profit. We must move to manage the morals of man, to renew man's relation to God which is our only assurance of remaining humane, decent or honest.

Our day must see as great a change inside men as man is capable of producing in his external world. In other words, we are called to be *redemptive.* And this call should have top priority among the important things there are to do in the world.

Says Harvard's Harvey Cox, "God has given man a thrilling responsibility for this world. But man has not fulfilled his assignment. God has placed the tiller of history in man's hand, but man has gone to his hammock and let the winds and tides sweep his ship along. Man has done things he ought not to have done, but even more importantly he has not done those things he ought to have done. He has refused to live up to the full stature of his manhood and has abdicated his crucial place in the scheme of things. This is what biblical tradition has called 'sin.'"

Cox also notes another interesting thing. He says, "In Adam, the man who at first will not and then cannot be man, the Bible sees all men. But with the coming of the Second Adam, Christ, that situation changes. Here was a man who would be and was a full man. In him the whole range of human responsibility is fully taken up again. He exercises the full prerogatives of manhood. He lives in vigorous reciprocity with thieves, prostitutes and children.

"In the stories that Jesus spins, one of the most frequent characters is the steward, the man who has the responsibility and exercises the power assigned to him by the master. The cautious or irresponsible steward, the one who hides his money in the earth or beats the servants in the master's absence, reaps the rebuke of Jesus. The Apostle Paul also sees the life that God makes possible for man as that of an heir who, putting childhood dependencies firmly behind him, assumes the duties of an adult. *It is thus quite evident that images of timidity, abdication, and irresponsibility should figure just as prominently in a biblical doctrine of sin as do images of rebellion."*

Pride and self-centeredness is indeed insubordination, but it is equally a rejection of responsibility, stewardship, management under God. Our sin is a combination of insurrection, irresponsibility, disengagement, uninvolvement — all because self has been made the center of life. It is the kind of moral distortion that may be illustrated by the days when men thought the earth was the center of the universe. This arrogance in science spawns its own brood of errors. But much more importantly, this arrogance in man breeds all the horrors we are acquainted with through the daily news media.

Well, so much for the reactionaries and the inactionaries. But the rebels, the revolutionaries, who are they? Or more precisely, who are the Redemptive Rebels, and what are they doing and what should they be about in the world? They are Christ's men. But it is not enough to say that.

Redemptive Rebels are the followers of Christ who deny that Christianity is or can be an "identification of piety with passivity." They accept as part of their commitment a "militant role" in this world. They accept responsibility for the world. They see the church's mission in part expressed under the symbol of an army. Constant dress rehearsal is not considered to fulfill their obligation. Saluting the flag, the recitation of national creed is not an end.

Too often the song, "Like a mighty army moves the church of God" is a parody rather than a praise of the church. Too often the church is a victim of the same conformities which have become normal to the society around it. It has made an accommodation with the world and fails to redeem it. The rebels of which I speak are committed to using the secular world for its own redemption. But the distinguishing mark of these rebels is their rejection of the ordinary tools of militancy and armies of nationalism. The redemptive rebel lives a revolutionary life because he adopts a way which is positive, constructive, transforming and fulfilling. Their mission is not to destroy, but to fulfill.

It is very important to observe their motivation. Unlike the reactionaries and inactionaries, they are *not* motivated by love and loyalty — by the love of God and loyalty to Jesus Christ. Because they are so motivated they cannot live and they *refuse* to live bovinely. They accept responsible citizenship in this world and in the kingdom of God for the very reason that they have a dual citizenship. They are citizens of another world. And because they are, they bring the exotic qualities of the world to come to bear upon the needs of this present world which God has given to us as our theater of action and responsibility. They are committed to involvement in this present world — this secular age.

These Rebels express their love and loyalty in concrete, practical and life-changing acts. Jesus and His followers make their approach to life by the cup of cold water, the visit at prison, the care for the uncared for and unloved. They are committed to a cross not as mere symbol but as a way of life. Their love is manifest toward the neighbor in our shrinking world; the neighbor may be next door, across town or overseas. They do not permit their love and loyalty to be spiritualized into something that finds its chief expression within the walls of a building designated "church." They follow God "outside" where the real work is done. Our Leader and Lord could never be cooped up within the four walls of a building and persuaded that this was the fulfillment of His mission. Just so, His Rebels.

It is this revolutionary love and loyalty which humanizes life and makes man truly man. The redemptive rebels march against injustice wherever man has imbedded it — in law, or in the social and economic systems. Laws and systems represent man's attempt to regularize a workable arrangement of society. The more complex society becomes, the more changes are necessary to secure justice.

It is dangerous to speak of economic, political or social systems as Christian. But it is essential that Christian people be involved at all times in securing justice within a prevailing system or even in altering the system to serve human needs. All systems past, present or future are the inventions of men, the functional means for achieving human ends. No divine right inheres to a system whether it is economic, social, political or even religious.

Concern for persons must constantly mold and remake systems whether legal or social. Jesus went to death because of His claims of authority over life which transcended the current religious system. He was a threat to security, to the status quo. He sounded like a revolutionary and was mistakenly identified even by his closest followers as a political reformer and redeemer. In a sense, He was. But His aims and methods were not understood. Jesus promotes revolution by transforming men, by releasing them from sin, the false center of life, and by use of non-military tactics and tools.

Jesus was revolutionary in His death. His very death — the most vulgar possible — became a symbol of victory. His followers have been committed to a comparable end and to the same way of life. It is a way of sacrifice and suffering. It is the order of service symbolized by basin, towel and cross. This is the way in which our responsibility to the world, our stewardship, our management is to be discharged. We are not lords; we are servants.

Let us stress now the word *redemptive*. The Christian way alone offers a better tomorrow with hope of realization. The Christian way *only* redeems all it touches, releases the best and not the worst in men. The Christian way accepts this world as God's good gift and as his personal responsibility. The Christian way accepts men where they are and however they are, and assumes a stewardship regarding their redemption. The Christian way is no escape from life. It is a plunging into life with head and heart. It is a profound involvement in life — the life of this present world.

The Christian does look beyond this world with hope because of relationship to Jesus Christ. But he cannot hope apart from the discharge of responsibility given him by virtue of his own creation and redemption. The day is past when we can be so heavenly that we are of no earthly use!

Some of us have stressed separation from the world, and too often the doctrine has been misunderstood and misapplied. Separation must not lead to isolation and non-involvement. It must not end in monastic withdrawal. It must not be identifiable by merely external marks. It must be identified by a new stance, style, method and spirit in an approach to the world. It must be identified by that good quality made known by Quakers — concern!

There are two significant New Testament words in this connection. One is the Greek "ecclessia" which is translated "church" and literally means "called out." The other is the word from which we get "apostle" and "apostolic" and means "sent out." Called out in order to be sent out or sent back. Redeemed *from* to be immediately returned *to*.

You will surely remember Jesus' great concern expressed in His High Priestly prayer. It was for the world. His concern for the church is as an instrument. He loves, cleanses, instructs, inspires the church but not as an end. It is all for a fallen world. True, He loves the church for itself, because it is a body of people and not a building. But He also loves the church as the means of reaching out and sharing His redemptive mission.

Christians belong to a sent, suffering and reconciling community. As such, they identify readily with known and self-recognized sinners.

How can graduating seniors of a Christian high school be redemptive rebels and prepare themselves to be better rebels?

First, I charge you with responsibility. If the U.S. believes that young men graduating from high school are old enough and responsible enough to fight in Vietnam, I also believe they are old enough to assume responsibility for the world in which they live in non-military concerns or areas.

Christ calls you to the continuation of a moral and spiritual revolution. The task is never finished. And the very fact that a million people are doing any given thing may well produce the question, "Then why should I?" All of us, I suppose, find ourselves torn between that within us that wants to conform and that which wants not to conform. We of an older generation feel the same pulls, though they may be about different matters. The problem is the same. But our concern must be for choosing the right things to change and to rebel against and in which to be nonconformists. This is why we need to live close to the biblical revelation of Christ.

You are called to be a Good Samaritan.

You are called to seek justice for all men in this world.

You are called to help the oppressed, relieve suffering.

You are called to work for better law and order in which there is justice and equality of opportunity.

You are called to root out prejudices born of artificial barriers between men, like color and accent.

You are called to suffer and be committed to a cross that God's way may be known and accepted in the world.

You will have opportunity to be a redemptive rebel if you go on to college, whether it is Christian or secular.

You will have opportunity to be a redemptive rebel if you go out to a job and do not seek further formalized education.

My challenge to you is to be all God intended in creation and redemption for you to be. May you be entitled to the designation "Man."

Above all, you are called to love, love in the New Testament sense. Love in the New Testament is not so much a sentiment, an emotion, as a rational concern. But in the New Testament we find Christian love is not only a rational concern for others; it is a concern touched by the emotion of Calvary.

It was this love which moved the early church forward, transformed society and changed civilization. We must once again believe there is power in that same love to transform society, our world, our institutions and the laws and customs of men around the world. I do not mean to Westernize. I do mean to Christianize.

Listen to a quotable quote: "There was a time when the church was very powerful — in the time when the early Christians rejoiced at being deemed worthy to suffer for what they believed. In those days the church was not merely a thermometer that recorded the ideas and principles of popular opinion; it was a thermostat that transformed the mores of society. Whenever the early Christians entered a town the power structure immediately sought to convict them for being 'disturbers of the peace' and 'outside agitators.'

"But the Christians pressed on, in the conviction that they were a 'colony of heaven' called to obey God rather than man ... But the judgment of God is upon the church as never before" (Martin Luther King).

In Fellini's film *La Strada,* the clown tells the girl Gelsomina to stay with the unlovable Zampano. "If you don't love him and stay with him," he asks, "who else will?" This is a parable of our calling in God's revolutionary world.

We are called to love this world and "... stay with it, to take upon our shoulder the responsibility for its reconstruction and renewal. This is the assignment that God has given us, and He will give us the strength to fulfill it" (Harvey Cox).

Regenerating Shudders

Is it nothing to you, all ye that pass by? Behold, and see if there be any sorrow like unto my sorrow (Lamentations 1:12, KJV).

1. In George Eliot's *Middlemarch* we meet Fred Vincy, fun-loving, irresponsible, volatile. He seems incapable of getting along with the serious business of living. But he is in love with Mary Garth. She is a person of homely goodness. His love for her is his one apparent redeeming feature. If there is a chance of making a man out of Fred it seems it could be in this attachment.

However, Mary is quite unaware of Fred's love. Fred is fearful that he may lose her for he is in no position to make his feelings known. In those days one needed first to establish a responsible position in the world to be free to ask for the hand of a lady.

So, in desperation Fred seeks aid of the young vicar, a Mr. Farebrother. The vicar is concerned about Fred, and so dutifully he attempts the delicate mission, though with a very heavy heart. For he too is an admirer of Mary, in fact in love with her. And he has not made known his love. But he proceeds because he believes it his duty to save Fred at any personal cost!

Despite Farebrother's delivering the message, Fred's conduct does not improve. In fact, it becomes worse. And the vicar is naturally tempted to pursue his own love for Mary. But he decides on one final effort to save Fred. He hunts him down and finally finds him in a joint, a dive. He brings him outside and pleads with him. Finally, in desperation he exposes his own feelings for Mary. And something happened to Fred. The author writes:

> Fred was moved quite newly. The contemplation of a fine act produces a sort of *regenerating shudder* through the frame, and makes one feel ready to begin life anew. A good degree of that effect was just then present in Fred Vincy.

And there is the source of the topic. The sequel is that Fred was indeed changed. He never looked back at the old ways. He went on to win and to deserve Mary's love.

2. Shakespeare gives a story with a comparable thrust. It is the story of Oliver and Orlando, sons of Sir Rowland de Boise in *As You Like It*. On Sir Rowland's death the younger son, Orlando, is given into the care of his older brother, Oliver. But Oliver hates Orlando, for he has a better disposition and bearing. Day after day he heaps shameful indignities on him. He finally decides on Orlando's death but fails in his murderous scheme.

Then one day Orlando's disappearance becomes known and the subject of comment and suspicion at court, and as a result Oliver is threatened with deprivation of the estate. To clear himself he sets out to find Orlando. He continues until he looks like a mangy beggar — hair long, clothes tattered and torn. Finally in exhaustion he falls asleep under an oak where he is threatened by a venomous snake and hungry lioness.

Oliver awakens to find Orlando has found him and has struggled with the beasts. Oliver looks with horror on the terrible wounds of his brother. He's overcome by shame and remorse. With bitter tears, passionate entreaties, he craves his brother's forgiveness. AND from that moment his character was transformed. *Regenerating shudder*!

Oliver tells Rosamond and Celia it was his "conversion." And looking back he regards the sleeping wretch under the oak, at the mercy of the snake and lioness as himself, YET not himself. Listen as he speaks:

> 'Twas I; but 'tis not I. I do not shame
> To tell you what I was, since my conversion
> So sweetly tastes, being the thing I am.

I was. I am. That is certainly the story of every convert! I am reminded of the true story of St. Augustine who before conversion led a rather riotous life. After his remarkable conversion he was accosted from the far side of the street by a former woman companion in sin. "Augustine, it is I," and though she tried with different tones and inflections he did not answer. Finally in exasperation she shouted it. Whereupon he turned in her direction and shaking his head shouted, "Yes, but it is not I."

3. Young St. Stephen. And let me now reach higher. There is a wonderful yet terrible story in the Book of Acts about a young layman of the new church. He was full of faith, courage, and conviction. Not afraid to stick his neck out, he would stick by truth and tell it! But by doing that, he got into serious trouble with the religious authorities and was hailed before the council.

It is recorded in Acts 6:15 (RSV) of Stephen as he spoke: *"And gazing at him, all who sat in the council saw that his face was like the face of an angel."* But they finally forgot the face as the truth they heard sawed their hard hearts apart. Their enmity reached fiendish heights until *"they ground their teeth against him."* Such was their rage that just grinding their teeth was not enough.

We read in Acts 7:55-8:1 (RSV): *"But he, full of the Holy Spirit, gazed into heaven and saw the glory of God, and Jesus standing at the right of God; and he said, 'Behold I see the heavens opened, and the Son of man standing at the right hand of God.' But they cried out with a loud voice and stopped their ears and rushed together upon him. Then they cast him out of the city and stoned him; and the witnesses laid down their garments at the feet of a young man named Saul. And as they were stoning Stephen, he prayed, 'Lord Jesus, receive my spirit.'*

"And he knelt down and cried with a loud voice, 'Lord, do not hold this sin against them.' And when he had said this he fell asleep. And Saul was consenting to his death."

So why do I tell this? In that moment Saul was seized with a *regenerating shudder* that only ended with his surrender to Jesus on the Road to Damascus. That surrender and subsequent change of Saul to Paul is more understandable when we associate it with the story of Stephen and Saul's relation to Stephen when he was murdered!

And now we have reached high indeed, from George Eliot and Shakespeare's story to that of Augustine and then to St. Stephen. But let's reach much higher than all that!

"Is it nothing to you, all ye that pass by? Behold and see if there be any sorrow like unto my sorrow" (Lamentations 1:12, KJV). This focuses on Jesus, the Messiah. I am told that these words are to be found either under or over granite crosses along country roads in Europe. Wayside Calvarys that the indifferent and preoccupied may get the appeal of the Cross of Christ!

I sometimes think about the Cross,
And shut my eyes and try to see
The cruel nails and crown of thorns
And Jesus crucified for me.

But even could I see Him die
I could but see a little part
Of that great love which like a fire
Is always burning in His heart.

Isaiah said of Christ prophetically: *"He had no beauty or majesty to attract us to him, nothing in his appearance that we should desire him. He was despised and rejected by men, a man of sorrows, and familiar with suffering. Like one from whom men hide their faces he was despised, and we esteemed him not"* (Isaiah 53:2-3, NIV).

No wonder that Jesus spoke that most pathetic of blessings: *"And blessed is the man who finds nothing that repels him in me"* (Matthew 11:6, paraphrase).

While a pastor in the Detroit area during WW II, I was returning home at dusk from calling and picked up a hitchhiker. He kept his face away from me and wouldn't talk. It was reported that some were using uniforms to gain access and rob.

Finally, after some minutes I got a fleeting glance at his face — horrible beyond description. He had been returned home terribly wounded to be treated. Revulsion quickly changed to compassion and love — why? Because he had been wounded for me! He was at the front for me!

Hear the poet:

The awful sorrow of his face,
The bowing of his frame,
Come not from torture nor disgrace:
He fears not cross nor shame.

There is a deeper pang of grief,
An agony unknown,
In which his love finds no relief —
He bears it all alone.

He sees the souls for whom he dies
Yet clinging to their sin,
And heirs to mansions in the skies

Who will not enter in.

Historically, there has been much discussion about the proper theory of the cross which best sets forth its meaning and significance. In fact, no theory can contain it. Certainly it was more than the exhibitionism of a martyr, as some would have us believe. Certainly more than an attempt to win me by pity! The best I can say is that it is indeed the self-giving of God in an unimaginable love which is my only hope of being changed. Changed until I am all He can make me. Changed until I live in a unity with Him closer than any words can describe. Changed until I am a person through whom He can work unhindered in His own redeeming task.

Let us note responses made by persons through the centuries.

The Three Responses to Christ

Dr. Paul S. Rees, writing of the three Christmas moods, says: Bethlehem and the Inn — **apathy**; Herod's jealous pride and hate — **antagonism**; the Wise Men — **adoration**.

Dr. James Stalker in his great book, *Trial and Death of Jesus Christ,* identifies three groups at the cross: Roman soldiers — **apathy**; Scribes and Rulers — **antipathy**; Friends of Jesus — **sympathy**. And he comments, "The living Christ is still in the world and meets with similar treatment."

Where do we find ourselves? Can one change from one group/attitude to another? One did that awful/wonderful day! A soldier ministered to Christ's thirst in apathy and ended the day in adoration. He said, *"Truly this was the Son of God!"*

Again a poet brings it home:

In evil long I took delight,
Unawed by shame and fear,
Till a new object struck my sight,
And stopped my wild career.

I saw One hanging on a tree,
In agonies and blood.
He fixed His languid eyes on me,
As near His cross I stood.

Oh, never, till my latest breath,
Shall I forget that look;
It seemed to charge me with his death,

Tho not a word He spoke.

My conscience felt and owned the guilt;
It plunged me in despair;
I saw my sins His blood had spilt,
And helped to nail Him there.

A second look He gave which said,
"I freely all forgive;
This blood is for thy ransom paid;
I die that thou mayest live."

Don't you think the writer experienced a *regenerating shudder*?

The Personal Response

The purpose of preaching is the personal response! Is it nothing to **you**?

Behold him, all ye that pass by,
The bleeding Prince of Life and Peace!
Come, sinners, see your Saviour die,
And say, Was ever grief like his?
Come, feel with me his blood applied
My Lord, my love, is crucified.

Then let us sit beneath the cross,
And gladly catch the healing stream;
All things for him account but loss
And give up all our hearts to him.

We must come to see the Suffering Saviour with our inner eyes. Three things will happen: **Arrest** of eye — we must be stopped. **Awakened** heart — our affections must be gripped. And the person must be **changed** — the will given over.

It's to this very end God in infinite wisdom planned Calvary to stab us awake and make us anew. No wonder the cross and the new birth are always inseparable. The one is in order that the other might be! My response to that doer and the deed is test and touchstone of eternity. Destiny determining!

Markham said, *"O friend, we never choose the better part until we set the cross up in the heart."*

Ah, the Master is so fair,
His smile so sweet to banished men

That they who meet it unaware
Can never rest on earth again.

Some may be able to identify with the poet:

I had walked life's way with an easy tread
Had followed where comforts and pleasures led,
Until one day in a quiet place
I met the Master face to face!

Then he tells his response:

And I cried aloud, "Oh make me meet
To follow the steps of Thy wounded feet."
My thought is now for the souls of men,
I have lost my life to find it again.
E'er since that day in a quiet place,
I met the Master face to face!

We are all at the Cross. It is our eternal confrontation! We are there now in apathy, antipathy, or adoration. Which? Remember that your response is eternity determining. Remember you can change to those who give Him life's adoration! You can know a *regenerating shudder* that makes one feel as Fred Vincy did, "Ready to begin life anew." And should you know a *regenerating shudder,* you will understand the wonderful words of Masefield's "Everlasting Mercy":

O glory of the lighted mind,
How dead I'd been, how dumb, how blind.
The station brook, to my new eyes,
Was babbling out of Paradise,
The waters rushing from the rain
Were singing, "Christ has risen again."
I thought all creatures knelt from
Rapture of the joy I felt!

A Relational Understanding of the Christian Life, Part 1

Responding to a request of the Light and Life Editorial Board, Dr. Lloyd H. Knox, general publisher of the Free Methodist Church, has prepared a series of three articles reflecting some of his current thinking under the general heading, "A Relational Understanding of the Christian Life."

Our Diamonds and Furs

Sears is a healthy, interesting company. In relatively recent history top management decided that a long, hard look into the future and current operations was essential. The chiefs of the organization took time out from daily functions to evaluate, predict, and decide. They plotted their future. They decided, like Dow Chemical, that they would orient to the future, not to the past. This meant taking seriously an affluent society. It meant new forms of management and creating new images. Today, according to Dr. Roger Blackwell, professor of marketing at Ohio State University, Sears is one of the best-operated large companies in the United States.

In their decisions, Sears selected two new symbols of their redirection: diamonds and furs. Who do you think is now the world's largest distributor of diamonds and furs? Sears — of course! This, incidentally, was an unexpected result, but a happy one.

The same sort of self-examination is needed in the affairs of the church. We, too, need to face the present and, more importantly, the future. And what about our "diamonds and furs"?

At Sears the symbols became translated into sales success. There was an unexpected merging of symbols and sales reality. That was possible because the symbols were, to begin with, also realities with potential.

What symbols can we lay hold of which are at the heart of

the gospel, which are rooted in reality and can be translated into the growth of the Christian community? Before answering that directly, let us ask what it is that really makes life. What is life without personal relationships? Life is not in things, though things can enhance life if our relationships are satisfying. The older one gets, I think, the more clearly one understands that it is our satisfying relationships which really make life. Without these we suffer personal deterioration.

Is there, then, more than a hint that what is basic to human life is basic to that life which has become Christian? We are becoming increasingly sensitive to the importance of interpersonal relationships. The pressure of population and the complexity of our civilization are prodding us into a keener awareness of our relational needs.

Must not, then, our symbols reflect these relational concerns? Indeed, are they not also the deepest concerns of the Christian faith and the biblical revelation? I answer, "Yes."

Our symbols, then, must reflect our deep desire for a personal relationship with God in Christ and our need for and desire of relationship with a community in which there is sharing in depth. Warmth and depth must characterize these relationships. Here we are at the heart of what the biblical revelation and the gospel is about. Everything else we talk about derives from or contributes to our understanding of these towering needs which are relational.

If we teach, we teach about what it is which enriches, develops, and promotes Christian relationships. That is doctrine. If we study our biblical history, we again are faced with the priority of relationships. If we talk of morality, it is the same. The Ten Commands of the Old Testament are committed to workable, satisfying relationships. There are four vertical (Godward) and six horizontal (manward) guidelines or principles offered. They are both personal and communal in objectives.

Our relationship, for example, to God is very personal, and yet is never completely so. We can love, worship, and devote ourselves exclusively to the God of revelation alone, all by ourselves. But always there is the implication that we will not, even *cannot*, for long be alone in this relationship. For the Hebrew, relationship and responsibility are always within the context of the community, never wholly personal. An example is the story of Achan (Joshua 7).

Our relationship to God takes priority. But our relationship to others so intertwines that Jesus makes it clear they are but two sides of a single coin. In fact, He reduces the guidelines from ten to two: love God, love one another. The Ten Commands tell us to love and not to covet. Immediately we are faced with the innerness of relationships. Relationships are established and grow or are dissolved in accordance with what goes on at the center, the core of the relationship. Our motives are basic in relationships.

The entire biblical revelation seems to concern relationships and shows that God's chief concern is the enabling of fulfilling relationships. And Christians have a special story to tell about God. Among the first words of our revelation are those telling us that God wishes a fellowship with man, the created, as real as a man has with his wife. And there is more to it. God seeks a productive partnership — first with individual men like Abraham, but also with a society like Israel. To this end, God makes agreements, covenants and promises. God is always the aggressive One. And that, incidentally, is what "grace" is really all about. God initiates, moves, seeks, gives always in love. He seeks our fulfillment in a partnership with Himself. Faith is our personal response which makes the relationship and partnership a reality.

Now, have I wandered? If so, it has been on purpose. For, you see, it brings us, hopefully, closer to answer, "What are our diamonds and furs?"

Like Jesus' reduction of the Ten Commands to two, we may be able to say that our "diamonds and furs" are really just one thing: fellowship. As "diamonds and furs" speak to and about our affluence, so "fellowship" speaks to and about our relationships. And like the Ten Commands, the fellowship has vertical and horizontal lines. We are offered, and in turn do offer, a purposeful relationship. The purpose? We are given the very purposes of God. We are called to a partnership aimed at enlarging the fellowship and thus redeeming society and helping to answer our prayer, "Thy kingdom come. Thy will be done in earth, as it is in heaven."

We must know what we have to offer.

We must help persons to understand, feel, and act upon that offer.

We offer a real, warm relationship with God in Christ. We

offer the friendship of God. A form of Christianity with anything less to offer is doomed. We offer a relationship in which we know deep inside that God loves and accepts us. Is that our "diamonds"? I trust so!

We offer a real, warm relationship within a community of the loved and accepted of God. It is a relationship of depth. In it we worship together, learn together, work together, praise and play together, share tears and joys. We offer a sense of community which rests firmly on earth, but the point of the triangle pierces heaven. Its apex is the very throne of God.

Hopefully, we have taken a long, first step in "a relational understanding of the Christian life."

A Relational Understanding of the Christian Life, Part 2

Metaphors and Crises

Relationships, we have said, are the *primary stuff of life.* Of all that matters to us, these matter most. In good relations we know happiness. In bad relations we know misery.

The biblical revelation has as its bull's eye the story of God's concern for a life of fulfilled, wholesome personal relations. Jesus and Moses both stressed that the best in life comes from a fine balance between vertical and horizontal relations. Moses reported four vertical and six horizontally aimed commands. Jesus reduced these to two, which in turn are like the two sides of a coin. They reveal what E. Stanley Jones refers to as "the grain of the universe." Go with the grain and life is beautiful; go against the grain and we suffer its slivers.

Bible and renewal of relationships

I consider it important that we view the biblical record as primarily the story of God's great efforts to renew relationships: man to God and men to men. This is the significance of Calvary, Resurrection, and Pentecost. The Holy Spirit, as the Enabler of relationships, uses the historical acts of God in Christ by making them inward realities which become the basis of renewed relationships.

A time for searching

I now offer a tour of my mental workshop with a warning. We are in need of a fresh look at our theology. If the primary thrust of the Scriptures is relational, then should not this fact provide us a new viewing platform regarding our Wesleyan theology? I am willing to say "yes" with a kind of *finality.*

But how then do we work it out? Here I am *tentative,* yet convinced. By this I mean I am prepared to modify the approach as readers are able to point to any false step. I write knowing full well that I run a risk. I aim, however, to call not for a hanging, just for dialogue.

I am certain that it is time for careful, honest searching for a biblical approach to the way we understand and present our teachings about the crises in the Christian life. Just how do we understand the beginning of the Christian life? And what about the crisis we Free Methodists call "entire sanctification"? What are valid expectations of the Christian in terms of growth in his new relationship with Christ, Christians, and others?

Twice I heard an overseas Christian leader say with vigor, "Entire sanctification no longer has the power to raise the dead!" Shocking? Yes. I think he was telling us that the phrase "entire sanctification" as an image in communication, and as it has often been broadcast and received, is inadequate. As a theological term, it appears stale and powerless. Conversations with both ministers and laity indicate great misunderstanding. The term does not excite response. Many have retired the emphasis to a secondary role or have ignored it completely. Much writing on the subject is still in the mold and language of the last century. To speak on the concept of a second major crisis in our relationship with Christ without the standard language, one may find himself accused of "not preaching holiness."

Or (and this is much more serious) I confess that once while pastoring in Rochester, New York, I had to ask forgiveness of my very young son, only to hear a parishioner say, "If we had a sanctified preacher he would not need to ask forgiveness." If a theology, or our transmission of that theology, contributes to such rigidity and lack of honesty, then we must certainly not abandon honesty.

Theological jargon does not change men; relationships do. We must deal with realities and not slogans or even specially loved scriptural words if they fail to help us understand and move toward the goal of Christian growth. We should also have discovered by now that some biblical terms need re-translating and interpreting, not to change their intent or meaning, but to understand them so well that we keep moving toward the realities the words suggest.

A new viewing platform

Unless we get a relational understanding of the biblical revelation and of the Christian life, we are likely to come out with a confused view and a warped Christian life. God's business (and ours) is relational business.

We must learn to think and talk about persons in terms of relationships with God, Christians, and others. I disclaim being very good at that. But I am willing to make a start. Others I am sure will do better. I am confident, at least, in the direction of the search.

Metaphors: "like" words

Every time we open our mouths we are faced with a serious communication challenge. The challenge is to transmit images I have to another so he can receive images very close to mine. How often have you experienced failure in this process? Then pity the theologian, the preacher, the speaker, the writer!

There is a "Metaphorical Theory of Language." Simply put, it suggests that words are pictures which one shows to another in an attempt to convey all sorts of reality. More precisely, a metaphor is a "like" word. I try to tell you about something you have never seen. I start with something you have seen, and I say, "It is like that, but it is not that." Remember the blind men feeling the elephant? Each had a different description of the creature based on the part he felt. But put all the descriptions together, and you are closer to the shape of the reality than with only one part. The Bible is full of metaphors which enrich our understanding of many things. Taken together they can give a fuller understanding of reality.

Think for a moment of the challenge which faced the New Testament writers. In their inspired attempt to communicate something so utterly new they had no choice but to use the metaphor device. Men were being made new all the time by becoming related to Jesus Christ as Savior and Lord. What was it like? How do you tell this wonderful reality? They constantly searched for "like" words, pictures, which would act as genuine pointers to reality.

New Testament metaphors

Immediately we will think of these words: adoption, new birth, regeneration, justification. There are many others. And these were used to say to persons of the first century and to us, "What is happening to people everywhere who receive the gospel is like ... ." And every time they used one of these picture words it was like adding another segment to a jigsaw puzzle, or like getting a clearer focus with the camera. And the New Testament cluster of metaphors enriches our view and understanding of a wonderfully inexpressible relationship.

Let us try to sort out the great initial reality the New Testament presents and for which its writers developed a magnificent cluster of metaphors. I think Paul's writing to the Romans puts it straight for us: *Christians are persons who are put into a right relationship with God in Christ by grace-faith.* The statement expresses both the major thrust of Romans and the great New Testament reality. The metaphors illuminate, enrich, and communicate this reality. But each has its own special appeal and comes with different force to different persons. Now look carefully at the italicized statement. *Christians are persons who are put into a right relationship with God in Christ by grace-faith.*

Put into a right relationship

First we examine "grace-faith." I think Paul forces us to create this hyphenated term. "Grace" is the initiative of God in an attempt to establish new relationships. It is the loving givingness of God. It is the word for the fact that God is always acting, moving toward us in love.

God wants relationship. Grace stands for all God does in that dark period of life when we have no relationship to Him. Some describe the period as "life of sin," which points up the reality that there is no relationship because such relationship has been violated, ignored, or never begun. There are other terms used by New Testament writers about this time in each life: alienation, rebellion, lost, unreconciled, unbelieving, and so forth. It is during this time that "the Spirit and the bride say, 'Come.'" That is, the church (the body of Christ) and the Holy Spirit link up to confront persons with Christ Himself in all His loving givingness (grace).

We have defined grace. "Faith" in this context is our response to grace, to the loving initiative of God in Christ. It is trust. It is our total response to the total giving of God in Christ. Now put the two words and the realities for which they stand together: grace-faith. Now we know how a relationship with God is effected. Wherever and whenever there is this joining of grace-faith something wonderful and new occurs in our relationship with God.

Crisis One – New life

Grace	+	Faith	=	Put into
(loving givingness of God in Christ)		(total trusting personal response)		right relationship with God in Christ (new life)

This is the central New Testament reality. The theologians are correct in referring to this as a "crisis." When Paul talks about "righteousness" he means the right relationship we have been talking about. Righteousness does not exist by our doing or not doing this or that. It is a right relationship. This is precisely what counts.

Look at the galaxy of enriching, sparkling, insight-giving metaphors related to "Crisis One." Two stand out: justification and new birth. The reality is like justification. This is the dominant metaphor of Protestants. You can hardly use it without thinking of Martin Luther. So it is an important biblical, historical and theological metaphor. But it is a metaphor.

The new reality is like: I am condemned, guilty, punishable, and suddenly I find I have a Friend at court who accomplishes freedom and removal of condemnation and guilt for me. The term is illustrative, not definitive. Anything definitive must be said in terms of personal relationships. But what a powerful figure the word presents! The danger lies in failing to recognize that the word is a legal illustration and has the limitations of any metaphor. It appears that historically it has assumed more than metaphorical significance and has contributed to a false sense of security which makes it possible to violate our relationship with Christ but to maintain a legal standing of "righteousness" which is not ours, but Christ's. The result is nonsense in terms of what is true in genuine relationships.

Nicodemus had trouble, too

New birth or being born again was a metaphor Nicodemus found hard to grasp. But our new relationship is like being born again. What a marvelous thing for someone who has a ruined life to hear that life can start over. The new relationship in Christ produces a brand new life. It is "like" that!

A recent writer would replace "justification" with "regeneration" as the great key doctrinal word which embraces every step in the Christian life. Again this seems to confuse reality and metaphor. But thank God for the "land of beginning again," for the washing clean of a sordid past.

Adoption: how this one sparkles in the cluster of metaphors. I was unclaimed, unwanted, unloved, unrecognized, unnamed. Suddenly I am loved, I am wanted, I belong. In Christ I have a Lover and come into a family in the body of Christ. How wonderful to be "accepted in the beloved," as Paul so tenderly puts it.

There are many other metaphors: lost, found, saved, redeemed. How many have felt the chains of slavery and the release of relationship with Christ! Perhaps this is enough to send you on a hunt for the biblical metaphors which when brought together, give you portraits galore of what it means to be in relationship with Christ.

It appears that all these metaphors speak of an initial relationship with Christ, the beginning of a lifelong walk to "glory." But we get "theological hang-ups" when we confuse metaphor and reality. This has happened, it appears to me, with the metaphor "justification" in all of Protestantism. It has likewise occurred with the phrase "entire sanctification," a metaphor dominant in those related to John Wesley's theology. The first metaphor is a legal picture. The second is ceremonial. Obviously, the two metaphors are addressed to different concerns in our relationship "in Christ." Both are pointers to reality, bridges to understanding. But they point to different realities.

Crisis Two – Beyond beginning

Thus far most of the time has been spent on the metaphors related to the establishing of a relationship with God in Christ. I believe this was necessary to establish an approach to the second concern. What, in broad terms, can we say happens thereafter?

The New Testament writers anticipated a relationship of increasing closeness and development. They also knew the tragedy of broken and/or declining relationships. "Walk" became an important descriptive word. Our Christian life is just that — a walk in partnership with Christ. They saw the unevenness or fluctuation in the relationship. But they saw something more. And that something more — and this I judge important — has been addressed by Christians for many years across denominational lines and with differing emphases which accorded with a particular theological perspective.

What they saw both in Scripture and in the life of many Christians was the development of a *"crisis" in relationship*. The crisis is a crisis because it demands decision. There are probably many smaller crises in our "walk." But viewers from trans-denominational observation points have seen a major, determinative "crisis." This crisis, it appears, may be precipitated in more than one way. It will vary as much as individuals vary. For example, with some it will come by the growing awareness and sensitivity developed in the relationship with Christ which makes one painfully aware of an inner resistance or drag which puts a brake on the developing relationship. Others may become aware of a subtle or not so subtle drive for their ascendancy in the relationship with Christ. There may be a resistance to the Senior partnership which slows growth.

Metaphors for Christians

There are, then, passages and words addressed to Christians in the New Testament which certainly cannot be said to be spoken to sinners (to those who have no relationship to God in Christ).

Wesley talked much of perfect love, entire sanctification, and Christian perfection. In the use of these terms he never had in mind the person without relationship to Christ. And, as Bishop L. R. Marston has observed, Wesley frequently confused entire sanctification with Christian perfection. B. T. Roberts with greater clarity saw the distinction, and that Christian perfection referred to the entire "walk" from beginning to end of the Christian life (i.e., perfect baby, child, youth, young adult, etc.).

But with the term "entire sanctification" Wesley talked about a major crisis in relationship subsequent to the establishing of that relationship. Others, with a different perspective, have emphasized being "filled with the Spirit" and talk of a life in the "fullness of the

Spirit." Others talk about the "baptism of the Spirit." Some have emphasized dying to self, which was understood as demanding a climactic point of "death" rather than a process of dying.

As in the establishing of a relationship, it appears that confusion has been created by labeling and by identifying metaphor with reality in discussions about a second major crisis in a Christian's relationship with Christ. I suggest we search for the New Testament metaphors which speak to the Christian about a second and major marking point in the developing relationships of Christians. I predict that we shall discover that the emphases which have become the more or less private property of sponsors may be more complementing than competing and that all the metaphors are needed to enrich our understanding of a radical deepening — heightening of our relationship with Christ.

Enriching our relationships

Our overriding concern is this: What can do most to forward the development, the enrichment of our relationships with Christ, Christians, and others? With this in view we may begin to see the role of such scriptural terms as "baptism of the Spirit," "filled with the Spirit," the "death" and "life" Paul talks about in Romans particularly, or "perfect love." There probably are other terms. But this is sufficient to illustrate the viewpoint. These terms seem to suggest that the Holy Spirit, who is always the Enabler of relationships, ministers to us in such a radical way that there are both negative and positive aspects to what is accomplished within us which releases us to uninhibited growth. Death and cleansing emphasize metaphorically the negative elements of the crisis. The other terms emphasize the corresponding positive elements. They exist and are known because they are the opposite sides of a single coin.

A failure to understand the metaphorical nature of terms relating to a major crisis (point of decision) "within" the person's relationship with Christ has, I believe, led to false talk about "experience," "states of grace," which in turn has led to unhealthy subjectivism on the one hand and a kind of eternal security for the "sanctified" on the other hand. It has been productive of emotional excesses on one side and rigid, legal concepts of the Christian life on the other.

Hopefully, we anticipate a new perspective for a rereading of our Bibles, an understanding of theology that encourages us to be honest about ourselves and others, a new concern for growth and ethic in terms of our love-relationship to both Christ and Christians, and a new dynamic in the body of Christ.

A Relational Understanding of the Christian Life, Part 3

Our Sets of Attitudes

Life works best when our concern corresponds with God's: the development of fulfilling relationships with God and others.

Relationships constitute the major thrust of the biblical record. They are dominant in God's acts in history: Eden, Exodus, Covenant, Law, the Christ Events, Pentecost. God chooses a man, then a nation, Israel, for partnership but always looks beyond to the goal of person-to-person relationships which will gather meaning and fulfillment in that each is related to God in a kind of sovereign love triangle. The goal is the enlarging church with Christ as Head.

We must therefore emphasize the overriding Christian concern to be the (1) beginning and the (2) development of the relationship of persons with God in Christ enabled by the Holy Spirit. *Crisis* we define as a major point of decision. Crisis is, we believe, associated with the beginning and the development of the relationship with God in Christ.

Two Major Hours of Decision

The first hour of decision is reached when we are confronted by Christ in His loving givingness. We face "crisis" because we must decide to receive or reject relationship. Our receiving is by faith (our total personal response). The result is that we are put into a right relationship with God in Christ (righteousness). The Holy Spirit is the Enabler.

The second hour of decision is reached when we are confronted by the pervasive lordship of Christ and a deep sense of need or lack in our relationship with God in Christ. The Holy Spirit is not only the Enabler of our relationships, He is the Sensitizer to our needs. He makes clear to us our inadequacies, our lack of power in service, an inner drag in our relation to the Lord — even friction, the difficulty in always accepting the moment-by-moment lordship of Christ and the pressure of the Holy Spirit in the direction of enriching our relationship with Christ, Christians, and others. There is a *radicalness* of adjustment required of us by this revelation of ourselves to ourselves that cannot be identified with the minor, though important, decisions which constitute the growing life of the Christian.

The confrontation of need produces crisis. That means personal response is demanded. Negative response cannot but result in a declining relationship. Positive response does something in me and in my relationships. There is a sense of release from inner drag, resistance, friction related to the lordship of Christ in every area of life. There is a joyous acceptance of the full lordship of Christ. There is a new sense of power and cope-ability provided by the deep indwelling of the Holy Spirit and my total consent to all required of my Senior Partner. There is, in reality, a deeper response to the givingness of God; there is a deeper commitment to His purposes for our relationship.

The result is an easier, more fruitful, fuller, and faster growth of the relationship with God in Christ. But the result is the thing. The crisis is but the means and not the end. Growth is the goal. The first crisis occurs in connection with the *beginning* of the relationship with God. The second crisis occurs *within* the relationship.

God Is Able

Our concern is, consequently, for a greater understanding of the nature of relationships than with technical definitions or proof texts. Wesley, the Keswickians, and others recognize in different language the common occurrence of a "crisis" within the ongoing relationship with Christ. There is likely more agreement on the conditions which produce the hour of decision for Christians than there is in language about the results. Some wish to talk about results as "entire sanctification." Others wish to emphasize the positive and talk about being "filled with the Spirit."

The full range of metaphors and language are needed. We

must guard against raising one specific term as definitive. Furthermore, talk about "experience" in connection with "crisis" is confusing. Experience is what occurs in relationships. Unless this is clear, "experience" becomes an "it," a "thing" persons seek. Our need is a fuller relationship.

Controversy over Greek tenses is likely not always decisive. More important are the plain words addressed to Christians in the New Testament which aim at securing a kind of wholeness, completeness, entireness which escapes many Christians. Important also is the testimony of many from different, even opposing, doctrinal perspectives that God *is able to set my relationship with Him on a permanently different angle of ascent toward maturity.* And as before, God initiates, we respond, and the Holy Spirit enables.

Maturing: The Goal

Maturing of relationships to God and others is the Christian goal (Romans 8:29; Ephesians 4:13). We must, therefore, discover and use every means we can to achieve this goal. The result of a faith response in the second crisis is a radical and pivotal means of growth. But of even greater importance are the daily practices and basic attitudes which characterize our behavior.

The accent falls on those simple, daily, undramatic acts and attitudes which enrich relationships: daily expressions of gratitude and love given to God and others; daily talks with God; reading of what our Friend has revealed to us of Himself and His purposes for the world; fellowship with others for purposes of learning, sharing, communing, proclaiming, serving, behaving in ways which please our Senior Partner; quickly mending the cracks which we create in relationships; asking forgiveness of Christ and others when He and they have been hurt inadvertently: admitting retarding or wrong attitudes; asking for help in our process of remaking; bearing one another's burdens, thus filling the demands of the purpose of Christ.

Consider a diagram consisting of overlapping circles, each circle representing a set of attitudes. Attitudes bring us to our motivating sources, that which drives or immobilizes us toward maturity and service. Attitudes form the foundation of our relations to ourselves, to others, to our environment, and to God. Imagine a diagram consisting of overlapping circles, within a larger circle.

Each circle represents an area of attitudes in which a person may respond in negative, positive, or mixed fashion. Growth is marked by a change of attitudes toward the positive. A change in one area affects the others, hence the overlapping of the circles. For example, a change of attitude toward self will reflect in attitudes toward others, God and environment. The encompassing circle suggests that it is the entire area of interrelated attitudes which motivates toward maturity or immaturity. We must develop understanding in each area and in the impact each area has on the other areas if we are to be growing persons.

The Non-Christian

Many non-Christians are concerned about achieving maturity in personal and interpersonal development. There is consensus that maturity is achieved as the individual is able to modify his attitudes toward *himself*, toward *others*, and toward his *environment*. It is, in fact, these sets of attitudes which produce good or bad relationships. Attitudes measure maturity and motivation and determine in large measure our ability to cope with life successfully. Often it may seem that the non-Christian has a better understanding of the needs and the techniques.

The Christian Dimension

The diagram of overlapping circles could be used in any secular setting by not labeling the center "God." The "God" area becomes the most important for the Christian because it is the most determinative. Attitudes toward God are decisive since they create the distinctive frame of reference for all other attitudes and consequent acts. In fact, we intend to suggest that attitudes toward God exert significant pressure on the other areas, reshaping them to conform "to the image of the Son." So let us take a closer look at attitudes toward God.

Attitudes Toward God

One's attitudes toward God cannot but reflect early views he has been taught about God. J. B. Phillips' book *Your God Is Too Small* is not amiss. Our view of God shapes our attitudes and expectancies. Our attitudes toward God affect the other sets of attitudes.

Not all Christians have healthy attitudes toward God. Some have difficulty in receiving love — God's love. Maybe this has something to do with the reception and treatment given by parents. One dear friend of mine in the late years of his marvelous Christian life still emotionally rejected the term "Father" applied to God. His physical father made it difficult for him to appreciate this metaphorical way of understanding God.

Our views of God form our attitudes toward God. For example, there were the saints who said to us when our children were small, "Don't love them too much, or God will let something happen to them!" What a well-intentioned caricature of the Christian's God! As though God was so jealous or parents were so prideful that there could not be full room in the heart of parent and God for complete love which embraced God, parents, and children.

Obviously, the attitudes of love, hate, and fear we have toward God do have an effect on our attitudes. The Christian, in fact, views his attitudes toward God as ultimately determinative. Recall the Apostle Paul's series of staccato exhortations in the letter to the Philippians (chapters 1 and 2). According to custom, Paul was probably pacing and dictating the letter. Suddenly he stops as his mind reaches for the highest, the most encompassing motivation he can conceive. What is it? Paul seems to say, "All of these exhortations I've been giving you will be fulfilled if you do one thing: Let this mind be in you, which was also in Christ Jesus."

May I rephrase the apostle? "Let the *set of attitudes* be in you which was in Jesus Christ." The transfer of these attitudes, I suggest, is the task we encounter in Bible study, prayer, fellowship, and activity, on behalf of our Lord. But it is also what occurs as the Holy Spirit ministers to us as we respond with sensitivity to the feelings, desires, and purposes of Christ.

In all honesty we must admit that many persons can achieve a high degree of maturity — interpersonal well-being — without Christ or the church. But it will lack much that Christ can supply. Furthermore, it often seems to the critical onlooker that more maturity is achieved by many non-Christians than by Christians. The observation is likely valid. But there are two things we can suggest. First, the observer should have seen the person before Christ began His work with him. Second, many Christians are growth-retarded because they have (1) an inadequate working picture of God, Christ, and the Holy Spirit, and (2) an inadequate understanding of all that is involved in their relations to themselves, to others, and to their environment. This may well explain why some persons are very devoted to Christ but are unable to successfully complete life's tasks, and/or relate poorly to others.

Some have condemned persons for being sub-Christian in their attitudes when actually they have been doing their best in light of a very limited understanding of their own attitudes, what formed them, and how they could be improved. No wonder we have exhortations to be extremely cautious in our judging of others. Christians must unite to bear one another's burdens, part of which may be a need for a fuller understanding of why they react and behave as they do.

Attitudes Toward Self

From the moment of birth we begin to form attitudes toward ourselves. The way we are received by our parents will be the first forming experience. An enlarging circle of contacts, relatives, neighbors, church, and others, will reinforce or modify our attitudes. Particularly powerful will be the roles we learn to play convincingly with our peers. There are other contributors to the self-image. But this is sufficient to make clear how dynamic is our self-portrait. Certainly Jesus understood the dynamic of a proper regard for self if one was to know a regard for others.

Attitudes Toward Others

This is the area of greatest "public" concern. Today, interpersonal relations receive enormous attention. There is consensus that we are all too ignorant of what makes for the best in human relations. There are many subtle factors at work: love, hate, desire for power, prestige and belonging, fear, jealousy, envy. Often these factors are hidden from view but are in fact shaping acts. Today when a person lashes out at others we may say, "He is seeking attention" or "He is crying for help." This illustrates the hiddenness of what triggers many actions.

Moses and Jesus both deal with our attitudes and relations to others. Moses in the Ten Commandments given to him for the guidance of the community Israel stresses the delicate relationship between the vertical (attitudes toward God) and the horizontal (attitudes toward men). Basically, the Ten Commandments say one thing: "It is essential to the proper functioning of life to *respect persons,* whether God or men." The forms of respect are given in broad outline.

Jesus did the same thing but in two words which really is but one word pointed in two directions: The word: LOVE. The directions: God and Neighbor! Again it is *respect* for persons. There cannot be this respect, care, and concern — which is the intent of the word *love* — without the conscious modifying of attitudes. Psychologists catch up with Jesus when, for example, they suggest that a low self-image will produce a low image of others. We must love (respect) ourselves if we are to respect others. Love casts out fear. Fear arises out of the different or the unknown. Much interpersonal tension arises out of observable differences or from what we do not know about others. Certainly the racial tensions of our time provide dismal illustration.

Movement toward Christian maturity involves the modification of our attitudes toward others. The greatest modifier is the love of God shed abroad in our hearts by the Holy Spirit. Yet given this gift of new direction we still must be exhorted to "love one another." Crisis and growth, the given and the cultivated, are of equal concern.

Attitudes Toward Environment

By environment I mean persons, not as separate entities, but as those involved in organizations, systems, or the establishment. I mean even more than that. It is the totality of the structure of the world about us: physical, social, economic, political, educational, and so forth.

Let us describe two extreme attitudes and responses to the environment. Imagine a line before you marked with numbers "0" to "10." Zero designates the person who views his environment as hostile, crushing, unbending, unyielding. It is like a stone wall. When he pushes his fist against it, the hand is hurt. It is hard for this person to believe that he, as a single individual, counts, that things can be changed for what he considers the good. It is even hard for him to believe in the ability of a group with which he identifies to change things. He waits for things to happen. He hopes it will be good but expects the worst.

On the other end of the scale is "10," which designates one who views his environment as friendly, responsive, changeable.

Whereas "0" is a pessimist, "10" is an optimist. He believes one person counts and things can be changed either single-handed or in cooperation with others. He does not wait for things to happen. He aggressively reaches out to his environment to make things happen.

It is not hard to deduce that "0" and "10" will have differing images of themselves, a different set of attitudes toward others, and probably a different attitude toward God. Perhaps faith comes harder for "0." Is it not more difficult for this person to see God as loving, helping, healing, enabling?

In every organization and community, however small, you can identify the persons described under "0" and "10." Every organization, including the church, is composed of people ranging somewhere between these extremes. Each of us has his own unique set of attitudes. It is wise to keep this in focus when persons seem resistant to change, hard to persuade to do the challenging and the difficult.

We Are Becoming

Several things, in light of this brief overview, are of importance. The maturity sought by the Christian has a special goal and framework. The goal is Christlikeness in attitude, response, behavior, and service. The framework is provided by the Christian community — the church.

What then are the specifics which loom important for the Christian? First, *the change of direction* produced by a change of attitude toward God. The change is repentance. The agents of change are the grace of God (loving givingness), my faith (total response), and the enabling Holy Spirit.

Second, the change of direction is essentially a *change in relationship* to God in Christ. Thus, the means of the maturing process is established. The change of relationship to God is not an end; it is the beginning of an exciting adventure in loving relationships.

Third, it is this new relationship which should be radically determinative in the *modifying of all our attitudes*: toward self, toward others, and toward environment. This is the process that shall engage us until we walk into His presence. Because of our relationship to Christ we should be developing a better self-image, better attitudes (and of course actions) toward others, and a more confident set of attitudes toward what needs changing around us (environment).

It is a life-changing, lifelong adventure which must engage the entire response and effort of every Christian. We are not in this changing business alone. This is the enterprise of the "communion of the saints." Support, strength, correction, and motivation should be expected from our associations in the "body of Christ," the church of Jesus Christ.

Changing attitudes which affect relationships is the task of the teaching-preaching ministry. We teach and preach for decision. These verdicts or decisions may be relatively small ones, but they contribute to the modifying process, to the change of attitudes. And whatever places a drag on our maturing in Christ must be denied a place in our lives. This means a positive response to the smaller disciplines of relationship and also "the big crisis" we have described.

To be "in Christ," to have a genuine relationship with Him, improves the self-image without producing selfish pride. We can see ourselves as His, as sons of God, as destined to the eternal best.

To be "in Christ" improves attitudes and relations with others. They are "neighbors," they are "the loved of God," they are the other side of "me," for Jesus calls me to love others as I love "myself." Island living is ended.

The maintenance and enriching of our relationships cannot be limited to the vertical. Cultivating a relationship with Christ involves doing the same with other Christians. Damage the vertical, and eventually it shows up in the horizontal and vice versa.

To be "in Christ" links us with purpose and meaning in and for the world, for our environment. It is God's world. The nations are God's. The cattle on a thousand hills are His. The end of all things is His. The means are His. In a confidence not my own but derived from my relationship to Him and to His people, I move out to meet and to change things for Christ's sake and in His name.

LHK's Note: This concludes a brief attempt to express theological views which I consider to be within a Wesleyan frame of reference. The relational approach to Christian theology would involve applying the basic view to each area of theology. Obviously, this has not been undertaken.

Bibliography

The Christian Faith, O. A. Curtis
Christian Holiness, Stephen Neill
Images of the Church in the New Testament, Paul S. Minear
No Longer Strangers, Bruce Larson
Time to Love, Eugene C. Kennedy

The Role of the Commands

What was the role of the ten commands in the life of Israel? What was Jesus' attitude toward them? What is the role of the ten commands in the life of the church and the larger society? Is there one basic principle underlying the commands? Let's see.

A Matter of Relationships

Each command speaks to some important phase of interpersonal relationship. The first four speak to our relationship with the God who reveals Himself as a person rather than force, energy, or power. Six commands address our interpersonal human relationships. The priority is significant. The significant passage for Israel is Deuteronomy 6:4-5 (KJV). *"Hear, O Israel: The Lord our God is one Lord: and thou shalt love the Lord thy God with all thine heart, and with all thy soul, and with all thy might."* The ten commands can be thought of as an expansion of this *revelation* and *command.*

There is but one God, and He is to be loved. That boils the matter down to utter simplicity. But man has introduced complications by his failure to honor either the *revelation* or the *command.* The violation of right relationships produces disaster, pain, and sorrow. Such violations are labeled sin. The relationship of persons is sacred and their violation is the very essence of sin. Sin is the word for all that is wrong in relationships. It is also the word for what makes relationships go wrong. It is the word for both the symptoms and the cause of moral disorder.

The Need for Commands

The ten commands were a necessary after-the-fact event. They were not needed in the Garden of Eden. They were not necessary as long as sacred relationships were not violated. But once they were violated, the entire dynamics of relationships were radically altered. The violation of sacred personal relationships perverted the thinking and intent of man. *"All have sinned and come short of the glory of God"* (Romans 3:23, KJV).

Man and God were in adversary roles. Trust fled. Secrecy was born. It seemed necessary to hide. Once man and God were in adversary roles, it was logical that man would also be in an adversary role with other men. All that is wrong in our relationships became operative. Here is the meaning of the Fall! And the need for the ten commands. No wonder the ten commands, along with the Deuteronomy 6:4-5 passage, are at the heart of the covenant relationship God effected with Israel!

When men cared enough about God and their relationship with each other, the ten commands were not needed. But given the inwardly distorting effects of the loss of love for God, it became necessary for God to spell out the laws of successful relations, both with Himself and among humans.

Olin A. Curtis, the famed Methodist theologian, uttered a sad lament about the Fall. He said, "Man did not care enough about God to do His will." That gets at the heart of the matter. The murder, hate, envy, malice, and so on which followed the Fall were symptoms of a great tragedy which continues as a disease of perversion engulfing man's every effort. The great sin and the great cause lying behind all the symptoms is found in Curtis's words, "Man did not care enough about God."

Nourished in a garden without an equal and enjoying daily walks and talks with God finally proved insufficient, because love grew cold. The loss of love gave rise to questions: Did God have limits that were unnecessary? Might not more autonomy enhance life? These are the continuing questions of man. The surge for autonomy opens the way to a diminishing trust, to a loss of love. The effect is to dethrone God. Man himself replaces God. Broken relationships begin with an inward loss of love. We, however, tend to focus on the consequences of that loss. We look on sins as symptoms. It is indeed right to label the symptoms as *sins*. But it is at least equally important to label the root cause as *sin*. Perhaps then the singular and the plural usages — sin and sins — become meaningful.

Reconciliation by Recovery of Love

Perhaps now we are ready to ask a daring question. In the face of the loss of love and man's accumulating sins, what can, what should, what will God do? Taking the entire biblical record into account, the answer seems to be that God intends to do those things which will recover the lost love. These we call His redemptive acts. Though offended, ignored, and disobeyed, God takes the initiative looking toward reconciliation. His grace — unconditional love — actively seeks to end our self-destructing course.

Covenant and Love

So God offers a covenant relationship with a people, Israel! The first requirement for Israel in establishing such a covenant with promise is that Israel renounce its autonomy and its competing gods and recognize Jehovah as the only God. The second requirement meshes with the first perfectly. It calls for a renewal of love which is comprehensive — "with all your heart, and with all your soul, and with all your might."

Let us take another look at Deuteronomy 6:4-5, for it is a key passage for both Jew and Christian. It is called the *Shema*, because it is the first Hebrew word of the passage and means "hear." Let me quote it, *"Hear, O Israel: The Lord our God is one Lord: and thou shalt love the Lord thy God with all thine heart, and with all thy soul, and with all thy might"* (KJV). It was the Jewish confession of faith. It got to the heart of what an Israelite believed and what conditioned his entire life. It is what set him apart from pagans. It saturated his culture. It gave purpose and direction to Israel as community.

Deuteronomy 6:6-9, 11:13-21, and Numbers 15:37-41 are in a sense part of the *Shema*, but they are an interpretation and exhortation. Heavy emphasis is given to the teaching of the confession and to what God promises if and when the covenant is honored. The ten commands are the specifics that accompany the confession. They are, by various teaching techniques and ritual, to be internalized by successive generations. Jesus came into, hooked onto, interpreted, and gave life to this tradition.

Love and Commands

Jesus said, "If you love me, keep my commands." Jehovah said to Israel, "If you love me, keep my commands." As the violation of relationships created the problems of the human race — first through loss of love and then through specific transgressions — so now the confession of love for God, along with His "only-ness" (no other gods), could be tested by specific *attitudes, acts,* and *restraints.* Attitude and restraint are both expressed in commands one through three — no other gods, no graven image, no vain use of the Lord's name, and number ten — do not covet. Actions are expressed in numbers four and five: keep the sabbath day holy; honor father and mother. Restraints are very specific in the "You shall not" commands: kill, commit adultery, steal, bear false witness. Keeping the ten commands became a sign of renewal of love and that God had priority in the life of the Jew and his community — Israel. "If, Israel, you love me, you will want to obey me. If you want to obey me, you will be guided by the law of relationships I now give you," seems to be what God is saying to Israel.

Commands as Absolutes

Now let me suggest that while the *Shema* and the ten commands were at the heart of the Jewish covenant relationship with Jehovah, the ten commands express the ideals for all relationships. That is, these are absolutes. They are the laws of relationships. They are *revealed* — not of human devising. Observed, they make life work rewardingly. Ignored, they produce personal and social disaster. And Israel was to be God's showcase for all mankind to see just how good a good life could be. The fact that Israel often failed in its "showcase" function in no way altered either the value or the absolute character of the commands for every member of the human race — then and even now for our global society.

Timeless Commands

Let me now suggest that while the ten commands do not specifically cover all the concerns of our relationships, they do provide inclusive, time-resistant principles from which to work out the specifics in any generation. They are quite adequate and valid for use by persons in every culture.

Respect for Persons

Years ago I began asking: What is behind the ten commands? What is behind the specifics? Is there one great principle underlying all of them? Then I asked the same thing about the two commands Jesus gave. I suggest that back of the ten is the requirement of *respect for persons.* First, respect for the supreme and personal God is required. Respect for another, be it God or another being like myself, produces "care-full," caring, thoughtful behavior. It involves not wanting to injure but wanting to fulfill the other person. Is that not exactly what Jesus was saying when He used the word "love"? And is that not what the Old Testament words of Jehovah meant when He commanded Israel to love? Note that both Jew and Christian are *commanded* to love. Love is a rational, purposeful response. We can will to love. It is no mere emotion. It is unconditional caring.

The Commands Are Inclusive

Now observe the broad meaning given to the four commands which point vertically to God. The commands are a *revelation* about God. They proclaim that He is (1) prior, (2) primary, (3) ultimate reality, (4) for knowing and reverencing. That is a lot to say about God. The commands indicate the response required of me. If God is prior, then my commitment is to make Him central in life; if God is primary, then He shall be my only Master; if God is the ultimate reality, then it calls me to reject hypocrisy and to respond in faithfulness; if God is for knowing and reverencing, then He shall be the renewing center of life, and to this end I will use the one day in seven designated as belonging to Him. My responses to the revelation of what God is constitute a specific spelling out of what it means to love God.

Now look at the six commands which point to man. These are broad directives implementing *respect for persons.* Number five — honor father and mother. But what about the drunken father or the prostitute mother? The child grown to adulthood may find a way to honor them. But the broader meaning calls for respect for experienced persons, for history, for the God-ordered life process. Teachableness is suggested.

Number six — you shall not kill. It is not merely an act forbidden but a reminder that the identity and continuity of persons is sacred. Number seven — you shall not commit adultery. It is a call for the recognition of the dignity of persons. Any degrading of self or others through improper use of sex is a denial of the dignity of persons, whether it occurs in or out of wedlock. Number eight — you shall not steal — recognizes the material rights of persons. Wanton destruction of property is a sign that the perpetrators do not respect persons. Number nine — you shall not bear false witness — the stealing of one's reputation is an act of disrespect. Just representation is required. Number ten — you shall not covet — calls for respect for one's self and for society. Love disciplines one's desires. All the commands aim at attitudes even when they seem to point at actions. But this last command specifically turns us inward to a close examination of our motives.

Jesus Commands Love

Jesus says that it all boils down to a single word. That word is love. But the word as used by Jesus and New Testament writers is primarily cool and rational rather than emotional. The love Jesus has in mind and the ten commands are not contradictory.

Careful Bible study shows two words which must always be associated: love and holy. Biblical writers kept their meanings together. The ten commands keep them together and so did Jesus. And well He should have, for they describe the character of both God and the Christian. It is more important to know the *character* than the *capability* of either God or a Christian. It is the character rather than the capability which determines what either will do.

So we can be sure that when Jesus boils down the laws of relationships to love for God, neighbor, and self, He has "holy love" in focus — an untainted, unconditional, pure, right, caring concern for other persons.

God has priority in the triangle of relationships. When any leg of the triangle gets mangled, it means one is reduced to less than a whole person.

Finally, Jesus gives greater and truer meaning to the ten commands than ever before. His concern then and now is to save — to fulfill — rather than destroy. He aims for the "abundant life" for each of us. A rich, continuous relationship with Jesus Christ as Saviour and Lord fulfills both the intent of Jesus and the Father who gave the ten commands and yields the full, rewarding life.

The Scapegoat: Complex or Confession

Leviticus 16

What is needed to deal with our sin problem? Are we so advanced that our needs can best be met by a bloodless form of Christianity? How does God intend to deliver us from our sense and reality of sin, our guilt? Can we be delivered — freed? Let's return to an Old Testament ritual.

1. The Scene Reconstructed – Day of Atonement

Leviticus 16 is a scene of great annual solemnity. It is a time of humiliation. *"You shall afflict yourselves"* (vv. 29-31, RSV). This is an acknowledgement of sin.

Aaron, the High Priest, clothed in sacerdotal robes, first killed a bullock in behalf of himself and his family. Then with a censer full of sacred fire he enters the immediate presence of God, sprinkles incense on the censer and thus sends up a cloud of perfume between the cherubim (vv. 12-13). Next, he sprinkled blood of his own sin offering before the mercy seat (v. 14). Thus he made atonement for himself and his house (v. 6). Then he performed a similar rite for the people.

What we wish to focus on are the two goats previously chosen (v. 5) for this service. In verses 7 and 8 we find one goat would by lot be destined to die. Its blood was to be sprinkled before the Lord — as the bullock's was before (v. 15).

After this, the propitiatory service extended to the tabernacle and altar — from which the people were prohibited until the ritual was complete — and the blood of the bullock and goat was sprinkled as before. In this way, the tabernacle was purified from pollution contracted from the sins of the worshippers (vv. 16, 18-19).

Now, and not until now, the living goat is brought. *"And Aaron shall lay both his hands upon the head of the live goat, and confess over him all the iniquities of the people of Israel, and all their transgressions, all their sins; and he shall put them upon the head of the goat, and send him away into the wilderness by the hand of a man who is in readiness"* (v. 21, RSV).

Israel had a visual representation with which they could identify. The ritual was a **pointer** to a reality, to the intent of God. Their sins were atoned for, guilt was transferred to another. They had not witnessed the blood, the killing, the sacrifice, but here was their assurance it had been completed in the Holy Place.

There has arisen what is advertised as a modern or contemporary interpretation of this scapegoat which reflects negatively on the entire Old Testament event. It suggests the scapegoat drama is not only outdated but bad.

2. The Scapegoat Complex

The late Methodist Bishop Gerald Kennedy wrote regarding this symbolism or parable of propitiation: "Long before this happened and ever since it happened there has been a terrible fascination in the idea of a scapegoat. We want to pour our sins on something or someone and send them into the wilderness never to return to bother us."

Kennedy continues, "The doctrine of the Atonement has often been presented in just this light. Jesus on the cross is regarded as a sort of divine scapegoat. By repeating a few words in a creed, men think they can be freed of their guilt and responsibility. It is no wonder that the very sound of 'blood' in connection with Christianity has an unreal, sentimental connotation for many modern Christians. It has been associated with ideas repugnant to men who have some understanding of the enormity of sin and its consequences, and have ideas of God beyond the mechanical, infantile stage. It is not so easy to get rid of sin. It takes more than passing it on to Christ orally."

Then Kennedy proceeds to point out the modern scapegoat complex and properly condemns it.

(1) In the **political area —** the tendency to find a scapegoat rather than confess a national guilt and seek ultimate remedy, i.e., the Versailles Treaty. (2) In the **social order —** once under Nero it was the Christians; for others the Jew, the black, the foreigner, the political parties. Social groups hurl accusations at rivals. (3) It's a **universal tendency** — John Gunther, after touring the South said

its greatest problem was the number of Southerners whose only profession "is being Southerners." But are they alone in clinging to a romantic, unrealistic picture of the past rather than to deal with obvious evils of the present?

Who has not known those who could have been saved if just once they confessed their own blame? Do husbands make scapegoats out of wives? Parents of children? Employers of employees?

Now if this Old Testament symbolism in ritual is only concerned with the kind of complex Kennedy is identifying, it's not only valueless, it is bad. The scapegoat complex solves nothing. Rather, it destroys the person with the complex. It can only postpone inevitable tragedy.

Psychoanalysis has shown how such pretence leads to twisted and ruined lives. So Kennedy correctly says that each man has to face his own sin. If he can't, it will haunt him like a black ghost until he cracks. How many are guilt-haunted! The time comes when all the guilt which we tried to send away, or put on another, suddenly descends upon our spirits like a thick fog. Kennedy again rightly says, "The only thing that will dispel that fog and lift that fear, **is an act of God**."

Exactly ... and how amazing that Kennedy misses the point of the ritual symbolism ... the acting out of reality as on a stage. He ignores, perhaps intentionally, that the ritual contains **two** goats! In the twin goats, the **act of God — past, present** and **efficacious —** is symbolized.

Because of that we can see this ritual, not as a lesson about scapegoats which symbolize our ways of passing guilt quite improperly to something or someone else. Rather, let us put on a new set of lenses and see the ritual as ...

3. The Act of Confession – Act of God in Deliverance

We must note that these old rituals and sacrifices do not continue, even now in Israel or elsewhere. They were visual aids for an untutored age. Hebrews calls them *"a shadow of good things to come."* The shadow becomes reality in Christ. Yet, modern as we think we are, we must admit that we and they are essentially alike, having the same sins and spiritual needs.

It is necessary to also note that the ritual and sacrifices were not in themselves of sacramental value. That is, they were **not chan-**

nels through which grace was conveyed to individuals or worshippers. They were **not designed** to gain God's favor.

Rather, the ritual and sacrifices were a recognition of the fact that God had already, by His own initiative, extended His mercy and His grace to the people. The ritual and sacrifices were the response of obedient faith to divine grace.

Of course there were those in Israel, and all those outside Israel, who viewed this as having a sort of magical efficacy. The law and the prophets challenged any such view. Along with sacrifice, the law demanded the confession of sin and humble penitence of spirit. If sin was against another and restitution could be made, it was demanded.

Author Ryder Smith says, "The intelligent Jew ... thought ... whenever in any sacrifice, the blood was offered, it symbolized both the fact of the Covenant and the truth that he had broken it, and also the further truth that, as he now came to God with a penitent heart and in His appointed way, the Covenant was renewed and was valid for him."

Why were two goats necessary? Only one could not complete the picture, the drama. God teaches the race even as we do children. Long ago, God knew the appeal and effectiveness of the eye-gate! Two goats represented two halves of a truth to be symbolized. **One speaks of sacrifice for sin; the other the effects of sacrifice.**

Sacrifice is the necessary condition for pardon, forgiveness. Forgiveness is costly! The Jewish worshipper did not see that the expiation for it was "within the veil." But as they saw the live goat heading for the wilderness, it was a visible token, a signal that indeed the sacrifice for them was complete. Feeble faith was thus helped. The unseen propitiation — a blessed mystery — was certified to them in this way.

Look again at vv. 20-22. See Aaron confess the **corporate** iniquities, transgressions, sins. *"The goat shall bear all their iniquities upon him to a solitary land"* (RSV).

For us the drama is deepened immeasurably because Christ fulfills all this (the two goats) in One Person. In fact, He is the Priest and the Sacrifice who with his own blood made expiation for sin, and He is also the goat sent away bearing the sin of the world into the land of forgetfulness, whence it can never return! Hallelujah!

John says that He is the Lamb of God who takes away the sin

of the world. *"As far as the east is from the west, so far hath he removed our transgressions from us"* (Psalm 103:12, KJV).

So the intent of the Old Testament ritual is no endorsement of any scapegoat complex where we transfer blame that we or others may have developed. That would mean we had only compounded our need for confession and pardon. Nor is the death of Christ to be seen as or treated as a way of easily, glibly passing over to Christ the sin we have not faced or renounced.

Should this appear "unreal, sentimental," to any professed modern, let us be reminded that historically it was not unreal or sentimental. Judaism was marked by a vivid consciousness of sin.

Was it exaggerated? Morbid? Well, the same consciousness is part of everyone, **but** so often it is mostly overlaid and stifled. However, when awakened by the Holy Spirit or by life's events, there is then a bitter sense of sin as **mine**, involving guilt; despair as to whether I can be delivered; and fearful thoughts of my relation to God which conscience itself brings.

It is the Bible — record of revelation — the authoritative revelation which brings us the message of hope.

In a day of mounting psychiatric needs ... wars, terrorism, strikes, barbarism ... it seems a silly, giddy veneer of refinement to shy from blood — blood that saves, not blood that any longer speaks of death. Rather, it speaks of life!

And we need to read and consider again and very carefully if we have any thought that this is an easy way to be rid of sin. We can't read the record and see beneath the surface without seeing **(1) the monstrousness of our sin; (2) the cost of Calvary,** and **(3) the promised real change in confessing hearts**.

I therefore suggest that the Scapegoat Ritual, far from being an easy-out complex, is in fact a hard to give confession ... **a confession of sin and of guilt, and, at the same time, a confession of the reality of pardon!**

Christ is our goat slain.

Christ is our goat sent into the wilderness.

1. We have a sufficient, efficient, efficacious way to treat our sin problem.

2. We have assurance that our sin problem can be treated with a permanent deliverance — a real change — so we are made:

New persons in Christ
Justified
Regenerated
Adopted

... and that this reality — a living reality — is witnessed to by multiplied thousands down through the centuries.

"Just as I am, without one plea,
But that Thy blood was shed for me ..."

Security for Believers

I was eighteen. I had a great desire to study about my faith. So I enrolled in a correspondence course distributed through a Bible institute in Los Angeles. I scored perfectly on each of the rather easy tests.

One lesson was labeled "The Position of the Believer." It taught an irreversible (eternal) security for anyone who accepted Christ. I gave the expected answers on the test. But I also wrote a letter expressing my objections to the teaching. I received a short letter assuring me that if I read the enclosed brochure I could not fail to be convinced.

The brochure said there were two views about the security of one's salvation.

One view was illustrated by the way a cat carries its young. The other view was illustrated by the way the monkey carries its young.

My Calvinistic friends who advocated irreversible and eternal security said their view was illustrated by the cat. A cat carries its kittens by mouth. If the kitten falls, it's the mother cat's fault.

The other view (supposedly mine) was illustrated by the monkey. If the little fellow fell off the back of its mother, it had no one to blame but itself. It should have hung on and been more careful.

That presentation demanded my response. So I wrote that the cat illustration probably was adequate for the view they taught. But the monkey illustration would never do for that which others and I believed.

Illustrations are helpful aids to understanding. But they must be carefully selected and carefully used. The Bible uses many illustrations. Often a single word or term is in fact an illustration, metaphor, or analogy. "Born again" is one of those illustrating words.

With this caution regarding illustrations or analogies in mind, I suggested to my teachers that their cat illustration taken seriously was a violation of plain biblical teaching. There could be no view of salvation which relieved the individual believer of responsibility for his relationship to God. Nor is it biblical or reasonable to blame God for our sins, apostasy, and neglect of Him.

Indeed, one cannot save himself, but neither can one be saved apart from himself. We were created by God to be responsible and "respond-able." Grace is the picture of God's givingness, of His reaching out to savingly touch us. Faith is my response to His reach. My faith response is an acknowledgment of my sin, my inability to save myself, my need of a Saviour. *"As therefore you received Christ Jesus the Lord, so live in him, rooted and built up in him and established in the faith"* (Colossians 2:6, RSV). What was required of me to "receive" Jesus is always required to continue and live (walk) in Him.

The cat illustration taken seriously makes God responsible for any break in the relationship with God. It relieves the individual of responsibility for continuing to respond to the grace of God. In many forms this error is spread today by well-intentioned but misled teachers. The Bible never relieves the individual believer of his responsibility for constant response to the grace (givingness) of God.

But what about the monkey illustration? It was a complete misunderstanding of what the Bible taught and of what I believed. Certainly I know of no evangelical who believes that my security is dependent alone on what I can do. But indeed my security is dependent on my response to what God can do for me. The monkey illustration is a distortion. God does not force me to be a believer or a receiver of Christ. But once I receive Christ and thereby begin a relationship with Him, I am not a little monkey hanging on for dear life. The illustration fails to indicate the believer's relationship to Christ.

I suggested an alternative illustration for what I and multiplied thousands believe. I said that while understanding the limitations of illustrations I would prefer that of the willing handclasp.

God offers His hand. He takes the initiative (grace). I respond by willingly placing my hand in His (faith). A new relationship is begun. He holds me as long as I want my hand to be in His. My security is illustrated by this common interlocking of hands by friends. The Bible vividly portrays the reconciliation which makes God and me friends.

But to suggest that God, having taken my hand, now says to me, "Ah, now I've got you; just try to get away; nothing you can ever do again can get you loose from me," is clear violation of the total biblical thrust and of the nature of relationships. My security is in the sustaining of our relationship, which has most of the characteristics of a human one, except there is one party to the covenant who is unfailing and unchanging. God is constant and unchanging in His attitude and acts of "steadfast love." The constancy of our Lord does indeed beget a growing constancy in us as we "walk" or "live" in Christ.

I believe in the security of the believer. But it is conditional rather than unconditional. I am secure while I keep on believing, trusting, responding. To be secure in any other fashion would violate all that is meant by personal relationship and covenant.

I believe in the "perseverance of the saints" if they persevere in their relationship with Jesus as both Saviour and Lord. I believe that all the resources for persevering that were available to Jesus — the Holy Spirit, communion with the Father — are available to us. Indeed, we have the Word of God, the grace of God, the ministry of the Holy Spirit, and the church to help us persevere. We should most certainly be secure. But at no point in our personal history does God intend to depersonalize us by destroying our will, our power to choose, our capability of responding positively or negatively to our relationship with God.

The Bible beautifully uses marriage as an analogy of relationship to Christ. Christ, the Bridegroom, wants to give Himself fully to the bride — the church. The meaning is both corporate (church) and individual. Commitment is two-way. The resulting covenant is two-way. The Bible also speaks of the violation of this relationship. Israel's going a whoring is an eloquent though horrible illustration of the facts of life. No one is unconditionally secure until he is ushered into the presence of Jesus to be with Him forever.

The teachers of unconditional security hold out false security in the name of the Bible. They appeal to illustrating Bible words. So they argue if you are once "born" you can't be "unborn." But "born" is used to beautifully illustrate the *newness* of life which the Christian experiences in a saving relationship with Jesus, not to erect a doctrine of false security. Once in a family as a son or daughter, always a member of the family is a distortion of analogy. In our natural life we had nothing to say about being born or becoming a member of a family. In our spiritual life we do, in fact, have the final say. We must be alert to the misuse of analogy, metaphor and biblical illustration.

Proponents of unconditional security often appeal to John 10:27-29. The clincher is *"shall never perish, and no one shall snatch them out of my hand"* (RSV). True. No force *outside* the person can break the relationship. The same applies to their appeal to Romans 8:38-39. Indeed nothing can separate us from the love of God, except *ourselves.* (Read the previous verses and discover that the words are addressed to "more than conquerors," not violators of a relationship with Christ.)

Appeal is also made to the theory of *imputation* of righteousness. That means that we are not responsible for righteousness but that Christ's righteousness is by religious magic made ours despite our own flaws, sins, or apostasy. This makes a farce of the Christian faith by removing it from reality. Advocates say, "When God looks at you He does not see you, for Christ stands between you and God. So your dirty rags are never seen, only the white raiment of Jesus." The trouble is that God sees us as we are at all times. We are not saved merely *positionally*. We are either really saved, transformed, and made new, or Christianity is hypocrisy. The righteousness of Christ is continually *imparted* to me as I respond to Him and permit the Holy Spirit to work within me. I can have a clean heart!

There are Bible passages which should shock those still clinging to the error of unconditional eternal security. Look at a few.

Examine the strong attack of Peter against false teachers who once clearly knew Jesus as Saviour and Lord. Second Peter 2:20-22 is a direct and conclusive contradiction of the teaching of unconditional security. Christians *"escaped"* but became *"entangled"* again in the *"defilements of the world,"* and their *"last state has become worse for them than the first."* Compare this with 2 Peter 1:9-11: *" ... if you do this you will never fall"* (RSV). Clearly, "to fall" is so possible that warnings are necessary. One need not fall "if"!

The book to the Hebrews was written as a check against threatening apostasy. Genuine Christians are addressed (6:10 and 10:32-34), nevertheless warning is appropriate. Note especially 10:23 which urges holding *"fast the confession of our hope without wavering"* and follows up with a severe picture of punishment if they do not (10:26-29).

Apostasy — utter and final — is possible for *"those who have once been enlightened, who have tasted the heavenly gift, and have become partakers of the Holy Spirit ... "* (6:4-6, RSV). No wonder the writer concludes, *"It is a fearful thing to fall into the hands of the living God"* (10:31).

Jesus twice said, *"He who endures to the end will be saved"* (Matthew 10:22; 24:13, RSV).

We observe Paul's anxiety for his converts who had received the Spirit (Galatians 3:2-5) and were running well, yet later they were not obeying the truth (5:7). He was alarmed. His labor could be in vain (4:11). See also 1 Thessalonians 3:5. Paul did not doubt the reality of his own conversion, but he still disciplined himself lest he should fail or fall (1 Corinthians 9:27).

And finally, the words to the church at Ephesus found in Revelation 2:4-5 should cause us to reject reliance in false security: *"I will come to you and remove your lampstand from its place, unless you repent"* (RSV).

The Bible teaches conditional security. But what a wonderful security it is. God is always for me — every moment. Christ died for me. Christ rose for me. Christ sits at the Father's right hand praying for me. The Holy Spirit is for me. The Bible is given to me as my guide. The church was instituted of God for me. What security!

But the Bible and reason tell me that if I ignore all that is for me I have no right to expect God to treat me as though He had given me a lifelong, irrevocable life insurance policy.

If we walk in the Spirit by faith and obedience — if we maintain our relationship with Christ — God and heaven are ours forever!

Relevant Passages of Scripture

The man who says, "I know him" but does not do what he commands is a liar, and the truth is not in him (1 John 2:4, NIV).

If we confess our sins, he is faithful and just and will forgive us our sins and purify us from all unrighteousness (1 John 1:9, NIV).

For the wages of sin is death, but the gift of God is eternal life in Christ Jesus our Lord (Romans 6:23, NIV).

How shall we escape, if we ignore such a great salvation? (Hebrews 2:3a, NIV).

Because he himself suffered when he was tempted, he is able to help those who are being tempted (Hebrews 2:18, NIV).

See to it brothers, that none of you have a sinful, unbelieving heart that turns away from the living God. ... We have come to share in Christ if we hold firmly till the end the confidence we had at first (Hebrews 3:12, 14, NIV).

Therefore he is able to save completely those who come to God through him, because he always lives to intercede for them (Hebrews 7:25, NIV).

... and, once made perfect, he became the source of eternal salvation for all who obey him ... (Hebrews 5:9, NIV).

Blessed are they that do his commandments, that they may have right to the tree of life, and may enter in through the gates into the city (Revelation 22:14, KJV).

... and those who formerly had the gospel preached to them did not go in, because of disobedience (Hebrews 4:6b, NIV).

We do not want you to become lazy, but to imitate those who through faith and patience inherit what has been promised (Hebrews 6:12, NIV).

For of this you can be sure: No immoral, impure, or greedy person — such a man is an idolater — has any inheritance in the kingdom of Christ and of God. Let no one deceive you with empty words, for because of such things God's wrath comes on those who are disobedient (Ephesians 5:5-6, NIV).

And to present her to himself as a radiant church, without stain or wrinkle or any other blemish, but holy and blameless (Ephesians 5:27, NIV).

Everyone who sins breaks the law; in fact, sin is lawlessness. But you know that he appeared so that he might take away our sins. And in him is no sin. No one who lives in him keeps on sinning. No one who continues to sin has either seen him or known him. Dear children, do not let anyone lead you astray. He who does what is right is righteous, just as he is righteous. He who does what is sinful is of the devil, because the devil has been sinning from the beginning. The reason the Son of God appeared was to destroy the devil's work. No one who is born of God will continue to sin, because God's seed remains in him; he cannot sin, because he has been born of God. This is how we know who the children of

God are and who the children of the devil are. Anyone who does not do what is right is not a child of God; neither is anyone who does not love his brother (1 John 3:4-10, NIV).

All of Ezekiel 18. *The soul who sins shall die* (Ezekiel 18:4b, NKJV).

The Lord replied to Moses, "Whoever has sinned against me I will blot out of my book" (Exodus 32:33, NIV).

All of Psalm 119.

The ordinances of the Lord are sure and altogether righteous. They are more precious than gold, than much pure gold; they are sweeter than honey, than honey from the comb. By them is your servant warned; in keeping them there is great reward (Psalm 19:9-11, NIV).

I tell you the truth, if a man keeps my word, he will never see death (John 8:51, NIV).

Shadows Flee Away

W*e tell you the good news: What God promised to our fathers he has fulfilled for us, their children, by raising Jesus from the dead* (Acts 13:32, NIV).

These are words of Paul to the Jews in Antioch of Pisidia. *"We bring you good news"* ... the words sound similar to the announcement of the nativity. Here is, in a sense, better news. The birth of Jesus was good news. But much had happened since then, and now — after ministry and death — there is Resurrection!

And without Resurrection we have no gospel. It is the capstone of the gospel message. It is what gives validity to the ministry and death of Jesus. The cross is glorious because of the Empty Tomb and the Risen Christ. It is the *sine qua non* of the gospel. It is that one element without which we have no gospel. No wonder then that we rejoice as we cry out, "Christ is Risen!" and the echo comes back, "Christ is Risen, indeed!"

James Denny writes, "The apostles did not preach the resurrection of Jesus itself as mere fact; what they preached was the *Gospel of the Resurrection*!" They knew the difference between good news and good advice. They were heralds.

Dr. Dale, the great theologian of Birmingham, England, believed in the Resurrection, at least in theory, until one eventful occasion when the truth burned into his heart with an entirely new conviction, and in almost a dazed way he continued to repeat the words, "Christ is risen! Christ is risen!" And in the years that followed, every service on the Lord's Day morning at Carr's Lane began with an Easter hymn — he felt he had to preach the only gospel that could save men's souls.

So on this day we preach Christ — Crucified, Risen, and Reigning! For gloom-ridden disciples, the resurrection of Jesus Christ meant that the shadows flew away! And so it is yet — NOW!

What are those shadows that flee away with the day of Resurrection? First there are ...

1. Shadows of Doubt and Uncertainty

Professor Warfield, speaking of the whole New Testament, says, "In the face of such evidence, spread broadcast over the New Testament, no one has been able to question that the founders of Christianity entrenched themselves in the fact of Christ's resurrection as the central stronghold of their hope, faith and proclamation."

Resurrection is profuse in the writings and preachings of Peter and Paul — the central heralds as recorded in Acts. A real and bodily resurrection was in their minds. Not just, as is in many places acccepted, that Jesus rose again in the souls of disciples, in resurgent faith and love, and that this alone gave birth to all the stories of the empty grave and the appearances of the Lord to His own.

Making the Resurrection a fine religious myth will simply not do. There is too much historical evidence in favor of bodily resurrection. The consequences worked out historically through the church down the centuries gives the lie to such shallow explanations. If we have no Easter message, then we have no Easter faith.

As Dean Simpson once declared, "Ghosts do not change the lives of men, inspiring the fearful with courage, the despairing with hope, the dying with life. Indeed, the apostles and those earliest Christians believed in an empty tomb, in a Risen Christ who is alive in the world."

Resurrection is the answer to ...

2. Shadows of Uncertainty as to Christian Experience

Christian experience in all its forms implies the Resurrection! Resurrection and Christian experience stand or fall together. Paul states it bluntly, *"If Christ has not been raised, then our preaching is in vain* [empty] *and your faith is in vain!"* (1 Corinthians 15:14, RSV).

Can we possibly imagine Paul adhering to a futile faith, devoting his life to a message which had nothing in it? On the contrary, the Resurrection informs his thought, colors his theology and impacts on his ethics.

a. Consider our experience of justification — being put into a right relationship with God in Christ. In Romans 4:25, Paul declares of Christ, that He was *"put to death for our trespasses and raised for our justification"* (RSV).

Justification then is clearly a Christian experience, a relationship with God which rests upon the historical foundation of the

Resurrection. No foundation, then no experience!

b. Consider this to be true also of an experience we may have of the sanctifying grace of God — His cleansing of heart and life. In the next chapter, Romans 6, he declares that we are set free from sin, have become slaves of God, and that we obtain *"sanctification and its end, eternal life."*

But as we read the chapter, it is clear that this benefit is based on our being both buried and raised with Christ — raised into newness of life in which we experience moment by moment sanctification. And in 8:11, we read, *"If the Spirit of him who raised Jesus from the dead dwells in you, he who raised Christ Jesus from the dead will give life to your mortal bodies through his Spirit which dwells in you"* (RSV).

Clearly then, holiness of life is utterly impossible apart from the mighty energy which raised Jesus from the dead. No wonder that Paul's cry voiced in Philippians and that we should all join in crying, *"That I may know Him and the power of His resurrection, and the fellowship of His sufferings"* (Philippians 3:10, paraphrase).

3. Shadows of Uncertainty as to Christian Conduct

Romans 14:9 declares it is Christ's death and resurrection that enforce on us the truth that we do not live or die to ourselves. Rather, we live and die *"to the Lord"* because in fact *"we belong to the Lord"* (vv. 7-8, NIV). And again this is echoed in 2 Corinthians 5:15. We live no longer for ourselves *"but for him who for their sake died and was raised"* (RSV).

The Resurrection is to impact our conduct, our selfishness, our ethics! The Resurrection takes the shadows from our conduct, and we live lives of gratitude expressed in our ethics. Resurrection removes the ...

4. Shadows of Uncertainty as to the Future

The resurrection of Jesus Christ is our most divinely authenticated "Intimation of Immortality," to use Wordsworth's lovely phrase. Of Christians it is written, *"He dieth no more."* The four Christians raised during His ministry did die again. But to us is the promise, *"If we endure, we will also reign with him"* (2 Timothy 2:12, NIV). See Him ... be like Him. Share His glory. Possess a resurrection body and ever be with the Lord.

O how glorious and resplendent,
Fragile body, shalt thou be,
When endued with so much beauty,
Full of health and strong and free;
Full of vigour, full of pleasure —
That shall last eternally.

Because of Resurrection ...

5. Shadows of Sorrow Shall Flee Away!

The Resurrection deals effectively with our sorrows. It was Longfellow who assured us that:

There is no flock, however watched and tended,
But one dead lamb is there;
There is no home, howe'er defended,
But has one vacant chair.

And Tennyson described the bitter anguish death can produce:

The stately ships go on
To their haven under the hill,
But oh! for the touch of a vanished hand,
And the sound of a voice that is still.

So St. Paul's profound apologetic for resurrection produced by the needs of those who wondered what had become of departed friends: *"If for this life only we have hoped in Christ, we are of all men most to be pitied"* (1 Corinthians 15:19, RSV). He goes even futher and declares, *"If there is no resurrection of the dead, then Christ has not been raised"* (1 Corinthians 15:13, RSV).

The triumph of Jesus and ours is inseparably linked. The first word of the Risen Lord was a challenge to a mourner, *"Jesus saith unto her, 'Woman, why weepest thou?'"* (John 20:15, KJV). The proclamation of the Risen, Exalted Christ is the best attack on the vagaries of Spiritism.

Dean Simpson declares, "The best defense of the Gospel of the Risen Christ is the power with which it enters lowly doors; the radiance with which it transfigures the lives of the poor ... It is not in our moods of criticism but in hours of need that the proclamation of the crucified and risen Saviour steals into our spirits, benediction in its breath and healing on its wings."

Because of Resurrection, the ...

6. Shadows of Weakness Flee Away

Nothing short of the power which raised Jesus can raise the sinner from the dark sepulchre of human guilt.

Recall that the Old Testament standard miracle of power was the deliverance of Israel out of Egypt. From Moses to Malachi, the appeal was to the Red Sea as the supreme demonstration of God's power to help and to save.

But now the resurrection of Jesus Christ is the New Testament standard of power — the empty tomb and the Risen Christ replace the Red Sea. The resurrection of Jesus Christ from the dead marks the greatest achievement of omnipotence in the Christian dispensation. It is also the standard of what God can do for them who believe.

Hear Paul in Ephesians 1:18-20 (NIV): *"... that you may know ... his incomparably great power for us who believe. That power is like the working of the mighty strength which he exerted in Christ when he raised him from the dead and seated him at his right hand in the heavenly realms."* When we want to know what God is able to do, we turn back to the resurrection of His Son from the grave.

Chadwick — the great Christian Holiness preacher of England — preached a sermon on "Many Infallible Proofs." It was, of course, about the resurrection of Jesus. In it he told of how his church was going nowhere, nothing was happening. Sermons, religious and social activity bore no fruit.

Finally, a few leagued together to pray for revival of the church and converts to Christ. Chadwick preached as one possessed regarding Lazarus and how Jesus raised him from the dead.

Then his faithful prayer partners united in praying for a modern Lazarus. They asked for the worst person in the community to be converted. At last it happened, and the one person no one had hope for was indeed converted. He flung himself at the communion rail and was gloriously captured by Christ.

At work, the new convert was fiercely, cruelly persecuted. He stood it all well until one day as they were blasting, a bar slipped and jammed his finger. Before he was aware, an oath escaped him. The men laughed but only for a moment. They released his finger and wanted to wrap it for him. Tears were on his face but not for pain. With broken voice he said, "Nay, I've a bigger wound than this; we'll have that seen to first." He prayed right there for forgiveness. Peace was restored. He said, "Now we'll have it wrapped."

Well, the news spread. When it was announced that this "new" man would tell the story of his conversion, there was not room for the crowd. When there was a Lazarus to see, they came to church. He became a standing proof of God's power. Scoffers and critics were silenced.

This, then, is the power the church needs. There is no substitute for it. The church languishes when there are no conversions. Let the church pray souls out of their graves. Then we can continue to celebrate Easter Resurrection appropriately and every week of the year.

Our most urgent need is that we should know the exceeding greatness of God's power in the resurrection of those dead in trespasses and sins. It was another Lazarus who wrote:

How do I know He's the Living God?
In corruption of sin I lay dead,
But life everlasting came into me when,
"Thy sins be forgiven," He said.

There's a Power Working

My brilliant professor of history at the university knew more about church history than most ministers. I was a pastor in the city. With serious sadness he asked, "Do you see any hope for mankind?"

That's a tough question. History and the daily din of news tell of human misadventure and human failure in the Church. Cynicism develops. How can hope flourish or survive when all we hear about is corruption, violence, and power struggles in every area and level of life?

Is there any basis for hope?

If we are locked into a material and natural explanation and understanding, we are hopeless. The best of humanism is a rope of sand. The Marxist hope is a distortion of God's dream. It denies at least 50 percent of reality, reducing it to matter only. And man is not doing well with bootstrap power and methods.

If there is hope it will enter by revelation, by the unveiling of a dimension of reality beyond the five senses. The Christian proclaims *revelation.* In Christ the secret of God for man, planet, universe, and church is now an *open secret.* Christ is the center, and the Bible is the carrier of that hope, that open secret.

Paul provides a condensed expression of the hope. God's purpose and dream for man and Church is for a holy, blameless, loving life — Christlike. Paul's report is utterly mind-boggling. God's purpose in creation is also the dream of re-creation. Re-creation embraces individual Christ-persons, believers, holy ones who together are Christ's body of fellowshipping Christ-trusters (see Ephesians 1:3-14).

Paul reports that the open secret promises that when the time is ripe — as God tells time — everything (every atom) that exists will be brought into unity by a new relationship to Christ as the center of the universe (verse 10). Verse 11 says we have a share in that heritage which God designed and toward which He now acts to bring fulfillment.

God has placed *everything* under the power of Christ (Ephesians 1:22-23). He has made Christ head of the Church in every single thing. If Christ is not Lord in *everything*, then it is not God's Church! The Church is Christ's body, His instrument for realizing the fulfillment of God's design which expresses His holy love. It is this planet's responsible community. But it is not self-dependent. Verse 23 says the God who fills the whole wide universe lives in the Body, the Church. What assurance, challenge, warning!

Paul proceeds to exhaust the magnificently expressive Greek language to picture the power of God as immeasurably strong, mighty, energetic, and great. Hope exists by virtue of that power.

How shall we understand that power? Look as it operates in Christ. It raises Him from among the dead ones. It seats Him in a place of supreme authority, power and control beyond any other or competing power. It is the power which will realize the dream of God.

It is the power which is available to individual Christians — our source of "cope-ability." We have access to resurrection!

It is the power of the Church as God's agent on this planet for reconciliation and the fulfillment of God's dream.

There's a power working. We know it by revelation. We experience its vertical insertion. It is a major reality in a moral universe. It is spiritual, supernatural, nonmaterial power. It shall prevail over material power, over sin power, and shall in fact bring the material and the moral to ultimate, God-designed fulfillment.

This is my Bible-based hope, my eschatology!

Understanding the Bible

Bible: Not an Easy Book

The Bible is not an easy book. Problems in understanding are created by the weakness of translations; by the cultural gap created by the centuries; and by the uncertainty of the language, on occasion, in the original language and in the best available texts.

This does not mean it is not for simple people. If simple people can read they can also study. Study is needed if one is to understand the Bible. Certainly, more study and more aids are needed in some sections of the Bible than in others. Christians cannot afford to be mentally lazy. If they succumb to that disease they may wind up — and guiltily — in the cults, in the false. The Bible itself never encourages mindlessness — the abandonment of reason, scholarship, or intelligence. The Bible and our Lord make great demands on the whole of our persons.

Principles of Interpretation

There is a theological discipline called hermeneutics, which means the proper interpretation of the Bible. So we need to be aware of a few interpretive principles:

1. Scripture interprets Scripture. The whole is necessary to a proper understanding of the parts. But careful study of the parts is essential to understanding the whole. Perhaps that is why Bible study offers a lifelong, exciting and rewarding adventure.

2. The New Testament has theological priority over the Old Testament. But the Old Testament is essential to the fullest, richest understanding of the New Testament.

3. Revelation is progressive — it moves in a historical line. It starts with peoples and individuals where they are and leads them upward. How else can we understand certain laws, for example, in Leviticus?

4. The same weight cannot be given to each part of the Bible. For example, Esther versus Romans.

5. The Bible is Christocentric. That is, Christians find the unity of the Bible in relation to the revelation in Jesus Christ their Lord.

6. The Bible is literature. Therefore the interpreter must give diligent and conscientious attention to its genre, words, and grammar. In other words, it seeks answers to questions: Is this poetry, history, sermon, parable? What did this word mean to its writer-reader? Did it always have the same meaning? How does the structure of sentences affect our understanding of the passage? What light does the context shed on a small section of the total document?

7. The true interpreter seeks to identify, understand, and interpret historical, cultural, language, world-view, and other gaps which may exist between the current generation and the generation in which words of an ancient document were penned.

8. The true interpreter seeks first to identify that which is clear and without question in any book of the Bible or any part of a book. He then moves to identify the difficult parts: words, ideas, sentence structure, etc. He never bases a rule of faith or practice on uncertain, unclear, or ambiguous portions of any book of the Bible.

Obviously, the preacher-teacher task in the church requires *ability* and *integrity*. But *each Christian* is under obligation, so far as his capability will carry him, to understand the Bible and interpret its saving story to his friends so that he may win, instruct, correct, and finally present them to Christ as a trophy of grace and inspired witnessing.

The Way to Right Relationship with God

Righteousness

But now a righteousness from God, apart from law, has been made known, to which the Law and the Prophets testify. This righteousness from God comes through faith in Jesus Christ to all who believe. There is no difference, for all have sinned and fall short of the glory of God, and are justified freely by his grace through the redemption that came by Christ Jesus.

God presented him as a sacrifice of atonement, through faith in his blood. He did this to demonstrate his justice, because in his forbearance he had left the sins committed beforehand unpunished — he did it to demonstrate his justice at the present time, so as to be just and the one who justifies the man who has faith in Jesus.

Where, then, is boasting? It is excluded. On what principle? On that of observing the Law? No, but on that of faith. For we maintain that a man is justified by faith apart from observing the law. Is God the God of Jews only? Is he not the God of Gentiles too? Yes, of Gentiles too, since there is only one God, who will justify the circumcised by faith and the uncircumcised through that same faith. Do we, then, nullify the law by this faith? Not at all! Rather, we uphold the law (Romans 3:21-31, NIV).

It seems to me that in these verses Paul deals with the most intimate and dynamic experience in the life of a Christian. It is **logical**, but the logic of experience and observation. It is **conservative** in that it retains the essence of true Judaism.

The law is not discarded, but is seen performing its intended function in man's moral and spiritual life. The true Jew, the only circumcised, are those who have had heart, or inner surgery. Without the inner surgery, the surgery performed on the flesh is futile.

It is **pragmatic**, for it declares that which has proven to be a satisfactory answer to man's deepest and historic problem — sin. The answer is grace-faith. The answer has been proven in the crucible (laboratory) of life itself.

It is **doctrinal**, but it is not theory imposed on life or Scripture; rather, grows out of both life and Scripture.

It is **dynamic**, for it points to the fulcrum, to the power, to the source of change needed to make man in the image of God, freeing him from sin, and setting his spirit soaring in a realm of victory through a right relationship with God.

The dynamic is further seen as Paul realistically faces man's greatest of dilemmas, the sin-righteousness dilemma. We are enmeshed in sin personally and socially.

Sin is deep within us. It is a seemingly inextricable involvement. We in sin — sin in us! None has escaped the involvement.

What can save us?
How can a man be good?
How can we be righteous, justified?

Paul's answer is grace-faith! What does that mean? Paul tries to explain. We are emancipated, justified, saved as a result of action and reaction, of initiation and response. Even as God is the principal actor in the Old and New Testament, so it is always in personal experience.

The Righteousness of God is not an abstraction. It is more than a quality He possesses. Vincent Taylor says it describes "His saving activity, His action in justifying men and so bringing them into right relationship with Himself."

Phillips translates grace as God's *"generous dealing"* with us. So His righteousness and grace are words of great good news about God. God is ever moving in upon us in generous and saving activity.

The purpose is to restore us to righteousness which is best understood as a right relationship. Primarily, it is a new relationship with God from which all other proper relationships must flow.

But while God acts out of an amazing love which has been recorded in its many facets in the Bible, this — even this — is not enough. Even the consummate act of the cross is not enough.

Nor is the law enough! Even though it is good. Law provides us a straightedge, a yardstick before which we discover our weakness and sinfulness. It makes us aware of how life works as God intended it to work. It makes us aware of how far short of this way we have lived.

It forces us to look outside, beyond ourselves for help. It can be useful in bringing us to the place where we, like the alcoholic, know we are at the end of our rope and must have a lift-up from Another. Every man knows he ought to be good. Before the law he knows what is good, and that he is not good.

Paul is by no means saying, "It is no longer necessary to be good." For God has not changed His mind about right and wrong, or goodness and evil. He is saying: if we are ever justified, righteous, or made good, it will be apart from any merit of our own or goodness we achieve by what we do for ourselves.

We are shut up to what Someone Else can do for us.

So God deals with us generously (grace) and is savingly active toward us. But even that is not enough. There is another essential factor.

Paul says that other factor is faith. What does he mean? He explains it. It is a very personal, intimate, positive, and full response to God's saving activity. Two actions meet — God's givingness and my outgoing, responding faith. Thus, faith is seen as the mighty, determining factor it really is.

Faith is no creedal response or recitation. It is the whole person responding to God's generosity and sacrifical love.

It is an attitude of **utter dependence**. (One has described sin as "a proud independence of God.") "Nothing in my hand I bring, simply to the cross I cling." I cling! I cling! For without that clinging I am sunk and forever.

It is humility.

It is the stilling of the cries of pride.

It is receiving.

It is accepting Another and all He brings with Him to effect my rescue, my change of mind and life.

It is my personal and total response to Jesus Christ.

It is a response I can make.

It is a response for which I have responsibility.

It is a response made possible by God's grace.

Do you know what it is to have faith in someone's promise, to have faith in a remedy, to have faith in a physician, a lawyer, or a friend? Then you know what is meant by faith in the Lord Jesus Christ, His redeeming blood and the Gospel.

The initiating action of God in His saving activity toward us (which is grace) continues in a new and dynamic manner in response to faith (our response).

Since we are dealing with reciprocating **actions** we may expect God not only to be in a position to **declare** us righteous and good, but to **make** us such in fact.

Quibbling about what word endings mean is pointless when the full impact of grace-faith is felt. However, Phillips' translation of verse 22 is of more than passing interest: *"It is a righteousness imparted to, and operating in, all who have faith in Jesus Christ."*

And Barclay's rendering of verse 24 (links with v. 23): *"But they are put into a right relationship with God, freely, by His grace."*

The **action** of God is in more evidence than a declaration or **proclamation** of our standing. Here is reality, change. Here is a new man *"in Christ."*

The context and Paul's logic make it clear that faith radically changes one. God knows what faith accomplishes and can safely declare us what we are not before the law, but are in and by His grace — and what we are becoming.

Understanding the **interaction** (grace-faith) is furthered by metaphors or illustrations. Three institutions are used: **law, slavery**, **sacrifice**. So by faith we are justified, redeemed and forgiven. Any merit gained by obedience could not produce these elements of salvation.

Man, guilty in court, is suddenly acquitted, treated as good, innocent, and a citizen. Man, who has been bad because of wrong relationships, is put into a right relationship. How? What happened so suddenly and dramatically in the court? God in Christ appeared in saving activity (grace) (verse 24). And by faith (verse 22) in the Advocate, something dynamic rather than legal occurred. And the man is not only declared right but knows himself to be made right, and instantly! His faith response to Jesus did it. Penitent and brokenhearted, he knows he is, after all, dear to God. A new relationship is established which is to ripen daily. He emerges from the court committed to goodness and life, rather than sentenced to sin and death.

Another metaphor: Man is in chains, enslaved. He is owned by sin. He lives under sin's sway and dominion. He exists in terror. His life is not his own. His wages is death. All is hopeless. A friendly Purchaser appears who will buy and release him. *"Redemption that is in Christ Jesus"* (KJV); *"deliverance which is wrought by Jesus Christ"* (Barclay, verse 24).

By Jesus' redemptive act, man is dramatically freed. Life is never the same.

Then another picture: (Sacrifices spoke of guilt.) Man is guilty. In times past he offered sacrifices to secure relief, avert wrath and punishment. But where can he go for an abiding sense of forgiveness, due to continuing right relationships?

Again, we note **action**. God sets forth Christ Jesus on the cross, and quite publicly, to be our propitiation, our atonement, our blood covered mercy seat.

So it is *"by faith in His blood"* that I have forgiveness. I am at ease in God's presence. I am at home among men. Enmity, resentment, fear and guilt are gone!

In each Pauline illustration emphasis is on God acting first: Christ, as God's special on-the-scene actor, acquitting, liberating, forgiving in the nick of time in response to personal trust in Him as a sufficient Savior.

And behold, the law is established in the heart and life by the new relationship!

Will you have this new life? It is yours in Jesus. It is yours by your response to Him!

What will you do with Jesus? Make Him both Savior and Lord of your life!

What God Wants Us to Know, Part 1

God Wants Me!

What God wants us to know about Himself, our selves, the world, sin, righteousness, salvation and the future are the most important considerations for human beings. Taken together, they constitute what is called *theology.* Theology for Christians is our word about God as it relates to ourselves and everything within the range of our knowing.

That means that theology is an attempt to answer the most persistent, pressing, important questions of our day or of any day. Does life have meaning? Is there purpose? Is history going anywhere or is it just one big repeatable cycle? Where am I from, and where am I going? What else is there of greater importance that any human could contemplate?

For the Christian, what God wants us to know is first and foremost found in a book! That book is the Bible. It is our primary source book for theology, which is to say, for the greatest concerns of any human being, living anywhere on this planet.

The Bible is the *unique* record of God's self-disclosure, and the meanings of that disclosure for each of us. That is why we speak of it as the record of revelation (the self-disclosing of God: what He is like, what He is about, what He wants).

We find that that self-disclosure reaches its climax, its ultimate, in the incarnation of God in Jesus of Nazareth — an event which occurred on this globe, in a specific location, on a specific part of history. This disclosure sets theology apart from philosophy.

Also, the Bible is the record of *drama* ... the drama of greatest concern to humans. It is a heavenly/earthly drama; a God/man drama. The central actors are indeed God and man.

Theology is the attempt to understand, to interpret, to apply that drama to our human situation, our dilemma, our potential.

Huxley once complained, "I object to Christians; they know too much about God." Of course he also wished he were a clock and only needed winding up, rather than living a life of difficult moral decisions. What often appalls me is how little Christians know, and how little I know about God.

Coleridge criticized so-called Christians, "They do not believe *in* God, only their beliefs *about* God." Too often the criticism is valid. *Job* discovered it was better to see (know) God than accept views about Him that did not square with reality. And he finally discovered if one really *knew* God one could trust Him even if some of life's nagging problems did not seem to be answered swiftly or easily by God.

And that leads us to the accenting of a point that needs underscoring: God wants us to know **about** Him in order that we may come to **know** Him!

Permit, then, one more word regarding theology. We need theology. But we need that which is (1) realistic and (2) relational, bringing us to a relationship with God and each other that is satisfying and ennobling.

And if in the process of thinking theologically we may for the moment seem abstract, we must very soon demonstrate that theology is for sidewalk, yard, office, store, industry, family, home, or hospital. That's why we keep coming back to our source book (Bible) to see if we are keeping on track with our understandings, our interpretations.

Let's take a look at the Book in a way that impacts on my subject. It begins with God **creating.** It ends with God **re-creating**. In Revelation 21:22ff, we see the portrait under the symbol of a new City. We humans, amazingly, are the center of concern at the beginning and at the end.

It ends with the Spirit and Bride saying "*Come*" (22:17). It ends with a plea, *"Amen. Come, Lord Jesus!"* (20). It ends with grace, not law, "*The grace of the Lord Jesus be with you all*" or *"with all his people"* (saints, Christ persons) (13). "*I am the Alpha and the Omega* [A-Z], *the First and the Last, the Beginning and the End"* (NIV).

This is the one we have to deal with all our lives and for all our destiny: So I want to know His intentions toward me, toward my species (race), toward all those like me.

For I am told it is in God that I live and move and have my being.

I want and need to know who I am, and to be certain of my identity I must **know** God (which is more than to know **about** Him).

I believe it is Adler who says the most important philosophical question is, "Why is anything?" I think he is correct. It is the question which precedes "Who am I?" "Where am I headed?" "Does life have meaning?"

The question I accept, but not the philosophers' answers. I turn to my source book and ask it. Why is ANYTHING? It tells me plainly. Right off we see a God who speaks and acts. And those are the characteristics of a person. It is the nature of a person to create. And so the Creator God does what is simply natural for Him to do. Why then is anything? It is because He wills it. It exists at His word ... this speaking God. As the old writings have it, "by divine fiat" (command).

Immediately I have another need created. I want to know what this Person God who wills everything, including myself, into existence is. What is His essence, His character? The Bible tells me much: He is Spirit; He is Light; He is Holy; He is Love. He is a person who is Holy Love. BUT what does that mean? Quickly, it means —

1. That He is Other than We: distanced from us, sovereign, supreme, and most certainly not to be confused with anything else that He made. He is the essence of morality, goodness (light, holiness, love). *Transcendent.*

2. That He is Also Near: with an indescribable closeness. He is the God out there. He is the God right here. Nearness of concern, of commitment to the man He made, nearness of self-giving — in short, of *Love.* Nearness of presence ... even though I make my bed in hell He is there. *Immanent.* Now that is the wonderful truth we Christians declare! Proclaim!

BUT how does God disclose all that to us? How do I know God's intent toward me? How do I know it is an intent of good will? Again, it's in the *Book.* But let me cite Article 2 of our *Articles of Religion:* "We believe the Father is the cause of all that exists whether of matter or spirit. He with the Son and the Holy Spirit made man to bear His image. By intention He relates to man as Father, thereby forever declaring His goodwill toward man. He is, according to the New Testament, the one who both seeks and receives penitent sinners."

So the ringing affirmation made on the basis of God's self-disclosure that you should leave with this hour, is something like this:

I affirm on the basis of God's self-disclosure that God wanted me; I am His wanted child; that He still wants me; that He accepts me; that He loves me. And that He accepts and loves me as the only way to a relationship between us, and to recreate us so that we and our life works are as He intended — which is for fellowship, personal fulfillment, creative, serving activity.

However can I make such an affirmation, confession? Again, only on the basis of the record of revelation found in our Bible. Let me say a word about the Bible as drama.

As soon as *our drama,* the drama of God and us opens — as soon as the curtain goes up — for the first act — the action begins. No long prologue — no description of the characters. But we are introduced to Him who provides the entire stage — our planet, Earth.

More. We immediately get two basic bits of information. Our *Creator-Partner* (our Great Other) in the drama is One who *acts and talks*! Genesis 1:1 "*God created*" and verse 3 *"God said."* And God has never stopped doing either. He is still the Creating God. Still the Speaking God. And like Him there is no other!

Then — watch this — we are immediately given the *key.* What we are to know about Him — our Maker-Partner — we will discover in what He *does* and in what He *says.* And the Bible is the record of exactly that!

God's acts and words are never divorced. Taken together they are or constitute our revelation (disclosure). What He says and does is always in sync. So on with the drama! *Action:*

1. God created — heaven and earth.
2. God saw that it was good.
3. God made man out of the elemental stuff of our earth home — our environment.

He made it for us; and us for it. *He,* not evolution, is the great Adapter. He created our home. He fitted us for it.

Then we come to Genesis 1:26 (RSV), "*Let us make man in our image, after our likeness."* There is our start, and what a start it is. God has a stake in us, an investment, and a very personal one!

And here is the answer to our (1) identity, (2) dignity, (3) value, (4) significance. Here is the beginning for everyone combating a poor self-image. *God wants me!*

Now, do we begin to understand why God doesn't give up on us — even when we give up on ourselves? There we have our identity established, regardless of subsequent inhumanities to each other. We are God's very special act of love.

But we must note that we are more than a plaything for an almighty, capricious and infinite despot. We are here because God wants us and has a working partnership to give us.

See Genesis l:24 which declares that all God created was given to us for our good and our use. See 1:28 (RSV) which declares that we were given responsible partnership in an on-going enterprise. God blessed and commanded, *"Be fruitful ... fill the earth ... subdue it ... have dominion ... ."* (Reminds one of the farmer who said, "Should have seen this place when God had it all alone!")

See Chapter 2 for additional information regarding ourselves and our relation to God. Verse 7 (RSV), *"... breathed into his nostrils ... and man became a living being"* — something more than animal. Rather, something distinctly and personally God-like. So we are indeed sons of God and by God's intention.

There is, in my judgment, a beautiful, powerful footnote which could not have been written regarding any other of God's creatures. It is Genesis 2:21-25 (NIV).

"So the Lord God caused the man to fall into a deep sleep; and while he was sleeping, he took one of the man's ribs and closed up the place with flesh. Then the Lord God made a woman from the rib he had taken out of the man, and he brought her to the man. The man said, 'This is now bone of my bones and flesh of my flesh; she shall be called "woman," for she was taken out of man.' For this reason a man will leave his father and mother and be united to his wife, and they will become one flesh. The man and his wife were both naked, and they felt no shame."

I turn in conclusion to the portrait of the **Creating/Re-creating God**. And I look at it in John's Gospel. The God who willingly identifies with us and discloses His good will in creating us now is seen disclosing His continuing intention/action. Again, we have as in Genesis 1 the combination of word and deed.

Turn to John 1. We will read verses in conclusion from this in a somewhat different order:

In the beginning was the Word, and the Word was with God, and the Word was God. He was with God in the beginning. Through him all things were made; without him nothing was made that has been made. In him was life, and that life was the light of men. The light shines in the darkness, but the darkness has not understood it.

The Word became flesh and lived for a while among us. We have seen his glory, the glory of the one and only Son who came from the Father, full of grace and truth. John testifies concerning him. He cries out, saying, "This was he of whom I said, 'He who comes after me has surpassed me because he was before me.'" From the fullness of his grace we have all received one blessing after another. For the law was given through Moses; grace and truth came through Jesus Christ. No one has ever seen God, but God the only Son, who is at the Father's side, has made him known.

The true light that gives light to every man was coming into the world. He was in the world, and though the world was made through him, the world did not recognize him. He came to that which was his own, but his own did not receive him. Yet to all who received him, to those who believed in his name, he gave the right to become children of God — children born not of natural descent, nor of human decision or a husband's will, but born of God (John 1:1-13, NIV).

The same wanting, yearning God reaches out to us now. We have marred the image He placed upon us. He still wants us. The cross was God's final way to try to tell me He wanted me.

What do you believe about God this hour?

What do you believe about yourself?

Are you satisfied with your present self?

Do you now want to be as near to the design of God for you as at this date it is possible for God to do in His re-creating mercy?

Do you want to know God as: **Savior ... Redeemer ... Lord ... Partner ... Friend ... Helper?**

What God Wants Us to Know, Part 2

God Wants Us!

You are a chosen race, a royal priesthood, a holy nation, God's own people, that you may declare the wonderful deeds of him who called you out of darkness into his marvelous light. Once you were not a people but now you are God's people; once you had not received mercy but now you have received mercy (1 Peter 2:9-10, NIV).

As indeed he says in Hosea, "Those who were not my people I will call 'my people,' and her who was not beloved I will call 'my beloved.' And in the very place where it was said to them, 'You are not my people,' they will be called 'sons of the living God'" (Romans 9:25-26, RSV).

We have spoken to the first and primary fact which should concern us. *God wants me!* You and I are God's wanted children. This comes through loud and clear in the biblical drama. It is clear in Creation, in Incarnation, and in the portrait of the future given in the last two chapters of Revelation.

God not only wants me and continues to seek me when I am not seeking Him, He is responsible for giving me my **value, identity,** and **dignity** as a person, an individual.

On top of that, He gives me a partnership with Himself — a task, mission, work-satisfying, productive, fruitful action. This adds immensely to the meaning and purpose of life — if we will have it so! If we will not have it so — not even God can do much about it, except to follow us and seek us!

This is our word to all who may not have a sense of sin but do sense meaninglessness, purposelessness.

But now we want to see what God does next and what He wants. He tells this by what He **says** and **does**. It is crystal clear that He intends to have a **people**, a **community** which centers in Himself and which will share in the fulfillment of His purpose on this planet.

The New Testament makes it clear that God is in the process of forming **a new race** with Christ as head! It is the formation of the new race of Christ-persons to which we are called to another kind of partnership — not only a planetary partnership, but a race-building partnership. We are humans *not* by choice. We belong to the **new race** *by* choice.

When we talk about evangelism, that is what we should have in mind — the extending of the Body of Christ, the forming of a new race, a breed of men who are redeemed by Christ, living in Christ and for Christ. God calls us to a holiness which is never entirely solitary but which is social. There is no such thing as solitary holiness or solitary holy love!

I think it is important that we look at the nature of our partnership with God. It is (1) environmental and (2) relational.

Let's talk a bit about what I mean by our relational partnership. God has given us (the church) the task of establishing, re-establishing, nurturing relationships in the body of Christ and among all men. This equals mission.

In the metaphors of St. Paul, we are agents of reconciliation, ambassadors, who on behalf of God plead for all men to be reconciled to Him and to each other.

Let us now carry this line of thinking out further. I suggest we need to see the Bible not only as I've suggested, as drama, but as a book about relationships — that's really what it is all about. Relational *drama!*

The entire biblical drama and message is one about relationships — to God, world, self, others. And for Christians, especially within the special community God creates, this calls into being Paul's constant emphasis on *unity.* Every act of God and therefore every act of the church should be aimed at doing something positive in this whole area of relationships. Our relationships — their nature and quality — make life a heaven or a hell. Our relationships cement or disrupt the social fabric whether it is in a nation, a local community, or in the church we attend.

Our situation is that of Humpty Dumpty who sat on a wall and took a great fall. All the king's horses and men were unable to put Humpty Dumpty together again. But God has called redeemed men to join Him in a partnership in doing just that. God intends to save the world — to restore and nurture relationships — through the use of restored, redeemed persons, persons He has taken hold of, redeemed, saved, and is in the procss of sanctifying.

Who are the saved? They are those who have come to know God, that is, to be in a reconciled relationship with God! They are those who, like Abraham of old, are **friends** of God.

So with that setting let's watch God ... what He does! Remember that is the way He discloses Himself to us. God does like any good missionary/evangelist — goes after one person, teams up and then gets others.

In that case it was a man and then a family, and then a nation — a broad community ... Abraham, then Isaac, then Jacob (Israel) — so God set about forming the "People of God." We watch God working patiently — and for the long pull! And the Old Testament is largely the story of that people — that community.

Now then we also see God developing some **Documents of Relationship.** What are they? They are Old Testament and New Testament. That is, Old Agreement and New Agreement. Important words those, for they divide our Bible into its two great parts of thirty-nine and twenty-seven books respectively.

Under the Old Agreement/Covenant it was God and Israel (His Community) — special, peculiar; called by God; chosen by God; and committed to God! Their special commission was to uphold and propagate God's Holy Law.

Under the New Agreement/Covenant it is God and Church — again a special, God initiated and formed community — **called** (ekklesia) ecclesiastical; **chosen** (elect); **committed** and **commissioned**. Committed to God in Christ and commissioned to "Carrying the Gospel and to Discipling!"

Church: God's community of messengers carrying God's message of Good News that men may be reconciled to Himself and to each other. There is our business in this world, the only justification of our existence!

Old Testament [Law] — told man how the good life functioned at its best.

New Testament [Gospel] — tells man the good life was made operational, actual, real by and through the Redeemer, Christ Jesus!

So it is when one is *"In Christ"* that life begins to function as it was designed to function, and lo and behold, the law is fulfilled! That is the message of Redemption.

In the Old Testament, Israel centered its life and mission around an act of God. That act, which is the very heart/core of the Old Testament, is called the *Exodus* which really has two parts: (1) The Egyptian deliverance; (2) Sinai: Law.

The Deliverance etched the consciousness of the people of God with the fact they could not deliver themselves. It accented faith/trust. Sinai — the Law — told Israel how a delivered people were to relate to God and to each other.

Now look at what St. Paul provides by way of contrast between the Old and New Testaments, between Law and Gospel:

Law	**Gospel**
written on tables of stone	written on heart
written code	Spirit of living God (internalized)
kills	gives life
dispensation of death	dispensation of Spirit
condemation	righteousness (right relations)
fading	permanent
veiled glory	unveiled glory; direct view of God's glory, He says, in the Face of Jesus!!

Now what we can begin to see is that under either Old or New Covenant the Agreements are always **relational**, always **conditional**.

Let me add one more thing to the Old Testament picture which accents the relational/conditional features of the People (Community) of God. The **offerings/sacrifices** of the Old Testament are always aimed at *establishing relationships; restoring;* or *enriching relationships.*

Then we learn from our New Testament that all that was included or implied by the Old Testament offerings/sacrifices is fulfilled in Christ and by our becoming related to Him as Savior/Lord.

Let us now take a further step. It is a word regarding the Holy Spirit and His role in the Church, Christ's Community. His role is to:

1. Enable wholesome, saving, fulfilling, growing relationships within the Body of Christ. It is in fact the Holy Spirit who forms the New Community. Man cannot do it.

2. Internalize the great historical/redemptive acts of God: Exodus, Sinai, and the Death and Resurrection of Jesus and Pentecost. Which means then:

a. a real deliverance/exodus by Christ (the central New Testament EVENT).

b. law of Moses moves inside us and finally reaches to our nerve endings, assisting our moral development, if you please!

c. die with Christ so the self that should die does die.

d. rise to newness of life in Christ.

e. filled by the Spirit who proceeds from the Father and is poured out by the Son.

f. put under the Lordship of Christ.

g. made God's communicators.

Let's quickly summarize how far we've come:

God wants me!

God wants us!

All His Acts

All His Words move toward making us

His own possession —

In restoring us to Himself.

In remaking us according to the original design.

God wants to use us to fulfill His purposes — to bring all men into His community — His church where He is Head/Lord. And where we are partners in both the grace and gospel of God.

Finally: **The Church as the only Community of Hope**

"Despite its faults, the church is the world's only hope for sharing the reconciling redemptive acts of God in Christ. Only thus can man recover his nature and destiny lost in the first Adam."

When the church is true to its nature and to the fulfillment of its mission, what it does in the world is the most important thing happening in history. This truth is and should be sobering. It should call us to new heights of holy love and redemptive suffering, if we are to contribute effectively to the new race God is creating in and through Christ Jesus.

Let my last word in this hour be ... *My longing for my Church.*

1. That together we let God have us if He wants us (and that He has made abundantly clear).

2. That we allow Him to:

cleanse,
enable,
empower,
activate me/us

In order that we may be His Partners in witness and winning the lost ones back to a loving Father.

The most important question facing each of us in this hour is:

Not what we have of God or the Spirit or of unusual or spectacular manifestations.

But what God the Holy Spirit has of us? Heart, Soul, Mind, Strength.

How do I — we — measure up as "the people of God"?

Who's Boss?

Whatever fills you has you. If your life is filled with booze, then booze is boss. It has you. If your life is filled with ambition, then ambition is boss. If you are filled with pride or envy or lust, then that is what has you.

If your life is filled with the Holy Spirit, the Holy Spirit has you. What fills you makes all the difference in the world — and the world to come.

The Apostle Paul was on target: *"Do not get drunk with wine, for that is debauchery (dissipation); but be filled with the Spirit"* (Ephesians 5:18, RSV). Here is both specific contrast and broad symbolism. Don't be filled with ... but be filled with the Spirit. Don't take into your life that which makes you less than you are. Don't take in that which demeans, degrades, destroys, or dulls. Of course that also includes the mind — pictures, reading, thoughts, imaginations, associations.

Are there pigs in your parlor?

E. Stanley Jones wrote, "Don't turn pigs into your parlor." Don't turn destructive beasts into the best rooms of your life. That is no way to enjoy the full life.

Scripture and life teach us that we are responsible moral beings. We are responsible for what fills our lives. We are responsible for the results of what fills our lives. If we are drunk, it affects our behavior. If we are filled with the Spirit, that affects behavior. So we have options.

I can escape life. Or I can embrace life in the fullness of the Holy Spirit.

Some escape with alcohol. Desire for success makes this almost inescapable to the salesman or to the climber. This false additive is too readily available. It is the primary escape.

Others escape with afternoon soap operas. They glide into the unreal world of the problems, exploits, and affairs of others. Real life fades.

Some drink from the bloating bottle of ambition and are filled to doom. Some consume the deadly, addicting stimulant called pride. Some fill their lives with things, with glitter, with a constant barrage of sounds — all which soon pass. Some escape with work. These "workaholics" deny themselves the cultivation of the highest values found in relationships and finer sensibilities. There are many escapes, many ways to fill life. But the end is always a deepening sense of emptiness.

Dare you live all your life?

The greatest challenge is to embrace life, to find true fulfillment. God wrote a book to help us to do just that. I can open myself to Life, to the Source, to the Holy Spirit. This is no escape. Here we are face to face with reality. The result is a life which is enlarged, enriched, intensified. I see more, feel more, understand more. I increase both pain and pleasure.

Now tell me, tell yourself — what fills you just now?

Whatever fills you has you!

It makes sense to be filled with the Holy Spirit. Since we belong to whatever fills us, why not belong to God? Especially when we think of what He did.

I have been bought with a price — not silver or gold, but the precious blood of Christ. And it is by the Holy Spirit that I trust in Christ. It is the purpose of Jesus to fill me with His Spirit. And I come into fullest possession of myself, I find my true identity, and I am made complete when the Holy Spirit fills me. Life takes on new meaning, satisfaction, and excitement. Filled with the Spirit, I am delivered from dependence on false supports.

Open your life to the Holy Spirit — gift of the Father and the Son. Receive the needed inward washing and regeneration of your life. This is what God pours upon us *"richly through Jesus Christ our Savior"* (Titus 3:5-6, RSV).

Open your life to the Holy Spirit. Receive renewal *"in the spirit of your mind,"* so you are a new person with a new nature equipped for a new life (Ephesians 4:22-24, RSV).

Open your life to the Holy Spirit. Receive assurance of the fullness of God, the love of Christ, and the strengthening force of the Holy Spirit.

What continues to fill you?

God is thinking of our greatest happiness when He says, through Paul, *"Be filled with the [Holy] Spirit."* The term *filled* is a present imperative verb. Literally, it means, "Be continually filled with the Holy Spirit." But first He must fill you. Then He must constantly fill you.

When the Holy Spirit fills you, He will push out everything incompatible with His presence and action in your life. He will do what Jesus promised, *"I came that they may have life, and have it abundantly"* (John 10:10, RSV).

What will you permit to fill your life from this moment on?

Miscellaneous Quotations and Poetry from Dr. Knox's Files

Love Him, and keep Him for thy friend, who, when all go away, will not forsake thee, nor suffer thee to perish in the end.

Thomas à Kempis

I went very unwillingly to a society in Aldersgate Street, where one was reading Luther's preface to the Epistle to the Romans. While he was describing the change which God makes in the heart through faith in Christ, I felt my heart strangely warmed. I felt I did trust in Christ, Christ alone for salvation; and an assurance was given me that He had taken away my sins, even mine, and saved me from the law of sin and death.

John Wesley

When we set out on this quest, we found ourselves moving in the midst of a mighty host, but, as we have pressed forward, the marchers, company by company, have fallen out of the race ... . And now, as we stand and gaze with our eyes upon the farther shore, a single figure rises from the flood and straightway fills the whole horizon. There is the Savior.

Arnold J. Toynbee

The life of faith is not a life of mounting up with wings, but a life of walking and not fainting ... . Faith never knows where it is being led, but it loves and knows the One who is leading.

Oswald Chambers

My most cherished possession I wish I could leave you is my faith in Jesus Christ, for with Him and nothing else you can be happy, but without Him and with all else you'll never be happy.

Patrick Henry

Winter is on my head, but eternal spring is in my heart: I breathe at this hour the fragrance of the lilacs, the violets, and the roses, as at twenty years ago. The nearer I approach to the end, the plainer I hear around me the immortal symphonies of the worlds which invite me.

Victor Hugo

For half a century I have been writing my thoughts in prose and in verse — history, philosophy, drama, romance, tradition, satire, ode, and song. I have tried all. But I feel I have not said the thousandth part of what is in me. When I go down to the grave I can say, like many others, "I have finished my day's work!" But I cannot say, "I have finished my life." The tomb is not a blind alley; it is a thoroughfare. It closes on the twilight, it opens on the dawn.

Victor Hugo

Besides theology, music is the only art capable of affording peace and joy of the heart like that induced by the study of the science of Divinity. The proof of this is that the Devil, the originator of sorrowful anxieties and restless troubles, flees before the sound of music almost as much as he does before the Word of God. This is why the prophets preferred music before all the other arts, proclaiming the Word in psalms and hymns. My heart, which is full to overflowing, has often been solaced and refreshed by music when sick and weary.

Martin Luther

Thou hast made us for Thyself, O Lord; and our heart is restless until it rests in Thee.

St. Augustine

Since my heart was touched at seventeen, I believe I have never awakened from sleep, in sickness or in health, by day or by night, without my first waking thought being how best I might serve my Lord.

Elizabeth Fry

Christ has made of death a narrow, starlit strip between the companionships of yesterday and the reunions of tomorrow.

William Jennings Bryan

One evening I invited Him into my heart. What an entrance He made! It was not a spectacular, emotional thing, but very real. Something happened at the very center of my life. He came into the darkness of my heart and turned on the light. He built a fire on the hearth and banished the chill. He started music where there had been stillness, and He filled the emptiness with His own loving wonderful fellowship. I have never regretted opening the door to Christ and I never will — not into eternity!

Robert Boyd Munger

Fear not that thy life shall come to an end, but rather fear that it shall never have a beginning.

Cardinal Newman

I cannot forgive God for the suffering of others; when I look abroad upon His world and behold its cruel destinies, I turn from Him with disaffection nor do I conceive that He will blame me for the impulse. But when I consider my own fates, I grow conscious of His gentle dealing; I see Him chastise with helpful blows, I feel His stripes to be caresses; and this knowledge is my comfort which reconciles me to the world. All those whom I now pity with indignation are, perhaps, not less fatherly dealt with than myself .... .

If I from my spy hole, looking with purblind eyes upon the least part of a fraction of the universe, yet perceive in my own destiny some broken evidences of a plan and some signals of an overruling goodness; shall I, then, be so made as to complain that all cannot be deciphered? Shall I not rather wonder, with infinite and grateful surprise, that in so vast a scheme I seem to have been able to read, however little, and that that little was encouraging to faith?

Robert Louis Stevenson

A man can accept what Christ has done without knowing how it works; indeed, he certainly won't know how it works until he's accepted it.

C. S. Lewis, Miracles

We are told that Christ was killed for us, that his death has washed out our sins, and that by dying he disabled death itself. Any theories we build up as to how Christ's death did all this are, in my view, quite secondary.

C. S. Lewis, Miracles

An ordinary simple Christian kneels down to say his prayers. He is trying to get in touch with God. But if he is a Christian he knows that what is prompting him to pray is also God. God, so to speak, inside him. But he also knows that all his real knowledge of God comes through Christ, the Man who was God — that Christ is standing beside him, helping him to pray, praying for him.

C. S. Lewis, Mere Christianity

The real Son of God is at your side. He is beginning to turn you into the same kind of thing as Himself. He is beginning, so to speak, to "inject" His kind of life and thought, His Zoe, into you; beginning to turn the tin soldier into a live man. The part of you that does not like it is the part that is still tin.

C. S. Lewis, Mere Christianity

If anyone would like to acquire humility, I can, I think, tell him the first step. The first step is to realize that one is proud. And a biggish step, too. At least, nothing whatever can be done before it. If you think you are not conceited, it means you are very conceited indeed.

C. S. Lewis, Mere Christianity

Christ takes it for granted that men are bad. Until we really feel this assumption of His to be true, though we are part of the world He came to save, we are not part of the audience to whom His words are addressed. We lack the first condition for understanding what He is talking about. And when men attempt to be Christians without this preliminary consciousness of sin, the result is almost bound to be a certain resentment against God as to one who is always making impossible demands and always inexplicably angry.

C. S. Lewis, Mere Christianity

"An unliterary man may be defined as one who reads books only once."

C. S. Lewis

"A book's no good to me until I've read it two or three times."

C. S. Lewis

I Don't Need A Why

I lay my "whys" before Your cross,
In worship kneeling.

My mind too numb for thought,
My heart beyond all feeling:

And worshipping, realize that I,
In knowing You, don't need a "why."

Anonymous

A Prayer for Courage

God make me brave for life,
Oh, braver than this!
Let me straighten after pain
As a tree straightens after the rain,
Shining and lovely again.

God make me brave for life,
Much braver than this!
As the blown grass lifts let me rise
From sorrow with quiet eyes,
Knowing Thy way is wise.

God make me brave — life brings
Such blinding things.
Help me to keep my sight,
Help me to see aright
That out of the dark — comes light.

Grace Noll Crowell

Why should we weep for those who die?
They fall, their dust returns to dust:
Their soul shall live eternally
Within the mansions of the just

They die to live — they sink to rise,
They leave this wretched mortal shore;
But brighter suns and bluer skies
Shall smile on them for evermore.

Alfred Tennyson

Thou canst not prove the Nameless, O my son,
Nor canst thou prove the world thou movest in,
Thou canst not prove that thou art body alone,
Nor canst thou prove that thou art spirit alone,
Nor canst thou prove that thou art both in one;
Thou canst not prove thou art immortal, no.
Nor yet that thou art mortal ...
For nothing worthy proving can be proven,
Nor yet disproven; wherefore be thou wise,
Cleave ever to the sunnier side of doubt,
And cling to Faith beyond the forms of Faith!

Robert Browning

A tenderer light than moon or sun,
Than song of earth a sweeter hymn,
May shine and sound forever on,
And thou be deaf and dim.

Forever round the Mercy-seat
The guiding lights of Love shall burn:
But what if, habit-bound, thy feet
Shall lack the will to turn?

What if thine eye refuse to see,
Thine ear of Heaven's free welcome fail,
And thou a willing captive be
Thyself thy own dark jail?

John Greenleaf Whittier

The Poet's Simple Faith

You say, "Where goest Thou?" I cannot tell,
And still go on. If but the way be straight
I cannot go amiss: before me lies
Dawn and the day: the night behind me: that
Suffices me: I break the bounds: I see,
And nothing more; believe and nothing less.
My future is not one of my concerns.

Victor Hugo

Life's Wounds

They say the world is round, and yet I often think it square,
So many little hurts we get, from the corners here and there.
But one sad truth in life I've found, while traveling to the west:
The only ones who really wound are those we love the best.
The choicest smile, the sweetest grace are oft to strangers shown.
The careless mien, the frowning face are given to our own.
We flatter those we scarcely know, we please the fleeting guest,
And deal full many a thoughtless blow to those we love the best.
Love does not grow on every tree, nor true hearts yearly bloom.
Alas, for those who only see this truth across the tomb!
But soon or late, the fact grows plain to all through sorrow's test:
The only ones who give us pain are those who love us best.

Anonymous

Friendship

Oh, the comfort — the inexpressible comfort
of feeling safe with a person,
Having neither to weigh thoughts,
Nor measure words — but pouring them
All right out — just as they are —
Chaff and grain together —
Certain that a faithful hand will
Take and sift them —
Keep what is worth keeping —
And with the breath of kindness
Blow the rest away.

Dinah Maria Mulock Craik

Speak to Him, thou, for He hears, and Spirit with Spirit can meet —
Closer is He than breathing, and nearer than hands and feet.

Alfred Tennyson

Peace

With eager heart and will on fire,
I strove to win my great desire.
"Peace shall be mine," I said; but life
Grew bitter in the barren strife.

My soul was weary, and my pride
Was wounded deep; to heaven I cried,
"God grant me peace or I must die."
The dumb stars glittered no reply.

Broken at last I bowed my head,
Forgetting all myself, and said,
"Whatever comes, Thy will be done."
And in that moment peace was won.

Henry Van Dyke

I shall grow old, but never lose life's zest,
because the road's last turn will be the best.

Henry Van Dyke

God, keep a clean wind blowing through my heart night and day.
Cleanse it with sunshine — let the silver rain wash away
Cobwebs and the smothering dust that years leave, I pray.

God, keep a clean wind blowing through my heart; wind from far
Green pastures and from shaded pools where still waters are;
Wind from spaces out beyond the first twilight star.

Bitterness can have no place in me, nor grief stay —
When the winds of God rush through and sweep them away.
God, keep a clean wind blowing through my heart night and day.

Author unknown

A Soul's Soliloquy

Today the journey is ended, I have worked out the mandates of fate;
Naked, alone, undefended, I knock at the Uttermost Gate.
Behind is life and its longing, its trial, its trouble, its sorrow;
Beyond is the infinite Morning of a day without a tomorrow.

Go back to dust and decay, body grown weary and old.
You are worthless to me from today; no longer my soul can you hold.
I lay you down gladly forever for a life that is better than this;
I go where partings ne'er sever — you into oblivion's abyss.

Lo, the gate swings wide at my knocking. Across endless reaches I see
Lost friends with laughter come flocking to give a glad welcome to me.
Farewell, the maze has been treaded; this is the ending of strife.
Say not that death should be dreaded — 'tis but the beginning of life.

Wenonah Stevens Abbott

He taught me all the mercy, for he show'd me all the sin
Now, tho' my lamp was lighted late, there's One will let me in.

Alfred Tennyson

Grow old along with me! The best is yet to be,
The last of life, for which the first was made.
Our times are in His hand, Who saith, a whole I planned.
Youth shows but half; trust God; see all, nor be afraid.

Robert Browning

Behold the Lamb of God

In evil long I took delight, unawed by shame or fear,
Till a new object struck my sight, and stopped my wild career.

I saw One hanging on a tree, in agonies and blood;
He fixed His lanquid eyes on me, as near His cross I stood.

Oh, never till my latest breath, shall I forget that look:
It seemed to charge me with His death, though not a word He
spoke.
My conscience felt and owned the guilt; it plunged me in despair;
I saw my sins His blood had spilt, and helped to nail Him there.

A second look He gave which said, "I freely all forgive;
This blood is for thy ransom paid; I die that thou mayest live."

John Newton

O glory of the lighted mind
How dead I'd been how dumb,
how blind.
Out of the mist into the light
O blessed gift of inner sight.

John Masefield

I think about God, yet I talk of small matters.
Isn't it odd, how my idle tongue chatters,
Of quarrelsome neighbors, fine weather and rain,
Indifferent labors, indifferent pain,
Some trivial style, fashions shift with a nod ...
And yet all the while I am thinking of God.

Gamaliel Bradford

The Hound of Heaven

I fled Him down the nights and down the days;
I fled Him down the arches of the years;
I fled Him down the labyrinthine ways
Of my own mind; and in the midst of tears
I hid from Him, and under running laughter.

But with unhurrying chase,
And unperturbed pace,
Deliberate speed, majestic instancy,
They beat — and a Voice beat
More instant than the Feet —
"All things betray thee, who betrayest Me."

And then there comes the time when the
fugitive was beaten.

Naked I wait Thy love's uplifted stroke!
My harness, piece by piece, Thou hast hewn
from me,
And smitten to my knee;
I am defenseless utterly.

"Rise, clasp my hand, come!"
Halts by me that footfall;
Is my gloom, after all,
Shade of His hand, outstretched caressingly?
"Ah, fondest, blindest, weakest,
I am He Whom thou seekest!
Thou dravest love from thee, who dravest Me!"

Francis Thompson

Lloyd Knox and his parents,
Robert and Bertha

Lloyd Knox and Harriet Boice
as school children

Lloyd (r), 13, next to Dale Cryderman at a
Southern Michigan camp, 1927

The cast of a Spring Arbor Junior College musical. Lloyd Knox played the lead role, front and center in dark suit and bow tie, circa 1935-1937.

Dale Cryderman, Lloyd Knox, Harriet Knox, and Dorothy Cryderman work on the YPMS (*Young Peoples Missionary Society* magazine), circa 1937.

Lloyd and Harriet Knox, 1936

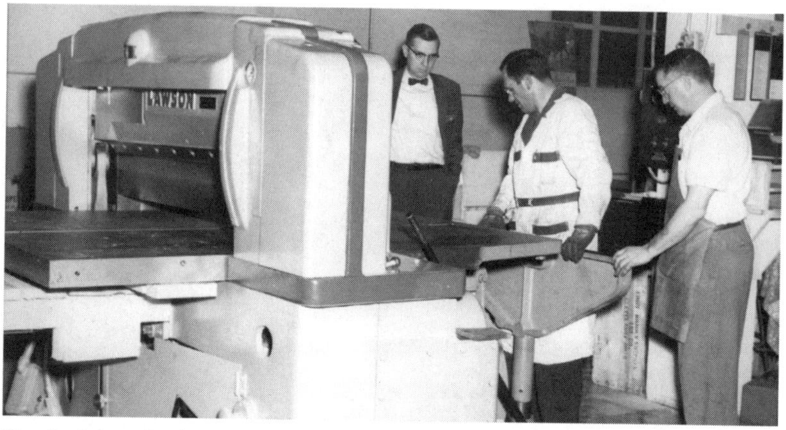

On the job at Light and Life Press, Winona Lake, IN, circa 1960s

At the entrance of Light and Life Press building, Winona Lake, IN, 1965

Bishop Charles Fairbairn, Bishop J. Paul Taylor, Lloyd Knox, Bishop Leslie Marston (at pulpit), and Bishop Walter Kendall at the Billy Sunday Tabernacle, Winona Lake, IN, 1960

Lloyd and Harriet Knox and their children Sylvia, Walter, and Edward, Winona Lake, IN, 1957

Senior Pastor Lloyd Knox at North Chili Free Methodist Church, North Chili, NY, 1983

Lloyd and Harriet Knox, circa 1970s

Bishop Paul Ellis and Dr. Knox, late 1980s

Lloyd Knox and his grand-
children, Layla and Lloyd,
1983 (in England)

Light and Life Press employees, Winona Lake, IN, 1978
Foreground: Lloyd H. Knox, Publisher

Harriet Knox, Lloyd Knox, Bishop Bastian, and friends at Lloyd's retirement party, 1979

Sylvia Knox Tugan, 1998

Walter and Barbara Knox and children, Jodi and Brandy, 1998

Edward and Claudia Knox, 1995

Layla Knox Ward and daughter, Alice

Lloyd Knox, Iraq, 1990 while visiting Ed and Claudia in Jordan

Lloyd Knox as a child

Lloyd Knox ... a man uniquely raised for ministry, "... esteemed by [his] peers as an outstanding preacher and writer and as a man with a dream who never allowed lesser things to dim his ambition for his church and his desire to bring glory to his Lord. ... we who have known and worked with you are better men and women because of your influence."

Tribute written by Dale Cryderman
upon Lloyd's retirement